POWERFUL LEADERSHIP

ISBN 0-13-066836-2

FINANCIAL TIMES PRENTICE HALL BOOKS

For more information, please go to www.ft-ph.com

Thomas L. Barton, William G. Shenkir, and Paul L. Walker
  *Making Enterprise Risk Management Pay Off:
  How Leading Companies Implement Risk Management*

Deirdre Breakenridge
  Cyberbranding: Brand Building in the Digital Economy

William C. Byham, Audrey B. Smith, and Matthew J. Paese
  *Grow Your Own Leaders: How to Identify, Develop, and Retain
  Leadership Talent*

Jonathan Cagan and Craig M. Vogel
  *Creating Breakthrough Products: Innovation from Product Planning
  to Program Approval*

Subir Chowdhury
  The Talent Era: Achieving a High Return on Talent

Sherry Cooper
  Ride the Wave: Taking Control in a Turbulent Financial Age

James W. Cortada
  *21st Century Business: Managing and Working
  in the New Digital Economy*

James W. Cortada
  *Making the Information Society: Experience, Consequences,
  and Possibilities*

Aswath Damodaran
  *The Dark Side of Valuation: Valuing Old Tech, New Tech,
  and New Economy Companies*

Henry A. Davis and William W. Sihler
  Financial Turnarounds: Preserving Enterprise Value

Sarv Devaraj and Rajiv Kohli
  *The IT Payoff: Measuring the Business Value
  of Information Technology Investments*

Jaime Ellertson and Charles W. Ogilvie
  *Frontiers of Financial Services: Turning Customer Interactions
  Into Profits*

Nicholas D. Evans
  *Business Agility: Strategies for Gaining Competitive Advantage
  through Mobile Business Solutions*

FINANCIAL TIMES

Prentice Hall

In an increasingly competitive world, it is quality
of thinking that gives an edge—an idea that opens new
doors, a technique that solves a problem, or an insight
that simply helps make sense of it all.

We work with leading authors in the various arenas
of business and finance to bring cutting-edge thinking
and best learning practice to a global market.

It is our goal to create world-class print publications
and electronic products that give readers
knowledge and understanding which can then be
applied, whether studying or at work.

To find out more about our business
products, you can visit us at www.ft-ph.com

Pearson
Education

POWERFUL LEADERSHIP

How to Unleash the Potential in Others and Simplify Your Own Life

Eric G. Stephan

R. Wayne Pace

FINANCIAL TIMES
Prentice Hall

An Imprint of PEARSON EDUCATION
London • New York • San Francisco • Toronto • Sydney
Tokyo • Singapore • Hong Kong • Cape Town • Madrid
Paris • Milan • Munich • Amsterdam

Library of Congress Cataloging-in-Publication Data
Stephan, Eric G.
    Powerful leadership: how to unleash the potential in others and simplify your own life/
Eric G. Stephan, R. Wayne Pace.
        p. cm. —(Financial Times Prentice Hall)
    Includes index.
    ISBN 0-13-066836-2
    1. Leadership. 2. Personnel management. I. Pace, R. Wayne. II. title. III. Financial times
Prentice Hall books
    (Computer science) I. Title. II. Series.

HD57.7.S734 2002
658.3'14—dc21   2001058242

Editorial/production supervision: Kerry Reardon
Executive editor: Jim Boyd
Project coordinator: Anne R. Garcia
Manufacturing buyer: Maura Zaldivar
Editorial assistant: Allyson Kloss
Cover design director: Jerry Votta
Cover designer: Nina Scuderi
Art director: Gail Cocker-Bogusz
Marketing director: Bryan Gambrel

© 2002 Prentice Hall PTR
A Division of Pearson Education, Inc.
Prentice-Hall, Inc.
Upper Saddle River, NJ 07458

Prentice Hall books are widely used by corporations and government agencies
for training, marketing, and resale.

The publisher offers discounts on this book when ordered in bulk quantities.
For more information, contact: Corporate Sales Department, Phone: 800-382-3419;
Fax: 201-236-7141; E-mail: corpsales@prenhall.com; or write: Prentice Hall PTR,
Corp. Sales Dept., One Lake Street, Upper Saddle River, NJ 07458.

All products or services mentioned in this book are the trademarks or service marks of
their respective companies or organizations.

Printed in the United States of America

10 9   8   7   6   5   4   3   2   1

ISBN 0-13-066836-2

Pearson Education LTD.
Pearson Education Australia PTY, Limited
Pearson Education Singapore, Pte. Ltd.
Pearson Education North Asia Ltd.
Pearson Education Canada, Ltd.
Pearson Educación de Mexico, S.A. de C.V.
Pearson Education–Japan
Pearson Education Malaysia, Pte. Ltd.

CONTENTS

2   THE FIRST ESSENTIAL CHANGE: 19 FREE PEOPLE TO TAKE THE LEAD

3   THE SECOND ESSENTIAL CHANGE: 43 PROMOTE CREATIVITY, INNOVATION, AND FUN AT WORK

4 THE THIRD ESSENTIAL CHANGE: 71 SWITCH FROM BOSS TO COHORT

5 THE FOURTH ESSENTIAL CHANGE: 95 MASTER THE 4E's OF INVOLVEMENT

PREFACE

Powerful Leadership embodies a new paradigm of leadership that respects and unleashes the potential of people. This is anything but a Pollyanna approach to a serious issue in organizations around the world. The development of more powerful leadership has been and continues to be one of the most concrete goals of society. In fact, having powerful leaders is a must for the survival of companies, institutions, governments, and even countries. Leadership development is a global issue.

This book identifies seven essential changes that elevate leadership and unleashes the latent potential of people in organizations. Leading people in new and invigorating ways must be the paramount objective in fulfilling the vision of the new economy.

We do not intend to survey all the literature on leadership or incorporate all of the current perspectives on leadership in this book. We have, however, included references and insights derived from the extant literature that supplements our perspective in a special section at the end of the book. Please study through those insights for additional ways of thinking about powerful leadership principles. The speeches in Appendix A are primarily examples of the thinking of contemporary individuals who have succeeded in leadership positions, and they deserve your careful reading.

We have avoided putting traditional reference symbols in the body of the book, such as names with dates in parentheses, but we have included publication data in the section on references. We have included some sayings and observations between paragraphs to provide further insights and to occasionally provide humorous interludes. In some cases the sayings are part of the folklore of the American culture and do not have specific authors.

This book was written to be read by individuals who serve in leadership positions at all levels in the organization, from chief executives to supervisors, as well as by leaders in the community who serve as administrators and board members of volunteer groups and organizations. Government leaders, business leaders, religious leaders, community leaders, educational leaders, and leaders in sports and entertainment will all find a new way to work with their cohorts if they follow the essentials described in this book.

Although the chapters of this book tend to follow in a logical sequence, the basic themes appear in every chapter. Themes like free people to take the lead, enable them to contribute more to the organization, help them grow and develop as well as enjoy their work, and keep yourself strong enough to withstand some of the frustrations and anxieties that come as you serve in leadership roles can be found in variations throughout the book.

The content overlaps in certain ways, resulting in positive repetition of the ideas right when you need the reinforcement. Though each chapter can be studied separately and will assist you in making some improvements in the way you lead, the full impact of these seven essential changes occurs when all of the topics are implemented simultaneously. Consider how difficult it is to encourage trust, risk taking, creativity, and innovation when you appear cool and aloof to workers. An awful clash occurs when you try to free people to take the lead but come down on them with criticism and fail to applaud their accomplishments. Occasional standing ovations thrill even the most staid workers and support them in making changes to improve the workplace or work process.

Leaders who free their cohorts to look at processes and systems more innovatively increase the effectiveness of their quality improvement programs. At the same time, working with fewer restrictions, cohorts implement quality improvement efforts more smoothly. When the structure of a work system is changed to introduce teams, cohorts will work more collaboratively and energetically.

Tensions in all parts of the world seek to undermine our confidence in leaders. Misdeeds and deliberate attacks on both our workplaces and our sensitivities shake the confidence we feel in anyone's ability to lead. This should encourage all of us to examine the mindsets that we bring into leadership positions. We know that much can be done to develop, improve, advance, and make progress in the way in which we lead. The seven changes proposed in this book restore trust, unleash the power of workers, and uncomplicate the lives of leaders.

ACKNOWLEDGMENTS

We acknowledge the enormous contribution of several individuals to this book. For their prior wisdom and special way of articulating their ideas, we thank Robert Staub, Warren Bennis, Paul Hersey, Steven Covey, Spencer Johnson, Jack Zenger, Stephen Robbins, and Gary Yukl for the wealth of ideas they have provided as background for our thoughts. We especially acknowledge the debt we owe to Sid Parnes and his work on creativity.

We appreciate the assistance and perceptive guidance of Tim Moore and Jim Boyd, and their staffs of diligent and dedicated individuals at Prentice Hall.

Finally, we recognize the wonderful transformational influence that occurs between our spouses and us whenever we prepare a manuscript. A thousand cheers to Sandra Stephan and Gae Tueller Pace—we love and salute you.

Eric Stephan
Orem, Utah

R. Wayne Pace
St. George, Utah

PROCLAMATION ON LEADERSHIP

Leadership may be understood in a multitude of ways, but powerful leadership is based on a philosophy of the nobleness of the human spirit and soul, and the persistence and doggedness of people in maximizing their potential. It has been written that "whatever their future, at the dawn of their lives, [people] seek a noble vision of [their] nature and of life's potential" and that "it is not in the nature of [people]…to start out by giving up, by spitting in one's own face and damning existence" (Rand, xi).

We choose to declare, therefore, that the prime purpose of leadership is to maximize the potential of people and assist them in kindling the fire within their souls in order to move the world and give meaning to life. Leaders should be undaunted in the face of corruption and fierce in achieving a sense of the proper stature in which people should be held.

This doesn't mean that everyone in a particular generation will comprehend these great underlying principles. Possibly only a few will grasp their full significance, but it is those few who will move the world and give life meaning. Nevertheless, powerful leaders at every level of the organization must learn to open wellsprings of insight, inspiration, and effort from the people with whom they work. They must see others as fellow cohorts and allow them to do everything within their power to succeed. We proclaim that leadership in the next decade must respect and release human potential in order for the new economies being thrust upon us to experience their greatest success.

Lead we must and lead we shall, but in a way that exalts the self-esteem of people and recognizes the sacredness of their happiness on earth. Powerful leaders demonstrate a resolute determination to give shape to the vitality of people and lead them in good purposes. Powerful leaders look within their own hearts, overcome their own ignorance, and face outward to move the world.

POWERFUL LEADERSHIP

1

HOUSTON, WE HAVE A PROBLEM!

For millions of workers around the world, the old gung-ho is gone. They talk and mutter and gripe about their frustrations at work. You don't even have to listen carefully to hear workers complain about managers, to hear managers complain about workers, and to hear both complain about the company. More than a decade of trying to run *leaner and meaner* has resulted mostly in meanness, making a shambles out of company loyalty of workers and throwing a blanket of distrust over every boss.

The complaints of most workers are usually about the boss, the infighting, the lack of support, and the boring tasks and restrictive rules and policies. A local beer-company employee expressed the pain, "It's just a job now, just a job. It used to be fun. When you made deliveries, you were the 'Pabst man or the Schlitz man,' and it made you proud. Now it's dog-eat-dog. The only things that anyone cares about are volume and money."

1

If you want loyalty, get a dog.

—Anonymous

Corporate loyalty no longer exists, faith in the hierarchy and bureaucracy is dead, the distressed employee is replacing the company man, and most organizations are experiencing difficulty in implementing quality improvement programs, simultaneous engineering systems, teams, and an assortment of strategic planning initiatives. The challenge of the decade is how to lead an organization of people who feel abused, feel confused, and don't want to follow.

What's happening? Alan Wolfe, a contemporary philosopher, passionately asserts that America, and other cultures as well, have become "decentered." Not only is life changing, which makes once-appropriate theories and ideals less relevant, but also the changes themselves do not seem to fit any recognizable pattern. Decentering means, simply, that the world around us is losing the center that holds it together and makes sense of living. We are living in a *quandary*.

Out-of-Sync Systems

Sometimes it seems like the whole world of work is out of whack. The company has one agenda, the worker has another, and the manager usually can't figure out either one. Company policies and procedures get in the way of doing the work in the most efficient manner. Core competencies are not in accord with changing customer needs. Everyone except the worker is defining the way in which work is to be done. Someone always seems to be restructuring someone else. Quality improvement usually ends up meaning doing more, faster, instead of doing less, more profitably. And no one seems sure anymore about what kind of "self-direction" will be rewarded and what will be criticized.

Living in a Quandary

Diversity, complexity, and contradiction surround us on every side. We are in the continual predicament of trying to get organized. The consequence, especially in the workplace, is an uneasy state of perplexity and doubt. Quandaries lead to a quagmire of anxiety and confusion. Inside each of us is a gnawing concern about how to handle daily decisions. Rapidly changing conditions and repeated chaos undermine our confidence in what we should think and do. The toll on all of us is heavy, but on managers and administrators who are supposed to be clarifying the situation and pointing the way, the burden is exceptionally damaging.

Confusion at Work

The number one difficulty of effective management today is confusion in the workplace. Following Wolfe's analysis, it is clear that the complexities of living in organizations mean that old patterns of social life and old expectations about how one will live one's life at work are replaced, not by new patterns and expectations, but by incoherence and ambiguity. This grappling with puzzling, bewildering, and knotty situations is illustrated perceptively by conversations with a wide range of managers. Listen in on one such discussion:

"How are things going here at Wonderful American Products International?" (Any similarity between this name and an actual company is a one-in-a-million long shot.)

"Pretty good, thanks."

"What's the mission of this company?"

"PEP, PEP, and more PEP!"

"What does PEP mean?"

"PEP stands for Productivity, Efficiency, and Profits."

"One of the PEP boys, huh?" (Bad comment, no laughter; in fact, not even a smile.)

"Those sound like fairly mainstream goals. So what's the problem?" (Asked in a redeeming tone of voice.)

"The people I manage are dumber than dirt—at least they act like it. They couldn't care less about productivity, efficiency, and profits, especially profits." (This particular comment seemed to be quite amusing to the other managers.)

"Frankly, our *be-nice-to-employees-and-they-will-be-nice-to-you* management approach hasn't been very effective. They don't trust us, and, truthfully, I don't trust them."

"Empowering first-line managers to make decisions and develop a few strategic planning initiatives has led to almost total chaos and was a huge and costly mistake."

Wishing to change the subject a little, we asked, "How is
employee morale?"

A manager in the midst (or should that be mist?) said, "They
are good people. They do their work and get their jobs done."
Over his shoulder another manager commented, "You know,
I really don't know how they feel. All right, I guess."
Leaning against a machine, a third manager urged, "Why
don't you go and ask them?"

As a matter of fact, we did act on the suggestion and talked to quite
a large number of employees. We were not surprised to find that they,
indeed, weren't too happy about their circumstances, but they needed the
jobs and were not anxious to quit. Strangely enough, when we asked them
what they thought of their bosses, almost unanimously and without much
hesitation, they said that their bosses were "JERKS!"

In a recent survey, employees of a high-tech aerospace manufacturer
were asked, "What is keeping you from achieving your goals at work?"
The clear-cut majority of respondents said that it was "management and
team leaders" who were the source of their problems, and the company
had too many chiefs.

Adding Misery to Confusion at Work

As part of his introduction to *Working,* Studs Terkel characterized a
second fierce problem plaguing modern organizations. He said, "This
book, being about work, is, by its very nature, about violence—to the
spirit as well as to the body." Workers sing both the blue-collar blues and
the white-collar moan. The two factors that contribute most to the blues
and the moans are the work itself and the manager.

As Komarovsky so poignantly describes in her account of the *Blue-
Collar Marriage,* the kind of work one is allowed to do serves as the
foundation of economic deprivations, anxiety about the future, a sense of
defeat, and a bleak existence: "The low status of the job, in addition to
low pay and unfavorable working conditions, is a frequent source of dissatisfaction.... Daily life is a constant struggle to meet the bills for rent,
groceries, a pair of shoes, a winter coat, and the TV set and the washing
machine."

For the white-collar worker, Freudenberger, a prominent psychiatrist,
has captured the dread of work in his impelling treatment of *Burn Out*:
"Many men and women who come to me in pain report that life seems to

have lost its meaning. Their enthusiasm is gone. They feel uninvolved, even in the midst of family and friends. Their jobs, which used to mean so much, have become drudgery with no associated feeling of reward."

Exhaustion from intense mental concentration, long hours in routine and repetitive tasks, and constant changes in tasks already completed lead to cynicism, irritability, paranoia, and mistrust of others. The demand to achieve more with less and less catapults us into voids of anguish and precipitates sudden outbursts of emotional energy designed to relieve us of the pressure of work, work, work.

Ripping Faces Off People

Scott and Hart, prominent authors in organizational theory and philosophy, place this malaise in the context of the "insignificant people." They argue that organization members are ruled by a managerial elite who, in order to maintain their place as rulers, must convince members of the workforce that, in relationship to the organization, the individual is *insignificant*. Workers are told how valuable they are, but they are then treated as invaluable and told to "quit if you don't like it here." The goal of managers seems to be to indoctrinate the workforce to understand and accept their insignificance in relation, particularly, to the superior goals of the system.

Further, misery and confusion arise because of the need in modern organizations to educate more members of the workforce to handle the increasingly more sophisticated demands of their jobs. Thus, even though the training may be simply technical, it encourages people to think. Thinking tends to lead people to reflect on the nature of their jobs. As they increase in technical expertise, they may recognize how dull, routine, and monotonous their work is and how antiquated the mindset of their bosses really is in this modern era.

The first rule of holes is when you're in one, stop digging!

—Anonymous

Managers Have Huge Blind Spots

One of the most distressing patterns in modern organizations is the apparent and long-standing view that *managers fail to recognize that employees are human beings who may be suffering at their hands.* Time after time, employees report in interviews and respond to surveys with essentially the same concern: People develop blind spots when they become managers.

Jaundiced Eyes

We've seen quite a bit of this yellow discoloration of the eyes in universities. When a faculty member is dragged, kicking and screaming, into the position of department chair, his or her initial understanding of problems is comfortably comparable with that of other faculty members. After being in the position for a few weeks or months, an alarming change occurs. The new chair seems to forget entirely what concerns he or she had as a faculty member. In only a short period of time, the new chair appears to exhibit a startling disregard for faculty concerns and a high regard for his or her new boss. Similarly, the move from worker to manager appears to short-circuit new managers' critical synapses so as to help them forget how little they really trusted their managers when they were workers. They forget how difficult it was to be listened to, much less how important it was to be rewarded and valued for their ideas.

How soon we forget that freedom is important in the lives of workers. Why do managers become consumed with the idea that they must direct and control the lives of others if they are to move up the corporate ladder?

After reviewing shifts occurring in business environments, Brandt observed that "unique events are increasingly the norm; at least they are common. And the correct responses are one-offs. *All the control systems can do in most companies is hamper the development of appropriate replies by the members of the enterprise.* Management heritage is aimed at order, not inventiveness or responsiveness."

The painful emphasis on control by managers led Macleod to identify factors that make employees feel like they are prisoners of the firm. They have little or no choice in their work lives. The range of options is very limited and the workers have little control over the conditions under which they work. They thus feel trapped and imprisoned. Additionally, like prisoners, they are under the control of people in authority who make decisions at their own convenience and by their own choice. There are rigid and arbitrary rules. Infractions of the rules are punished severely. Employees quickly learn about the negative consequences of disobeying or even speaking up in opposition to the orders, rules, and norms of the corporate culture.

Employees are also regulated by imposed time schedules and unwavering routines. Specified starting times at work dictate when the individual rises, has breakfast, and leaves for work. The worker may also need to meet a fixed train, bus, or commuter schedule both before and after work. The employee's time may almost be completely regulated from rising on Monday morning to arriving home on Friday evening. At one prominent company, employees are asked to work at least 50 hours each week. Commuting time takes an hour to get to work and another hour to return home. The train schedule adds an additional hour, and lunchtime tacks on another hour. Employees devote about 70 hours to work each week. Incredibly, this company takes great pride in advancing family values and encouraging employees to spend more time with their families.

At work, employees may be deprived of their individuality, be separated from their family and friends, occupy offices and quarters that have a lack of privacy, and labor in unpleasant physical conditions in workstations with limited space. The temperature, humidity, and cleanliness of the air is carefully controlled for computer equipment rather than for employees. Finally, appraisal systems implemented by powerful people who have secondhand, sketchy, and often inaccurate information, but whose decisions are final, may have a decisive and highly negative effect on employees' futures.

No wonder employees watch the clock, daydream, and expect little stimulation from the workplace. On the job, they only do what seems absolutely necessary, stay out of trouble, and try not to rock the boat.

Old Management Logic

Despite all the rhetoric about new age management styles, managers, as well as too many others, are still locked into an elitist, outdated "management logic." The old management logic runs something like this: The ideal system for creating products and delivering services is to take human beings and coerce them into following a specific set of procedures that hopefully minimize the risk of failure. At the same time, managers can pursue other policies that mold, shape, change, and control workers on the misguided assumption that management is responsible for making decisions for them.

At first glance, this doesn't seem like a terribly bad approach, at least for managers. In practice, however, it is fraught with difficulties. The first difficulty stems from having employees perform the same procedures day in and day out, week after week. Employees become bored out of their minds because they are not able to use their minds. Soon morale declines, energy levels dip, and in fact workers begin to discover ways to impede the work and strike back at managers and the company to compensate for the mindless, insensitive ways in which they are being treated. They begin to feel frustrated, tired, and imprisoned. Isn't it interesting that managers trap themselves in this old management logic and then turn right around and trap their workers in the same mindset?

The second difficulty that comes from following traditional management logic is that the demands on management make it impossible for them to figure out new procedures for workers to follow when the market changes. Thus, changing customer needs, the development of new technologies, and widespread decentering can't be responded to in order to ensure maximum profits and implant a no-failure effort.

Managers have tried in the past to keep employees interested in their work by such practices as rotating them from one job to another. Rotation doesn't work very well, because each job quickly becomes boring and doesn't use the workers' potential any better than the first one. When rotating workers resulted in even more complexity and contradictions, managers were urged to add more variety and depth to the work. Unfortunately, the variety is limited and the depth is restricted to fit the company's already existing rules, regulations, and processes. So, that doesn't help very much. It leads again to the popular metaphor of the workplace as a prison.

An Old View Restated

Workers are human beings who are ready to contribute to the company. They are intelligent and caring. They work, laugh, and cry like the rest of us. They have hearts and souls. They want to use more than just their hands to make the organization successful. They want to devote their minds, courage, wisdom, and spirit to helping the organization do its very best. The challenge, as managers, is to figure out how to release the energy of workers in order to encourage them rather than discourage them.

For employees, workplaces should be quite different from prisons, not only for the sake of the employees, but for the sake of better corporate competitiveness, effectiveness, and success.

The difficulties won't be easy to overcome, but it will be worth the try. Remember, you can only downsize so far before you go out of business. Costs can be cut only so much before profit margins start to flat-line. And one final thing is for sure—you will never get things right if you keep separating profitability concerns from people concerns.

Teams: The Panacea?

Some consultants have suggested that we put workers into teams to solve the problems of low productivity, quality, and morale. As Musselwhite and Moran point out, that seems to ease the pain for a while, but eventually teams begin to wear off and the same difficulties return.

We don't want to parade out all of the latest research on the failure of teams and other techniques, but we just reviewed a report from employees of a rather large healthcare operation. When asked to rate the effectiveness of their teams, these healthcare employees rated them about 40 percent effective. Obviously, they were underwhelmed by teams. Some organizations have abandoned teams and reverted to various forms of discussion and problem-solving groups. Incidentally, most teams ultimately fail in organizations because the work of the organization doesn't require people to work in teams.

A New View Restated

At some point we need to stop running from one management fad to the next, from one management philosophy to another, and move forward by going back to the fundamentals of managing people so that they feel valued and significant. At the risk of sounding too idealistic, we believe that it is possible to change what's going on inside of our heads by listening more carefully to our souls and leading a little more from the heart than from some set of unnatural prescriptions for management success. If we don't change, we'll continue to have more days like this humorous sign describes:

> *There are days when as soon as you open your eyes,*
> *you know you are in over your head.*

—From *Me Mum Sez*

We had to chuckle a little bit when one of our manager friends replied to an inquiry about how his work was going. His voice rose about an octave, actually just short of a scream, and he said something to the effect that "it's an H-E-double-hockey-sticks-week at work. Stress doesn't begin to cover what I'm experiencing. I'm lucky if I can squeeze in lunch and a call to my wife. When I finally get home, it's well after dark, and I'm so incredibly cranked up that I can't get to sleep."

Hell-week-at-work accompanied by new responsibilities and a plethora of new management techniques is not uncommon in today's organizations. New buzzwords pop up almost every day: diversity, time-to-market, collaborative individualism, 360-degree appraisals, de-jobbing, right-sizing, flexible compensation, internal strategies, and so forth.

Place all of this in the middle of a decade of downsizing, mergers, plant closings, leaner-meaner managerial organizations, restructuring and reorganizing, and it's no wonder that managers begin to question their own sanity about whether they should continue on as managers, or why they even became managers in the first place.

Deep down inside of each manager is a desire to feel more joy and serenity while at work. At the same time, managers realize that a multitude of personalities, talents, and skills must properly mesh if their business enterprise is going to succeed. At the end of a particularly frustrating day, many ask themselves, "Isn't there a better way? Is this really what management is all about? Am I truly enjoying what I am doing?"

At the present time, managers seem more confused and befuddled than they have ever been. Although their knowledge of management processes and techniques is greater than ever, this knowledge is, in a way, less satisfactory, for in every direction they are faced with contradictions, clouded issues, and immense ambiguity.

We are reminded of the debate about the difference between management and leadership and whether you can have one without the other. The cry on one side is to build brilliant competitive strategies, while on the other side people are urging, "Don't compete with anyone, focus on your customers." At a time when some companies are touting TQM, others are writing articles about why TQM doesn't work. To top it all off, we just read a document about how identifying and building upon "core competencies" can hinder a company's progress! What is the world of management coming to?

Managers find themselves in a position where the world has become so complex that they know very little outside their own areas. Explosions in technology, new forms of analysis, and sophisticated systems of doing business are usually only known by the people directly engaged in those activities.

Managers frequently hold meetings with other managers and administrators and try to make decisions about how employees should do their work and how problems should be solved. To make matters worse, they often spend hours encouraging each other to believe things that they don't know a lot about and to develop policies and directions that won't work.

Synergistic Ignorance

We call this phenomenon synergistic ignorance: the development of enthusiasm for plans from people who simply don't know, who have pooled their ignorance behind closed doors and developed a set of directions, rules, and guidelines that are supposed to help guide a group of frustrated employees who know more about the operations and their areas of expertise than do the managers.

Cheer Up!

This state of affairs should not be discouraging. On the contrary, it can be extraordinarily stimulating. Unrest provides the fuel for change and revolution. Our difficulties can be resolved by letting our imaginations and common sense construct and identify a few certain things that every manager can do to tap into the unused power of organizations. Managers and workers together have the power to turn organizations upside down and bring harmony and direction out of chaos. As you proceed forward in your quest, please keep in mind that failing to use the immense and unlimited potential of individual workers is extremely wasteful and is a travesty to society, to the organization in which the individual works, and to the individual.

As a tentative first step, we suggest that everybody—employees and managers alike—try "softer" rather than "harder." Ponder this oriental fable for a clue:

A young man traveled across Japan to the school of a famous martial artist. When he arrived at the dojo, he was given an audience by the sensei.

"What do you wish from me?" the master asked.

"I wish to be your student and become the finest karateka in the land," the young man replied. "How long must I study?"

"Ten years at least," the master answered.

"Ten years is a long time," said the young man. "What if I studied twice as hard as all your other students?"

"Twenty years," replied the master.

"Twenty years! What if I practiced day and night with all my effort?"

"Thirty years," was the master's reply.

"How is it that each time I say I will work harder, you tell me that it will take longer?" the young man asked.

"The answer is clear. When one eye is fixed upon your destination, there is only one eye left with which to find the way."

So it is with many things! The harder we try, the poorer the result and the more frustrated we become. This seems to be particularly true when working with people. The day-to-day effort of trying to keep everyone and everything moving forward while at the same time trying to meet your special commitments as managers, supervisors, and administrators often leaves you breathless and fatigued.

Yes, Houston, We *Do* Have a Problem

But unlike Apollo XIII, it is not an oxygen problem. We know that the problem is low worker morale, lost faith in the bureaucracy, and failure to take innovative actions to improve management practices. Over the years, we have surveyed Fortune 500 companies about their human resource practices (Stephan, Ralphs, Mills, and Pace). In our last survey of 300 managers, the most frequently reported difficulties they experienced were motivating workers to take more responsibility for their jobs, taking care of customers, making prudent decisions, being more innovative, and correcting mistakes without running to the boss for advice and direction on every issue.

Managers reported that they felt like they had to overmanage just to keep everyone going. But the more managers managed, the less initiative employees took. Inadvertently, managers found themselves worrying more and working harder and longer trying to meet productivity and efficiency goals. The managers found themselves trapped in a vicious cycle they hated. The more they managed, the less enthusiastic the employees were about using their own brainpower. The ultimate irony of all of this is that managers frequently feel just as frustrated as the employees.

Fortunately, because managers play such an important role in the lives of workers and are the single greatest influence on the job performance and satisfaction of workers, managers can pretty much clean up this mess by helping workers take more responsibility for winding themselves up each day and feeling more confident about making valuable contributions to the organization's success. You, as the manager, are the employees' only hope. You can buffer them from much of the organization's chaotic machinations and the accompanying confusion and drudgery at work.

When fellow workers are allowed, encouraged, and enabled to contribute their ideas, hearts, and hands more fully to the success of the organization in which they work, morale goes up, productivity increases, more prudent decisions are made, and collaboration is strengthened. Best of all, your efforts to help employees stand on their own two feet and feel more confident at work will allow you to worry less about what they are doing and spend more time doing what you need to do. And, of course, play a little more golf!

A close friend of ours was just made a senior manager in a large media organization. When he asked the president of the corporation for advice, the president gave him three succinct suggestions: Make a profit. Be honest. And have fun! The new senior officer realized that he could not achieve this interesting mandate by himself. Employees would need to share their ideas, dreams, and hopes in order to make a profit; they would need to have confidence in the company in order to make honest decisions; and they would need to feel more enthusiastic about their work in order to have fun.

His first challenge was to infuse confidence into his fellow workers by eliminating organizational restrictions that might inhibit their best efforts. He didn't waste much time in doing everything he could to show employees that they were free to improve the business.

If you want to fire up your people and get them more involved in sharing their ideas, like our senior management friend, we suggest that you do three things:

First, call a meeting of all employees and explain that they are to try out new ways of doing their work, without fear of penalties for fouling up.

Second, announce a policy that promotions will be based on demonstrated abilities to help and coach other employees.

Third, enthusiastically accept changes in their work and support them in their decisions.

Gradually, you will be able to withdraw from attending meetings where employees are making decisions. The momentum will begin to shift. Teams of employees will take responsibility for managing their own jobs. You will have time to meet with employees, treat them more friendly, and coach them to improve their work. Your life will become simpler as decisions are made closer to the work itself.

The Japanese have a wonderful saying: "Better to have many engines pulling the train than to have one engine pulling the train." Leadership is not for the few anymore, but for the many. Literally tens of thousands of supervisors, managers, and administrators are searching for ways to "spread engine power" among their employees, and at the same time, uncomplicate their own lives as managers. Unlike Apollo XIII, the space-craft doesn't have to be brought down and relaunched. What you have to do, however, is rethink and retool your present management approach to focus your energies on helping employees seize responsibility for their own work, which will unleash the power of organization members and the workforce.

Houston, We Have a Solution

In this small but insightful book, we will describe and advocate seven essential changes that you can make in your style of managing that will transform you into a powerful leader. Managers who have made these seven essential changes have noticed that their employees quickly lost their fears about raising thorny issues and "rocking the boat." Organizational members gained confidence in their abilities to confront problems and resolve them. The managers were pleasantly surprised to find that employees were able to streamline their work, reduce costs, and make their work more enjoyable. In addition, they discovered that they had more time and energy to do their work. The managers were on the path to powerful leadership.

Now, we'll provide an overview of the seven essential changes that will help you to become a powerful leader. These seven essential changes free you to do your own work better, with fewer complications and with more personal satisfaction.

The First Essential Change frees your immediate reports—employ-ees—from every unnecessary rule, process, procedure, and constraint that prohibits them from making changes in their own work to improve the efficiency of the workplace. We just talked to a manager at one of the top three computer companies in America. He said that workers sometimes refer to coming to work as "day prison." This perception is prevalent in hundreds of organizations throughout the world and needs to be changed as quickly as possible.

Rene McPherson, CEO of Dana Corporation, pared down its bureau-cracy by cutting 350 people from the corporate staff of 500 and replaced a 17-inch set of standard operating procedures with a slim, concise poli-cy statement. He stopped over 400 pages of management reports each month and prohibited managers from sending memos to their subordi-nates so that they had to meet face to face, and he removed all time clocks from the premises. He said that he didn't believe in corporate procedures because they were counterproductive and restricted the flexibility of people to cope with the unpredictable.

Managers tend to overmanage their employees. This practice creates more work for the manager and imposes severe constraints on workers. Overmanaging means that you are not allowing your employees to take the lead. You can free yourself up by freeing up your employees.

The Second Essential Change helps employees engage in more creative thinking and carry out more innovative actions. Most top executives realize that innovation is the key to survival. Making unique, interesting, exciting, and profitable changes is what keeps a company competitive. Unfortunately, few managers are taught how to release their own great creative potential and lead employees to experiment with innovations. Getting employees to examine their own work creatively and innovatively places the emphasis where it belongs. Harold Geneen, ITT's exceptionally successful CEO for many years, says that good ideas are hard to come by and "I always felt that as chief executive, it was incumbent upon me to welcome and foster creative thinking." Most top managers say that the most wasteful time you can spend is trying to get employees to do things well that shouldn't be done at all.

The Third Essential Change switches your relationship with employees from that of "boss" to that of cohort. The simplest truism in the world of leadership is that it is a lot easier to lead a friend than an enemy! And much less complicated. Roberto Goizueta, the CEO of Coca Cola, feels that to get people to do their best, you have to know them; bosses should not be regarded as gods, because they aren't. He described his management style with the acronym of CIO—coordinator, integrator, orchestrator. Goizueta, like so many very effective executives, spends much time coaching, teaching, counseling, and developing management talent, realizing that this talent is Coca Cola's greatest asset.

John Stollenwerk, president of Allen-Edmonds Shoe Corporation, never uses the term *employee*. He says he works at the plant just like anybody else. There are no reserved parking places for Allen-Edmonds workers, including the president, who had to park a great distance from the main door of the plant because he was late getting to work.

The Fourth Essential Change shifts managers' focus from delegating and trying to motivate people to the more powerful concept of "involvement" by mastering an energizing and dynamic approach that we call the 4E's of Involvement: envisioning, enabling, energizing, and ensuring results. As chairman and CEO of 3M, Allan Jacobson says that managers shouldn't be too narrow in their focus. They should "get other people active in and supporting your plans in order to make them real." You have to have a lot of people doing the right thing to get the job done.

When you have tried a thousand ways to motivate and reward people and you find out that people really aren't increasing their productivity in any significant way, you may want to alter your management style to incorporate the more natural 4E's approach for involving people.

The Fifth Essential Change helps managers avoid criticism and reprimands and moves them to the almost magical approach of applause and redirection. Criticism is absolutely useless in the workplace and reprimands have always been associated with punishment. Applauding and redirecting is definitely more useful and less harmful to employees. Robert Haas, CEO of Levi Strauss & Co, explains that his job is to create an environment for employees in which they feel that they can contribute, that their ideas are heard, that their opinions are taken into account when decisions affecting them are made, and that they understand the importance of their contributions to business success. Haas emphasizes listening rather than telling, and this listening should be accompanied by a relentless curiosity directed toward making things better. Being critical of others is totally antithetical to powerful leadership.

When Robert Kirby was CEO of Westinghouse Electric Corporation, he reflected on the old style of management and observed that a few years ago, a manager would fire you on the spot if you told him or her you had lost five million dollars. Then, the next time you made an error, you wouldn't go and tell the manager. That's no way to run a company. When people came to Kirby with bad news, it was his job to help them out, not ship them out. The manager should be the repository for bad news rather than the employees' worst critic.

The Sixth Essential Change insists that managers take the high road in making decisions. Taking the high road is the simplest way to restore trust and good will between the manager and workers and among the workers themselves. And, of course, save the company from a pile of legal troubles and lawsuits. Robert Haas of Levi Strauss does not do business in countries with lists of human rights violations. He has an unprecedented affirmative action policy and an outstanding employee benefits package that supports his "high road" approach to employees. As CEO of Phillips Petroleum, Pete Silas imbued the company with the spirit of volunteerism, encouraging employees to be involved in community activities and permitting workers to take time off from work to participate. He considers involvement in local communities to be a corporate responsibility. Taking the high road in both personal and workplace decisions is critical to exercising powerful leadership.

The Seventh Essential Change places managers on the peaceful path. A powerful leader has a willingness to confront adversity and the ability to deal with it calmly. Powerful leaders strengthen themselves so that they don't become fatigued and overwhelmed while trying to be effective. Walter Williams, CEO of Rubbermaid, says that being physically fit pays off for a manager's mindset. If you stay in good shape, you are going to be healthier, more astute, and more tuned in. Kay Koplovitz, CEO of USA Network, is an avid camper and hiker and prefers to spend her off-hours in the wilderness. She feels that when you get away from what you do every day, you come back much more relaxed. As CEO of Westinghouse, Paul Lego engaged in a number of practices to ensure time for himself to strengthen his mental and physical well-being. For example, he rose at 4:45 a.m. and ran every other day. He got a lot of ideas as he ran and actually had time to think them through. While John Hall was CEO of Ashland Oil, he maintained a robustness by speed walking, weightlifting, and golfing—mostly playing golf. He set a less hectic pace than other CEOs and encouraged employees to have a more balanced family life. Making this essential change is really the key to personal survival and peace of mind, both at work and in daily living.

Managers who are willing to make these seven small changes in their management style can significantly improve employee performance and morale, and at the same time uncomplicate their own lives as managers. In fact, we always chuckle a little when managers report that by implementing these seven essentials, they have eliminated most of their "brilliant management failures!" Allen Jacobsen, CEO of 3M Corporation, says that 3M looks for people who have a fairly good balance between work, family, and community. In addition, he feels that his father's statement, "Provide your own leadership," is sound advice.

Powerful leaders regularly implement these seven essential changes. You too can increase your influence as a powerful leader by following their example.

2

THE FIRST ESSENTIAL CHANGE: FREE PEOPLE TO TAKE THE LEAD

The highest and best form of efficiency
is the spontaneous cooperation of a free people.

—Bernard Baruch

Time magazine devoted its December 7, 1998, issue to the most influential business geniuses of the century. "Managing to be best" was one short section touting the talents of the century's smartest bosses: Coke's Roberto Goizueta, General Electric's Jack Welch, Wal-Mart's Sam Wall, and Panasonic's Konosuke Matsushita. After characterizing their accomplishments, the author, Ram Charan, asked the question, "Do these four share common traits other than their leadership and superb business acumen?" Charan's answer was yes: "They were curious folks and hence lifelong learners. And they paid attention to people, realizing that the potential of

19

any enterprise hinged on giving subordinates the maximum opportunity to succeed." Then, Charan made this prediction: "Even in the 21st century, these characteristics will still be required of great managers."

Most organizations are land-mined with various devices that restrain, confine, and restrict employees from contributing their best efforts at work. Poll-taker Gallup reported in March 2001 that 55 percent of employees have no enthusiasm for their work, while 19 percent are so negative about their work that they poison the workplace to the point where the companies might be better off if such pessimistic employees called in sick. Workplaces are laden with constraints that repress, limit, regulate, restrict, bridle, check, curb, and put down employees.

Although this book tends to focus most directly on managerial practices, one element of the work system, three other elements—the guidelines or policies, the work itself, and the structure of the system—exercise powerful constraining influences on workers. In order to free your people, it will be necessary to make adjustments to each element in the total work system, not just in managerial practices. Remember that what you do as a leader should allow others to take the lead in making adjustments in the work system.

If you demand good work from your people, *you must free them* from any rule, procedure, policy, routine, approval, report, job description, structure, bureaucratic expectation, and workplace process that doesn't make sense and limits employees from growing, developing, and contributing their very best at work.

As you read about this first essential change, you will be absolutely shocked at how many restrictions and constraints have been placed upon employees. In too many organizations, we have not only bound and gagged our people and stifled efficiency, but we have also put employees to work for the boss and the bureaucracy rather than for the customer.

Let Them Take the Lead

Why free your people to let them take the lead? Because most, if not all, human beings have brains and a surprising amount of untapped energy. It is unnatural to squeeze a human being into a milk carton. Besides, if you demand effective work from your people, they have the right to demand the freedom and resources to do it well.

There is also a very practical reason why you should liberate your people from organizational constraints. If your people are free to think and act, to innovate and figure out better ways of doing things, your managerial burdens will become lighter. You will succeed or fail as a leader, not by what you do, but by what you encourage and allow others to do. The question that you must ask yourself each day is not what did I do as a leader today, but what did I do to allow others to take the lead today? Quite obvious, isn't it? The more you encourage others to take the lead, the more growth, development, and responsibility they have, and the more time you have to figure out long term goals and, of course, to engage in some leisure-time activities. Ultimately, as you make each of the seven essential changes that we suggest, you will learn how to point the way and then get out of the way. This may be quite a turnaround from your present method of management; however, it is being done by other managers and leaders, and you can do it also. Now back to the first essential.

When you free up employees to take the lead, they discover new and innovative approaches to increasing profitability and achieving customer satisfaction. Banks have been deregulated. Airlines have been deregulated. Utilities have been deregulated. Start now to deregulate your workers by believing in their great potential and eliminating restrictions.

Today's employees want not only the freedom to redesign their jobs, but also a say about the way things are done in the organization. You need to create an environment in which people can contribute, in which their ideas will be heard, and in which their opinions will count when decisions are being made.

Robert D. Hass, CEO of Levi Strauss & Co., has commented that at Levi Strauss 36,000 pairs of eyes and ears are tuned to the marketplace all the time. Haas wants to involve as many people as possible in making Levi Strauss a world-class company that shapes the future in its markets. Levi Strauss is trying to develop a management style that gives the workers the confidence to respond in real time to changes rather than wait until some spiral-bound study works its way up to the chairman's office.

We believe that if you kick down a few doors and knock over a few walls that get in the way of your people, you will find your workers much more fulfilled and energized by the work that they do. You may discover that your own people have the best ideas about product and service improvement and about creating an environment where work is more fun than drudgery. As an effective manager and leader, your best opportunity to free your people will come as you **encourage them to take the LEAD!**

Stop Strangling People

It wasn't long ago that a subtle change began to appear in the workforce. It wasn't noticeable until the 1980s when Yankelovich, the polling company, discovered emerging trends in business and industry. The surveys revealed that

> the leaders who run our institutions do not really understand today's workforce: tens of millions of well-educated [workers], proud of their achievements, zealous of their freedoms, motivated by new values, with substantial control over their own production, and ready to raise their level of effort if given the proper encouragement.

The concept of allowing employees to think creatively and implement solutions to problems that arise has not yet been widely realized. In a few paragraphs, we will outline a better way to manage the people who will be leading in the future. With this different paradigm for understanding the contemporary workforce, a more effective form of leadership can emerge.

Although the workforce landscape may be slightly obscure, revealing only glimpses of a figure here and there, it is striking enough to signal a shift in conditions necessary for exercising effective leadership. Follow along for a moment.

Consider these six characteristics of members of the contemporary workforce identified by Yankelovich:

1. well-educated,

2. proud of achievements,

3. zealous of freedoms,

4. motivated by new values,

5. wanting substantial control over production, and

6. ready to raise level of effort with proper encouragement.

What implications do these characteristics have for organizational leadership? For leadership in general? Consider some basic assumptions that must be overturned when trying to lead that kind of workforce.

First, you must relinquish any thoughts of having a stranglehold over those who work with you. The current workforce is more highly educated than any previous workforce, and the importance of freedom in decision making is understood.

Second, you must give up traditional motivational techniques, such as rewards and punishments. The fact is that with proper encouragement, workers will extend their own efforts and take responsibility for their own lives. So-called rewards should be used simply to confirm the good work done by employees.

Third, you must give up thinking that you have an advantage over employees in initiating actions, getting new ideas, and creating innovations in the workplace. Members of the workplace have the talents, abilities, and interests to do a better job of improving the workplace than you do.

Fourth, and lastly, you must never constrain, restrain, restrict, hinder, or hamper your cohorts in their pursuit of excellence, high quality, outstanding performance, and enjoyment in the workplace. The clarion call is fourfold: Let them work free, let them move ahead, let them aspire to great things, and let them want more and more and more of the abundance that comes from success.

Leaders in the new economy free their workers to aspire, to move, to want, and to achieve. In turn the new leaders free themselves to be supportive, helpful, and sustaining. The new leaders walk side-by-side with those whom they work with in the organization. They facilitate, encourage, empower, capacitate, allow, permit, aid, assist, support, and benefit those with whom they work. They free those with whom they work from the mundane, the routine, and the anguish of organizational trauma. The new leaders are mindful of the needs of their colleagues and free them from organizational constraints.

As President Franklin Delano Roosevelt so cogently expressed,

> We look forward to a world founded upon four essential human freedoms. The first is freedom of speech and expression—everywhere in the world. The second is freedom of every person to worship God in his own way—everywhere in the world. The third is freedom from want—everywhere in the world. The fourth is freedom from fear—anywhere in the world.

Freedom to express oneself in the workplace, freedom to feel uplifted and spiritual in the workplace, freedom to feel secure in the workplace, and freedom to feel confident and respected in the workplace are the standards that must guide the very thoughts and actions of the new leaders in the workplace. The new leaders have new paths to trod, new roads to travel, and new freeways to cruise, where they must relieve sorrow, tribulation, doubt, and turmoil. They must inspire, succor, share, inquire, enlist, and facilitate. These new concerns are no longer reserved for the weekend. These new concerns are no longer reserved for religious leaders. These new concerns are no longer relegated to social events. These new concerns are no longer part of the myth and warp of the weak. These new concerns are now the obligation and the opportunity of leaders of the new economy. They must move from run-of-the-mill managers to powerful leaders of people. The longer we wait to move to the next level, the greater the risk of declining morale, profits, and efficiency.

Avoid Sheep Dog Management

Most organizations have been designed around the concept of command and control rather than around the concept of freedom. Too many managers still practice a form of tailkicking to get the work done. They improve their management styles by strengthening their legs with a little weight training and consulting a martial artist on the most sensitive parts of the anatomy to kick, rather than by making the seven essential changes. They become better tailkickers, but they don't become more powerful leaders.

> *Bark-and-bite management is also out,*
> *unless you are trying to be a sheep dog.*

> —Anonymous

Excessive numbers of managers are trying to think, plan, and organize without employee input; then they try to tell the workers what to do to change and improve. This directive style of management is out, or at least it should be. It simply doesn't work well. Today's workers are better educated than in the past, and more able to contribute their own thinking to the job. Some jobs have become so complex that the workers actually know how to do the work better than the manager does.

Rene C. McPherson, famous for his leadership style at Dana Corporation put his faith in his employees and argued that in a 25-square-foot manufacturing setting nobody knows more about how to operate a machine, keep it running, maximize its output, and optimize the flow of materials than do the machine operator and the maintenance people responsible for it. Nobody.

The competitive nature of the marketplace requires quick change in the way we do work, produce products, deliver services, and respond to the needs of customers. The people who do the work need to be able to make the decisions and implement changes so that everything is done with maximum directness and efficiency. Managers can't decide everything anymore, and no one has time to wait for a feasibility study. We are talking about real-time actions and decisions. No manager can hope to succeed in today's workplace trying to micromanage the work life of their reports. Powerful leaders don't make the employees' decisions. Effective leaders let the employees tell them the decisions that they have made. If the leader suspects a problem with the decision, the leader simply asks the employee how the decision was made. This gives the leader an opportunity to see if anything has been omitted from the employee's decision-making process. If the leader has some information that needs to be conveyed to the employee, the leader shares the information and asks if the employee wants to modify the decision. Notice again that the best leader doesn't make employee decisions but allows and encourages the employee to come up with solutions. This is another way to encourage employees to take the lead.

The Work System Is a Major Constraint!

When we talk about a work system (see Figure 2–1), we're referring to key elements in the organization that surround the workers. Nearly every constraint on workers may be associated with some feature of the system in which they work.

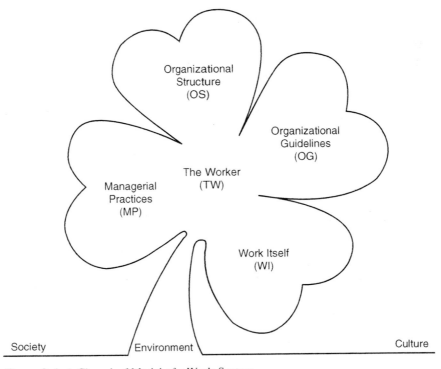

Figure 2–1 A Cloverleaf Model of a Work System.

In our depiction of the work system you may have noticed that we placed everything in the form of a cloverleaf. This is what we call an *organic model*. The four leaves touch each other and have a common stem system, representing a work system that is alive, can be made to grow healthy, and has flexibility. Removing constraints in one part of the work system usually contributes to the health of other parts of the system. For example, when you eliminate an unnecessary policy, it may facilitate changing the way the employee is allowed to do the work. Changing structure frequently opens up the opportunity to get rid of a restrictive policy and increase the efficiency of work processes.

As you pursue the elimination of constraints in your work system, do not overlook restrictions placed on contacts among people. It is important that workers be able to make regular contact with others when they need to. Some ways of making contact may be stipulated by organization policies. In fact, the old "open-door" policy was an effort to allow employees to get around some of the specified reporting relationships by making contact with the boss just by walking into his or her office. You may want to revisit each element of the work system to discover how your workers are being constrained from contacting coworkers and others with whom they would like to associate.

In order to help you recognize constraining influences that affect the worker, we shall briefly describe three critical elements of the work system: the guidelines of the organization, the work itself, and the structure of the organization.

Let's talk about the guidelines first. The **guidelines of the organization** consist of all of the policies, rules, regulations, mission statements, and other statements that control the thinking, actions, and decisions of organization members. Decisions are based on "policies," another term for guidelines, and rules and regulations, whether expressly stated or just implied. Organizational guidelines create some of the worst constraints, restrictions, checks, curbs, and repressive actions that occur in work systems. Organizations that operate with a book full of rules and regulations are often called bureaucracies, which has taken on a pejorative and negative connotation because of the myriad of abuses when rules are adhered to rigidly. Although organizations need some guidelines to function a little bit consistently, the bulk of the guidelines are generally restrictive and unnecessary.

Examine with us an organization that you are probably familiar with and which seems to function in a loosely coupled state or with few tight controls, regulations, and rules—that is, until you look closely at how it actually carries out its business. We call it a college or university. The reality is that students, faculty, and support staff work within a heavy framework of rules, regulations, policies, and guidelines. For example, what determines who gets into a university? What determines which students get into which academic majors? What determines which courses and activities students must complete in order to graduate? Almost everything about the lives of students is governed by a policy or rule. Guidelines for entrance into a university, rules for courses required to graduate, and even regulations such as how to stand in line at commencement control and determine just about everything that happens to a student.

The lives of faculty members are likewise controlled and directed by policies, rules, and regulations. For example, policies limit when and how faculty members may give final exams, how grades may be assessed, and when grades are to be submitted. There are rules about office hours, treatment of students, and attendance at faculty meetings. Faculty members are governed by retention, promotion, and dismissal policies, as well as by contemporary harassment and discrimination policies.

In the past, employers were able to make any regulations, rules, or policies that they felt were desirable, but now there are lists of practices that are prohibited as a result of federal and state statutes. This results in adjustments to policies and practices and often requires employers to add more rules and regulations.

In formulating guidelines, companies should avoid three problems: (1) creating excessive or unnecessary rules and regulations that restrict what employees can do and that discourage creativity and innovation—too many restrictions provoke resentment among employees; (2) having too few rules, leaving employees uncertain about what constitutes acceptable workplace conduct; and (3) failing to clearly explain rules and policies, encouraging employees to bypass them because they do not seem necessary.

Powerful leaders in the new economy examine the organization's policies, rules, and regulations to make certain that they are not excessive, that they adequately describe acceptable workplace conduct, and that all of them are clearly explained in terms of what they are designed to achieve. The practice should be to cut out all policies, regulations, and other guidelines that unnecessarily restrict employees.

The most important principle to extract from this discussion is that it is the perception of the value of the rule that affects the behavior of employees. For example, a rule prohibiting employee use of a telephone may be viewed as unnecessarily inhibiting, but a rule about when employees are to come to work may be considered a positive act.

One way to identify unnecessary rules and regulations is to encourage employees to challenge any rule they feel is silly or unnecessary and then review the rule to see if it can be modified or eliminated. I remember when I was in the army being assigned to the standard operating procedures (SOP) office. My main task was to open the on-post mail and lay out all of the changes in the standard operating procedures for the day. I then went to an 18-foot shelf, located the appropriate binder, and replaced the description of the old procedure with the statement of the new procedure. We were comforted by the fact that, with so many rules and regulations, no one would be able to determine whether or not a person was doing the job correctly. The outlandish detail represented by the shelves and shelves of standard operating procedures was overwhelming.

Work with your employees to eliminate any rule, procedure, policy, or practice that prohibits the best efforts of anyone. For starters, try these powerful suggestions:

1. Become freedom fighters. Simply declare war on bureaucratic red tape. Remember, you are in this war together. You are fighting with your workers side by side. You have a common enemy, and there is no question that you are going to win.

2. Eliminate the invisible restraint called "they." Encourage everyone to identify who or what is "they." When someone even thinks or speaks about "they won't allow it," identify and destroy the "they" and find out who or what the real restraint is.

3. Use various forms of information technology to share ideas and exchange information. This is the quickest way to work around the bureaucracy and find better ways to do things. Even forming ad hoc groups at lunch to discuss creative ideas to enhance one's work will provide an opportunity to think outside the red tape. Then, perhaps, the new idea will make the restrictive policy pale in light of better ways to perform without the policy.

4. Focus on the customer and the customer's needs, not the appeasement of the people who enforce the rules and policies.

5. Finally, meet together regularly just for the purpose of identifying and eliminating unnecessary policies and practices that seem to be getting in the way of freedom in the work place.

The **work itself,** another important element in the work system, consists of the ways in which work is done, ought to be done, and could be done, as well as the tools and methods by which work is accomplished. Machines, assembly lines, and traditions tend to impose restrictions on activities of the workers and make them feel like prisoners of the work.

The location of equipment, the manner in which materials are acquired and processed, and the procedures used in completing work are all sources of serious constraints on workers.

When you encourage employees to study, analyze, and review their work to find ways to be more efficient and effective, you are encouraging them to identify and eliminate constraints. When you free employees to make changes in the way they do their work, you may find it necessary to change some of the guidelines that have been restricting them from making improvements in the work itself.

One way to make changes in the work itself is to help employees redesign the work. In the sales office of a large computer software company, for example, morale was low, the work was boring and routine, and the employees were on the verge of revolt. The work was task-oriented and fragmented. The flow of paperwork seemed at random, with files floating from desk to desk and with forms being checked and rechecked. Forms were never processed faster than the slowest worker could complete them because each individual performed only part of the process. Decisions that seemed complicated were sent to senior staff who failed to provide feedback on what they decided should be done.

An analysis of the workflow resulted in a reorganization of the work process. Each sales clerk was assigned a group of clients organized by geographical area. The sales clerk was able to take personal responsibility for accounts in that area. Notices were sent to clients, identifying the clerk directly responsible for their account. Clerks then established personal relationships with contacts in client organizations, signed their own letters, and spoke directly with their contacts. The result was a shift in perspective, from an impersonal clerk to that of an account manager. Errors were associated with specific individuals who were responsible for checking their own work. The account manager now followed up on his set of clients. The reorganization of work was around geographical areas with accounts managed by specific individuals. Employees were more motivated and found that they could more easily get helpful feedback about how they were doing, and the company increased its sales. The employees' feelings changed. They didn't work for the company any more. They *were* the company!

Recently we consulted with a large company in the hospitality industry. Among other things, we helped employees identify various methods of doing their work better and at the same time having a little more fun. We gave our final report in a large conference room where the general manager had gathered all the department managers. As part of our presentation of findings, we reported that in the "sweat shop area" of their organization, where part-time and full-time minority members were cleaning dishes, utensils, and pots and pans, the employees had made some dynamite suggestions about how to redesign the work to be less repetitious and faster. Also, these same employees made some excellent suggestions about how to improve the general working conditions in their area.

We were absolutely startled when the department manager over that area of the business said rather vehemently, "Are you telling me that I'm supposed to ask those part-time blankety-blank employees how they should be doing their work?" With probably more than normal volume, we replied, "That is exactly what we mean." Had this manager been a little more teachable, we would not have said anything else. However, as he continued to fuss and grumble, we revealed another aspect of our research, which showed that he was the least liked of all the managers in the room. You would have enjoyed the laughing and joking from the other managers who had received higher ratings from their employees. The point is that there seems to be a direct correlation between listening to your employees and helping them incorporate their ideas into the way that they do their work and their positive perceptions of you as a leader.

Leaders in this new and changing economy should examine work processes, enlist the help of employees, and assist employees in redesigning their jobs so that employees can be more productive while their jobs are made more interesting.

The **organizational structure,** the last element that we need to review, consists primarily of reporting relationships and contacts among members of the organization. Structure is often portrayed in the form of an organization chart, but the real structure of an organization consists of who actually reports to whom, with whom you are obligated to have meetings, and whom you are prohibited from contacting. Every organization structure tends to restrict or constrain who may contact whom.

A restricted set of contacts makes employees feel that they are living in a prison; it is usually a function of too many restrictions on whom they may contact and how they may make contacts.

Supervisors and managers introduce restrictions on employee contacts out of fear that they will lose control of their people. Workers who are allowed, or even possibly encouraged, to visit with employees in another part of the company may find out what others are doing and make a fuss when they get back. Anxiety over what employees might think and do if they are turned loose to talk with other employees can impel managers to promote a form of isolationism that thwarts the best intentions of serious and thoughtful employees.

Managers often derive a feeling of power from administering rewards, allocating resources, making decisions, and telling their employees how best to do their work. Controlling and exercising power in this manner is the opposite of what an effective manager should be doing. Employees should talk to other employees and supervisors about problems that they have solved and methods by which they obtained resources to carry out a project. They should also discover what kinds of rewards and benefits others have received as a result of their efforts. This kind of information empowers and enables employees to function more efficiently in their own area of work. Resources and significant rewards are often scarce in organizations. This form of freeing people enables them to discover ways and means for improving their work and being recognized that have eluded the manager.

A high-tech organization with which we worked as consultants enforced forms of contact so that employees were restricted from leaving their workspaces at any time except for emergencies. The employees resented their inability to see what other employees were doing in their work. They were openly hostile to other employees. The question was raised concerning what the consequences could be if employees were able to mingle and observe the work of others. At worst, there might be some lost time and a temporary slowdown in production. At best, employees would understand total plant operations, create friendships among individuals in other parts of the plant, and discover ways of doing their work that might be an important improvement.

Over the years, practices have been introduced to remove some restrictions from the workplace and create a structure that is designed to foster more contacts. For example, a traditional open-door policy illustrates the value of lifting contact restrictions. An open-door policy should say to employees that they are free to discuss any work-related problems with their immediate supervisors. If a matter is not resolved or if sensitive circumstances prevent discussing the problem with the immediate supervisor, employees may go to the supervisor's manager or to the manager of human resources. Nevertheless, the employee should not be penalized for using this open-door practice.

Such a policy specifies the structure in which employees are to function: The first contact is with the immediate supervisor; the second contact is with the supervisor's manager, and the third contact is with the human resources manager. The matter would probably stop there, unless the HR manager took it to another level. Employees would not likely make contact with someone more than two or three levels above their position in an organization. The open-door policy is an interesting first step, but far too restrictive. Managers must overcome their own personal fears about letting employees freely inquire of anyone in the organization about making work more efficient and more rewarding.

By the way, in the hospitality industry company that we examined, the plant maintenance people who were keeping every mechanical and electrical system functioning properly reported to the housekeeping managers, who were trying to give orders and directions to the maintenance people. These managers knew nothing about plant maintenance or preventing problems, or even redesigning antiquated heating and cooling systems. Everyone was frustrated with everyone else. The solution was simple: Redesign the work structure. That is, change the reporting relationships. In this case, the plant engineers wanted to report directly to the assistant manager of the hotel, who could understand reasons for updating some physical facility equipment and systems, and who could not only give permission but could obtain the resources to make the changes. Needless to say, the housekeeping managers were more than happy to get rid of issues about which they knew practically nothing. A simple structural change was made.

The restructuring of an organization by a powerful leader is illustrated by the work of Bob Martin, vice president of AT&T phone centers. When he took over, five levels of managerial staff existed between the sales associates and the vice president, with 5 regional managers and 10 area managers. Another 300 people provided support services to the stores, and the corporate staff consisted of 150 additional people.

Four years later, all regional vice presidents and staff had been eliminated, and the area managers had been reduced to 5, with only 30 people in staff-support positions. The total overall headcount was reduced 50 percent. The cost for staff functions was reduced from $1,000 per month to $400 by the second year. In addition to their regular work, middle managers took on the work of staff people. The division initiated a yearly meeting to talk about staff issues. The structure was flattened, and the division was able to respond more quickly to market demands and was more flexible in its work. The division had gone from being phased out in 6 months to contributing to the profits of the business. Only leaders who recognize the waste contained in weak work structures are able to achieve these kinds of goals.

Creating a Topless Paradigm

The *big* item on the agenda of the powerful people leader, and the best manager, is to help others succeed and grow. A new set of guidelines is required. A new paradigm is required. A new mindset must be acquired. The new leader in the new economy must lead with charity in order to energize with vigor. Faith, hope, and charity appeal to our inner selves and can make the world of work a better place. Charity that embodies goodwill, humanity, compassion, benevolence, tolerance, and graciousness and that rejects ill-will, hatred, selfishness, and malice is the charity with which the powerful leader is endowed.

Lilia Cortina and her co-author reported at the American Psychological Society meeting in Toronto, during the summer of 2001, that rudeness is poisoning the U.S. workplace. Seventy-one percent of workers surveyed said they'd experienced put-downs or condescending and outright rude behavior on the job. Researchers report that such disrespect causes employee anxiety and lower productivity. The worst off were lower level employees who were abused by powerful bosses. The message is clear: If workers are treated shabbily and bosses use the stick to get short-term organizational performance increases, workers will try to retaliate by undermining the organization and the boss. Morale goes down just about as fast as productivity.

Managers must move their styles to the next level, to a higher level, to a more effective level, to a level of less effort and greater results, to a level that produces increased quality, productivity, enjoyment, and profits. They need to learn from the past and move forward.

It is possible for you to transcend run-of-the-mill management and become a more powerful and effective leader only if you have a renewed commitment to human beings, not as resources to be used in organizations, but as partners in the process of building organization effectiveness. You must accept the inevitable conclusion that people who work in organizations are capable. Thus, your goal must be to help them get the best out of themselves.

Everyone Is a Genius at Something

Human beings are amazing organisms. As symbolic beings, they are both creatures of and creators of the culture in which they live. They are capable of remembering, imagining, hoping, and choosing. They are vulnerable to both their own choices and the choices made by others. They define both themselves and the world in which they live. Human beings are not constrained in their development, as are plants and animals; their instincts and drives do not limit them. They do not live in the immediate present alone, responding only to the forces and influences that impinge on them now. Every person has unique gifts, talents, and skills. Each person can think of things in unique ways, and can in fact do something better than others.

Human beings increase their capabilities as their choices or options are increased. At the same time, increasing people's options increases their capabilities. Thus, it is imperative that you capture the impelling principle that **the enhancement of people's capabilities frees them to achieve more**. Powerful leaders have the quintessential task of increasing workers' options, which naturally enhances their capabilities and allows them freedom to achieve more.

When you increase the capability of those with whom you work to achieve more significant and meaningful goals, you provide those same people with new access to freedom. The new workforce, the workforce of which the new leaders are part, cherishes freedom. As human beings, access to greater freedom is critical. As W. Somerset Maugham, English novelist and playwright, so gloriously declared, "If a nation values anything more than freedom, it will lose its freedom; and the irony of it is that if it is comfort or money that it values more, it will lose that too."

Lawrence A. Bossidy, Allied Signal's chairman and CEO, voiced his feelings that "this is America, after all. We're a freedom loving people, a democratic and entrepreneurial people. Americans don't like to be managed or treated like children. They want to be asked for their ideas and are willing to take accountability for their decisions."

Such is the challenge of effective leaders. Above all, they must develop the capabilities of their people and enhance their freedom. We join with Alfred Austin, English poet laureate, in asserting that

> So long as Faith with Freedom reigns,
> And loyal Hope survives,
> And gracious Charity remains
> To leaven lowly lives;
> While there is one untrodden tract
> For intellect or will,
> And men are free to think and act,
> Life is worth living still.

No more worthwhile path can be trod than to be instrumental in making people free to think and act and lead. This is no abstract and worthless platitude. This is a call to action. This is what will ultimately reenergize and possibly save someone else's work life and make your own life worth living. Be a leader who uses gracious charity to leaven lowly lives.

The Road to Freedom is Filled with Potholes

Through small steps, little acts, and simple movements, workers lose their freedom in the workplace. As James Madison so perceptively enjoined in a speech during the Virginia Convention, "I believe there are more instances of the abridgment of the freedom of the people by gradual and silent encroachments of those in power than by violent and sudden usurpations." Small decisions by run-of-the-mill managers have crippled so many in the workforce that Scott and Hart have reported that most employees find "routines and monotonies that are corrosive of life…within a week, [they] find the job dull, routine, and personally unrewarding."

Corrosive workplaces are places of lost freedom. Monotonous workplaces are places of lost freedom. Organizations cannot survive management styles that restrict, corrode, and destroy the freedom to think and act.

In late 1993, the *Monthly Labor Review* reported that there were about 15 million managers in the United States and probably more than 100 million managers worldwide. No small numbers, my friend. The question is, what are they all doing? And what do employees think about what their managers are doing?

In our research efforts to find out what employees thought of their managers, the most interesting and not uncommon response from employees was "I think my manager is brain dead!" When employees were asked why they thought their managers were such dummies, the most frequent comment was "My manager doesn't listen to what I say and doesn't encourage me to try out new ideas." What we are finding is that most managers who have been on the job for a few years are having a difficult time giving up control and converting their styles from that of a boss to that of a leader. Our prediction is that those managers who fail to change will ultimately become discouraged, be less effective, and finally lose their jobs.

While researching low morale of employees in several major companies, we asked a manager in the aerospace space division of one of America's Fortune 500 companies how things were going. We knew that this company had spent the last few years implementing a Total Quality Management program and had, in fact, spent tens of thousands of dollars making sure that it was done right. After a quiet pause, he answered in a thoughtful but rather direct way, "Same old crap." This manager continued, "We sit in groups and hold meetings and once in a while come up with some pretty good suggestions for making things better. But nobody listens. In fact, a few weeks ago we almost killed a couple of guys trying to do something the company way."

People are devastated when they spend time and energy trying to figure out a safer, simpler, more cost-effective way to do something and their ideas are not allowed to breathe the fresh air of life. Workers, however, become quite excited about following powerful leaders, not managers, because leaders have a wonderful way of making their people feel needed and valued. Moving your management style to the highest level means that you must become quick to acknowledge the talents, experience, and uniqueness that everyone brings to the workplace. As a manager, you must work hard to ensure that your workers make fulfilling and significant contributions at their place of work; you must free up your people to allow them to contribute and take the lead.

If your workers still see you as a classic, run-of-the-mill, talking but not listening manager, then you may be the major obstacle blocking their freedom to think and act, to create, and to enjoy their work. One acid test of whether you are a leader is to look around and see if you have any followers.

Take a Deep Swig for a Violent Jolt

Workplaces led by powerful people leaders are invigorating, energizing, animating, inspiring, and elevating. Workplaces led by powerful leaders excel at every level in the organization in quality, productivity, enjoyment, and profit.

We concur with Walt Whitman's rhetorical question from *Leaves of Grass*: "What do you suppose will satisfy the soul, except to walk free and own no superior?" Indulge us as we present a bit of humor about freedom at work, couched in American commentator Irvin Shrewsbury Cobb's description of Corn Licker. Paraphrasing, we say that the freedom to take the lead is like Corn Licker,

> When you absorb a deep swig of it, you have all the sensations of having swallowed a lighted kerosene lamp. A sudden, violent jolt of it has been known to stop a person's watch and snap his suspenders.

Recently, a special task force of about 10 people from a western steel company asked for an appointment to discuss some concerns within their organization. We met with them in a conference room where each person took a chair around a rather large table. For the next 45 minutes, members expressed their frustrations with how each division of the organization had declined in profits, efficiency, and morale. It became quite evident that top management, middle management, and the employees themselves were quite discouraged with what was happening in the company and feared that they might have to shut down the company and find employment elsewhere.

When members of the steel company task force had pretty well vented their feelings, there was a long pause. No one seemed sure that they had defined the problem well or knew how to begin solving the problem.

Knowing that people can't contribute to the achievement of organizational goals unless they know what they are, we asked the group to articulate the company's goals and any strategy it had for achieving the goals. Not one person in the room could respond to the question. It seemed apparent that they had little direction.

One thing that managers do is give a group or organization some initial direction. Managers "prime the pump." They get things started by helping people understand what they are supposed to do. Once things get underway, managers need to make sure that the forward motion is sustained by removing every possible organizational constraint.

The Two-Million-Dollar Listener

We have a young friend with a high school education who owns two very expensive cars and lives in a two-million-dollar home. When we asked him what he did to earn his millions of dollars, he related this informative story.

> I call myself a consultant. Generally, I can promise to increase business volume and/or profits by 10 to 30 percent for anyone who will let me interview a few people in the company. What I have found out is that the person who works on the job, eight to ten hours per day, day in and day out, week after week, month after month, not only knows the problems but also knows the solutions to the problems.

"Most managers," he continued, "don't realize the great value and potential of the worker and, consequently, discover neither the problems nor their solutions."

We asked, "So what do you do?"

The answer was, "I ask the employees the right questions and then listen to their answers. Then I take their answers back to management and show how they will save thousands of dollars over a year's time if they just implement the workers' ideas. And, of course, I suggest that they recognize and share some of the profitability of the workers' ideas with the workers."

"Sounds like a win-win idea," we said, "but couldn't the managers or the bosses do this themselves?"

The self-made consultant's answer was classic: "They could, but they don't."

We visited a major computer software company and asked about 700 employees to share their perceptions of what it was like to work for this company. By the way, this particular company believed that they were following Steve Jobs and the Apple culture, where people were encouraged to be creative, focus their efforts on being customer-friendly, and remove tons of bureaucratic red tape. The results were astonishing. The employees were not about to leave the company because of the very high pay, but they felt totally restricted in contributing their insights to help the organization accomplish its projected goals. The demographic section of our research project with this company showed that a substantial number of the employees in the surveyed division were college graduates. When interviewed personally and asked about their feelings concerning their work, the most common reply was "It's just lip service. We are asked to contribute our ideas, but nothing significant comes out of it. It's almost as if we don't exist."

We presented our findings to the appropriate manager with the warning that people were of a mind to revolt because they were unable to use their insights and talents; we predicted a wave of low morale and decreased efficiency. Nothing much changed in this organization with the exception that more and more decisions were made by top managers and passed on to lower levels of management and employees as "the best way to go." Many bright employees were laid off. Profits continued to decline. Soon the company was sold. Without oversimplifying, poor leadership contributed heavily to the fall of a once mighty company. The irony is that quite a number of highly educated and very able employees and first-level supervisors tried to speak out, but they were left mumbling to themselves in the company hallways.

Freedom First

Creating a generation of employees who take the lead is an exhilarating challenge. It is the first thing that must be done to release the full power of an organization. Freedom isn't something superficial. Freedom isn't a triviality. Freedom isn't to be taken lightly. Freedom must be given and taken without reservation and without compunction. Freedom in the workplace has a critical meaning.

Freedom in the workplace means being able to decide how the work is to be done. Freedom in the workplace means being able to make changes in the way in which work is done to make it more effective. Freedom in the workplace means being able to talk back to the supervisor or manager without fear of reprisal. As a manager, you must allow workers to talk back. Workers must be able to say what they think and feel, in a kind and gentle way of course, and without rancor on their part.

Freedom in the workplace carries with it the responsibility to care, to be concerned that the work gets done, and that the workplace is safe and attractive. Freedom carries with it the challenge to perform at your best level, to excel at what you do. Freedom in the workplace carries with it the obligation to be truthful and honest. When you are free, you are obligated to do all you can to advance the position of the company in which you are working.

Freedom in the workplace, however, offers every employee the opportunity to be greater, to aspire to greater things, to care and to want and to achieve beyond what they had anticipated before joining the company. Freedom is exhilarating, stimulating, invigorating, and enlivening. Life is fun when you are free. Life is sad and tragic when you are bound and gagged. Life is enjoyable when you are free. Life is depressing and disgusting when you are fettered and shackled. This realization of the fundamental nature of freedom in the workplace as the most critical underlying perception to active workplaces and productive employees has eluded most managers.

Most managers just do not realize that freedom in the workplace may be the most important element in a global environment where immediacy— spontaneous decision-making, direct action, and continuous analysis— must be contended with every moment of the working day. The freedom to think and act on behalf of the organization, the freedom to think and act on behalf of the customers and clients of the company, the freedom to think and act on behalf of the best interests of all employees in the organization, and the freedom to think and act on behalf of future generations of employees is a solemn responsibility and obligation. Nothing can be more important than taking every step possible to free employees to live and work at this level. This must be the first and primary concern of every leader.

I Hate this Place

We had an opportunity to be involved in some analysis and proposals for freeing employees in a company that was involved in the manufacture of aerospace equipment. Things had not been going too well, and one afternoon the plant manager was replaced by an experienced manager from another part of the country.

The new manager was knowledgeable about applications of the theory and practice of the social sciences in industry. In fact, he could quote most of the significant social studies in industry and explain their consequences and effects. He spoke positively about the importance of the people in the organization and in industry in general. Confidentially, we were advised that he was new to the area, and we might find that his actual management practices might be different from his expressed philosophy.

After a period of analysis and several visits to the plant, we were ready to offer some suggestions for ways to stabilize employee relations and put the plant back on target for achieving some of its stated technical goals, like reduction in the production and delivery of airplane parts. We met with members of top management, who deferred to the plant manager more frequently than usual, and began to introduce some of our ideas. The first suggestion was met with intense questioning about its relevance and possible difficulty of implementation. Although we had about 10 general suggestions, by the time we got to the third idea, we had the distinct impression that freeing employees was of very low priority. In a private meeting off the premises, a member of the management team expressed a deep apology for the manner in which our ideas had been received and indicated that an effort would be made to implement some of them in spite of the plant manager. Things did not progress as the new plant manager had expected. In this case, as with many others, freeing the employees would have been much more important to accomplishing the technical goals than new equipment or new work procedures.

I Love Working Here

Let's take a minute and talk about some of the things that can happen when you free up your employees. We were working with a healthcare organization that had a state contract for services comprising over 60 percent of its business. One afternoon, the state decided to change its way of doing business and canceled the contract. The CEO was devastated. With 90 employees, that meant laying off almost 50 of them. Maybe he wasn't a tough businessman because when he returned to his office, a tear trickled down his cheek as he contemplated what he had to do.

The next day, he called a meeting of all employees and presented the awful news to them. As he explained the serious loss of business, he sensed some rumbling among the group assembled. Eventually, one of the more outspoken employees asked for the floor and offered a plan. She said, "If you'll turn this problem over to us and not discharge any employees, we'll share the income loss and build the business so that it is better than it was when we had the contract." As the CEO, he was not certain what he should do, but given the serious state of affairs, he agreed to the proposition.

Immediately, employees organized into teams to consider ways in which business could be increased. Every employee was intently involved in discussions. Employees talked to their spouses and friends, reviewed the nature of the services they were providing, and sought out new contacts. Within a few short weeks, although the weeks seemed a bit longer to the CEO, business began to improve. In a couple of months, the company was breaking even. At the end of 6 months, the business had increased by one-third over what it had sustained with the state contract.

Incidentally, company headquarters were located in a rented building that was not particularly appealing. One of the committees created by employees concerned the maintenance of property. Although the CEO had tried for many months to get the owner of the property to landscape and improve the looks of the building, nothing had been achieved. However, the employees met with the owner of the property and explained their role in the revitalization of the business. The property owner was so surprised that he agreed to immediately landscape the area and paint parts of the building. The general appearance of the corporate headquarters was significantly enhanced through employee meetings with the property owner.

At the latest count, employees numbered over 160, and business was prospering better than it had at any time under the management of the CEO. At our last meeting, the CEO said, "Now, I just ask our associates what they think we should be doing. I concur with their suggestions and leave the office to visit other units while they get on with the business. We're having a great time. I just love working here."

Regardless of what you may have thought in the past of the idea of freeing up your employees, today you must reconsider. Today is, as a poster down the hall announces, the first day of the rest of your life. You don't have time to procrastinate on this issue. The decision to grant clemency to the employees with whom you work and give them more freedom, regardless of what they currently have, may be the most important decision you have ever made, and it may be the most important landmark of your career. Give it a try. Even though it might go down a little hard at first, you and your employees will enjoy the energizing "jolt" that will occur. Even though you may truly snap a suspender in the process, you'll like it.

What Comes Next?

In this chapter we described the first essential change that you need to make to take your management style to a level that will unleash the power of your organization. Freeing your people from organizational constraints that don't make sense in the first place will start to turn your organization from a jail into a house of freedom and new opportunity. We referred to the perception that people have of their manager as a boss who really doesn't value their worth to the organization. Freeing your people will change that perception in the quickest way possible.

Now we turn to another workplace challenge: How can you get people to be more innovative and creative at work? We all know there are easier, simpler, faster, and more cost-effective ways to do things. How can we take the tedium out of our places of employment and have a little more fun? As we achieve the "spontaneous cooperation of a free people," is there a way to encourage spontaneous creativity and enjoyment at work?

Creativity and innovation are freeing for workers. Paraphrasing quality guru Phillip Crosby, creativity is "an honest-to-goodness profit maker." Too many good ideas are not finding fertile work environments in which to grow. The next chapter is about making creativity and innovation certain and the steps that should be taken by managers to make it happen.

3

THE SECOND ESSENTIAL CHANGE: PROMOTE CREATIVITY, INNOVATION, AND FUN AT WORK

Show me a man with both feet planted firmly on the ground
and I will show you a man who can't even get his pants on.

—Anonymous

Welcome to the world of creative thinking and problem solving. This is where you live, just as we all do. Why? We all have goals to achieve, challenges to overcome, and problems to think through each day of our lives. Because today's organizations face numerous problems trying to meet customer demands for quality, speed, and low cost, they must have members who are able to think up new ideas and put them into practice on a regular basis.

Never tell people how to do things. Tell them what to do and they will surprise you with their ingenuity.

—General George Patton

Because unique products, services, and the means to produce them are more likely to come from individuals who are closest to the process rather than at the manager's level in the organization, it is infinitely more important to stimulate and encourage creativity at the workers' level than at the management level. As we pointed out in the last chapter, you should free your people and encourage them to take the lead. That great principle can be applied directly in creating a climate in which you foster creative thinking and innovative actions in individual workers. When organization members are free, they have a foundation for becoming creative and innovative. If they don't have that foundation, no matter what you do, individual workers will be unable to experience the thrill of thinking creatively and doing things innovatively.

In a recent interview reported in *USA Today*, George Lucas, the director of the highly technical *Star Wars* films, says that he knows how technology works, but as things have gotten more and more digital, he has gotten more and more lost. Startling as that revelation appears, George Lucas admits that he doesn't know as much about new technologies as the people who work with him, and he is totally lost when it comes to hammering out computer codes to bring to the screen a powerful vision of the high-tech future through his *Star Wars* creations. Lucas explains that in every enterprise there is a person who points and says, "We are going to do that, and I guess I'm the guy who points." Not only does he point the way, as we emphasized earlier in this book, but he gives his followers exceptional latitude to be innovative and creative. Indeed, he asks for their best use of technical information that he doesn't possess as well as the constant use of their own creative minds.

The most aggressive and successful companies are making creativity part of their business strategy. The 3M Company is famous for encouraging the development of innovative products by allowing employees to bootleg time and resources. The invention of the Post-It notes came out of just such a climate. While 3M simply encouraged creativity on the part of workers, Toyota directly asked each team of employees to contribute at least eight suggestions each month for improving the way in which their cars were manufactured. The employees responded enthusiastically, although probably not expecting much of a response from the company. As the suggestions flooded in from all sectors, managers began the process of determining whether any of the ideas could be used. To the astonishment of everyone, almost 90 percent of the suggestions were implemented. Employees did come up with creative *and* useful ideas. By the way, the simplest way of getting ideas from employees is just to *ask them*! Try it; you'll like it!

One extraordinarily effective international, multilevel marketing company spends an enormous amount of time and money finding new product lines to sell to its customers. Its strategy is to replace a product as soon as it reaches peak sales, before sales begin to fall off. If that means replacing a product at the end of 6 months or less, that's what the company does. Down lines continue to grow. The salespeople end up with more sales. And, of course, the company is a profit leader in the industry. This means that every employee must be constantly engaged in thinking about new products. Every employee must be thinking creatively. Every employee must have the goal of innovating new products. Not every company can change its products every 6 months, but every employee can be encouraged to think and act creatively in order to find an exciting and profitable innovation that can be used tomorrow.

What Is Creativity?

Arthur Koestler, in his classic text *The Act of Creation*, refers to creativity as the *actualization of surplus potentials*. Other experts call it adeptness in making fresh observations, or seeing something in a new way, or as applied imagination. The idea of creativity as applying your imagination to discover new products and services is particularly appealing in the organizational setting because it extends the concept of artistic creativity to practical matters. No matter how many new ideas you come up with, they contribute far less to the success of the organization if they can't be put into practice.

Some discussion still exists about whether there is a significant difference between creativity and innovation. Theodore Levitt, a distinguished faculty member of the Harvard Business School, defines creativity as thinking up new things, and suggests that innovation means doing new things or implementing new ideas. The origins of the two words suggest that being creative means to bring into being, to originate, design, or invent. Innovate means to introduce new methods, practices, or devices into the organization. Sometimes we use the term *creativity* with problem solving, meaning that we seek new ideas for solving a problem.

Frequently, the term *innovation* is used to suggest the generation of new ideas around products or services or processes present in an organization. You'll notice that sometimes the terms creative and innovative are used interchangeably. What you may need to remember as a manager and leader is that until the idea is put into action (innovation) in some way, shape, or form, it may be of little value to anyone.

When we review the tremendous strides that work technology has made in recent years, it is appalling how little progress has been made in unleashing the creative capacity of people in the organization to use the technology to improve work processes. Although you might be able to store machines for a while so they can be used in some other function, people's ideas can't be stored for future uses. When the ideas of people are stored, delayed, and filed, the ideas become useless and the people become frustrated, angry, and disconsolate. The fun of being creative is lost, sometimes for good.

Does Creativity Lead to More Fun at Work?

Boredom has long been recognized as a source of unhappiness and dissatisfaction at work. The people who are free to be creative at work are never bored. Being creative is fun. Without it, organization members experience constant frustration and unrest. If you look at the day-to-day disappointments and troubles that typically uncreative workers have at their places of work, and consider that creative workers are coming up with wonderful arrays of interesting, if not slightly wacky, ideas for accomplishing their goals, then there is little doubt that creative people are a lot happier and excited about their work than uncreative workers.

Naisbitt and Aburdene, authors of *Reinventing the Corporation*, have argued that people know intuitively that work should be fun, but only a few corporate innovators have created an environment in which fun, profit, and productivity flow. Here then is the challenge: *Move* yourself to the level of management that promotes creative thinking and unleashes the natural energy of organization members to achieve both personal and organizational goals.

Beyond fun, profit, and productivity, a workplace characterized by creative innovations explodes with interest and excitement. Naisbitt and Aburdene have said that the reinvented corporation is a workplace where people are working on what interests them most, although it also means stretching to learn new tasks related to your job or working in new departments to get a feel for the company as a whole.

We're certain that creativity leads to fun in workplaces and makes them stimulating, inspiring, animated, and alive. What we have discovered by looking at organizations that have successfully implemented a powerful leadership philosophy of management, like we are describing, is that they are in fact more productive, more profitable, and more enjoyable places to work.

George Carpenter, for example, left his family's dairy farm to work with his wife at Ben and Jerry's ice cream factory where, Janice Clurman says, "they run the risk of getting a free back rub or having a hilarious run-in with the company's Joy Gang." The Ben and Jerry's company has acquired a reputation for high quality and competitiveness.

A creative and innovative business climate not only enlivens employees and gives them new life in the workplace, but it also enables the business itself to survive and grow. Businesses are shaped by the innovations being implemented every day in the world. To be competitive, businesses need to keep up. The amount of creativity and innovation by members of an organization make the difference between whether that organization or business achieves great or moderate success. All of our upper management colleagues unanimously agree (in fact, there are so many that we are not even going to try to list their names) that innovation is the key to meeting one's core business goals and achieving competitiveness in today's marketplace. The most interesting statement we heard from top managers was "Innovate or Die!"

Helping Others Find Joy in Their Work

Yankelovich made a searchingly pointed observation when he asserted that "it is astonishing how little it takes for most people to feel wanted, needed, challenged, and useful in their work." To overstate somewhat, he suggests, "It is possible that there are few inherently undesirable jobs. But in millions of jobs today people are treated shabbily and paid poorly besides. It is this combination that makes their job undesirable." The evidence is so incredibly powerful that we find it almost unbelievable that anyone would even consider leadership and management practices that do not free people to use their surplus potential.

Being creative and having fun means that organization members respect one another enough that they are able to relax, let down their hair, and behave like real people. A spirit of creative wackiness allows organization members to offer exciting ideas that may revolutionize work processes and make organizations much more competitive. *Inc. Magazine* reported that employees in the 500 fastest-growing small and midsize private companies in America were more satisfied with their jobs, and had more respect for their companies, than the employees of corporate America. Those employees, *Inc.* reported, found themselves in jobs that offered challenges and a sense of accomplishment. They experience a company culture that values initiative and ideas, and they are confident that they work for companies that put out quality products, treat their employees with respect, and compete effectively in the marketplace.

Creativity and fun tend to free organization members to show their enthusiasm for their work and to release hidden energies suppressed by traditional management approaches. Galagan, editor of *Training and Development* magazine, explained, "More and more companies are realizing that you can't do good business without that indefinable extra [spirit] that people bring to a job." Spirit, enthusiasm, and commitment spring somewhat naturally from an environment in which organization members are encouraged to enjoy their work, have fun, and contribute to the well-being and spirit of others.

A big problem that we have been trying to point out in this book is that managers need to develop the skills for leading people so as to unleash the potential of employees. These skills are quite different from traditional management skills. Powerful leaders must learn how to coach and allow their employees to take the lead. However, this cannot be done using a do-as-I-say approach. This is particularly true about promoting innovation, creativity, and fun in your organization. You must take a do-as-I-do approach. You must be prepared to support your people in their creative efforts and be an example of a manager who champions his own and everyone else's efforts to be creative and innovative.

Powerful leaders like Robert Eaton and Robert Lutz of Chrysler were described in *USA Today* as getting lots of attention by cavorting in yellow rain slickers and smiling out from huge cereal boxes in stunts staged to launch Chrysler's new products. The Bobs, as they were called, were listed in *Business Week* as the world's best executives, and Chrysler was identified as *Forbes'* company of the year.

Commenting on six management tips that made them effective leaders, they listed as their number one tip to have fun and encourage creative wackiness, which Bob Lutz says "nurtures an atmosphere of laid-back creativity." Bob Eaton adds, "You have to have a good time. That's what it's all about." Stimulating creativity and fun are two important goals of powerful leaders.

It's Okay to Laugh at Work!

Another reason to stimulate, support, and encourage creativity at work is that creative people look at situations from different angles, some of which may be oblique and humorous, if not downright festive. People who use their imaginations frequently and spontaneously tend to laugh more at life and at themselves. Almost every dark cloud has a silver lining if we take a moment to find it creatively. Paul Harvey, renowned commentator and newscaster, frequently reports some of those incongruous and imaginative solutions. During one noonday news broadcast, Paul Harvey talked about a lady who advertised a late model Porsche for sale at $74.50. The first caller asked if there had been a misprint in the paper. There was not, she reported. He asked if he could buy the car. Come and get it, the lady responded. Finally, unable to contain his curiosity, the potential buyer of the Porsche asked why the car was being sold at such a ridiculously low price. She said that her husband ran off with another woman, called her on the phone, and said, "Sell my Porsche and send me the money." So the lady did just that. How about that kind of creative thinking!

Workers who aren't free won't be able to experience fun at work and engage in high-level and even profound levels of creativity. But, even if workers are free, they must be encouraged to have fun because it represents a degree of risk. *USA Today's* cover story a while back was entitled "Employees encouraged to lighten up." Julia Lawlor, the author, explained that companies like Nickelodeon use rubbery floors and wacky decorated workspaces to encourage employees to enjoy themselves at work.

Why should workers have fun? Most people who have seriously studied the consequences of the work environment say that if employees can lighten up on the job, they will increase productivity, improve morale, and boost profits. Beyond sheer profits, a happy, fun environment releases the creative juices of employees. Such a milieu reverberates with joy, meaning, and a fuller lifestyle, contributing to a greater sense of freedom by employees.

You can't coerce employees into having fun on the job, but an organization can open the way. The mission statement of Levi Strauss, for example, indicates that all organization members want to derive satisfaction from accomplishment and friendships, balance personal and professional lives, and have fun in their endeavors. National Computer Systems offers an Out on the Limb Award for employees who take risks, and an NCS manager also maintains an open-door policy for complaints as long as the employee with the gripe *sings* the complaint. A systems manager for a San Francisco financial institution encourages employees to wear 3-D glasses whenever a system goes down. A manager of a company in Berkeley, California, tapes a candy bar to each long memo with the suggestion to eat it to relieve the boredom of reading the memo. Another company livens up meetings by banning coats and ties and requests that everyone don a loud Hawaiian shirt from a rack provided by the company.

Fun and creativity go hand in hand; just as Ben and Jerry's has a Joy Gang, powerful leaders should express the fun things that characterize their personalities and their organizations. Having fun, enjoying work, being creative, and showing spirit at work are intimately connected with enduring success and enduring profits.

Cultivating creativity should come as a natural extension of a free and joyful workplace. Sid Parnes, director of the Creative Problem-Solving Institute in Buffalo, New York, explained years ago that an organization is creative primarily when its leaders subtly stimulate the creative productivity of the individual members. Managers who are strong leaders certainly adopt different approaches to subtly stimulating the creativity of their organization members, but they seldom leave that stimulation to chance. Authentic leaders cultivate imagination, ingenuity, initiative, and resourcefulness to undergird the discovery of creative solutions to daily problems.

Creative people are reacher-outers, thinker-uppers, and fix-it rather than nix-it types. This implies that they are optimistic rather than pessimistic. They think that problems can be solved, and they constantly work on them. Creative workers are more self-confident because they can adapt to changes and new situations. This means that creative people must be free to explore, to wander, and to discover what makes the organization tick. As the leader, you must assume the obligation to nurture creativity throughout the entire organization.

Jump Out of the Box; Pop a Cork

Regardless of your list of great management characteristics and skills, *Training Magazine* lists three concepts central to the way in which Hewlett-Packard works:

   1. Freedom and belief in people in the organization.

2. Respect and dignity for the individual.

3. Cultivating creativity and the ability to stay out in front with new ideas.

Fun and wackiness are simply ways of expressing the ultimate courage to demonstrate creativity in the organization. Without creativity, an organization may be okay, but it can never be great. Organizations that free their people to engage in creative activities and have some fun make their own openings in marketplaces.

Most organizations have been captured by the cult of competence and limit themselves to doing an adequate job. Thus, allowing or even encouraging organization members to think and, heaven forbid, act creatively appears to require too much courage for some, and some also fear that they do not have the innate ability to seek such a state in an organization. Nothing, however, could be further from the truth. All it takes is a conscious effort to implement principles of creative problem solving and innovation in the organization.

How Does a Leader Support Creativity, Innovation, and Fun?

There are some simple basics that free people to be innovative and to have fun in an organization.

1. To begin with, have confidence in and show enthusiasm for being creative. Innovative leaders demonstrate that they want ideas. There is very little in contemporary organizations that is perfect, making an ever-present demand for quality improvement, reduction of labor costs, simplification of work processes, elimination of wasteful actions, reduction of scrap, prolonging the life of tools, materials, and worker enthusiasm, and for new uses of old products.

2. The people who should think about the way in which work is done are those closest to the work. Every idea, no matter how small, builds a bridge to another greater idea. The happy, energetic, enthusiastic, productive workers are those who are using their ideas on the job.

3. One of the primary goals of powerful leaders is to establish an atmosphere of creativity and fun in the organization. Dudley

Lynch, partner in a Dallas, Texas, consulting firm, says that "Companies don't kill ideas, managers do!" With the pressures of contemporary competitive climates, managers desperately need the innovativeness and creativity of employees, especially those who are closest to the job. An employee who completes a task several times a day, 5 days a week, and 48 weeks a year knows more about the details of that job than a manager or executive, but those employees are seldom, if ever, asked how to improve the job.

4. From managers' points of view, there are usually good reasons in their minds for not entertaining ideas from employees. Here is a good list of reasons for rejecting employee ideas; don't use them.

It isn't in the budget.

It won't work in this department.

We tried that before and it didn't work then.

It's too radical a change for us at the present time.

I just don't have the time to follow up on it.

The price is too high for us.

Our group is too small to absorb it.

This will make our current ways obsolete.

The executive committee will never go for that idea.

We're doing all right without it.

No one else is doing it that way.

It's against our policy.

5. Building confidence in creative thinking is accomplished most effectively by implementing some simple fundamentals of being creative. Teach yourself and those with whom you work to enjoy being creative. Never reject an idea until it is completely formulated, then look for modifications that will improve the idea. Encourage everyone to try for simple ideas first, looking for ideas that accomplish the most for the least expenditure. Consider a number of ideas before selecting one to pursue. Shoot to achieve Rule 25: Try to think up 25 ideas to improve a process before you pounce on one idea to use.

6. When you are looking for ideas, alternate thinking with relaxing. Think hard, then relax and let your subconscious work for you. This allows you to think loosely, avoid preconceived solutions, and get out of the thinking ruts of the past. A key question that keeps you directed toward being creative is, How could the process, product, or service be made, completed, or designed *differently*?

7. To get started answering the key question, study the process, product, or service, then set a goal to come up with 25 ideas for doing it differently. Keep trying until something clicks. A way to get new ideas is to use a checklist. Rule 26 says that you should use the most obvious, common, and effective checklist around: the alphabet. Start with A and think up an idea, then go to B. By the time you have completed the alphabet, you will have 26 ideas. That's not a bad start.

8. Powerful leaders must encourage others to think up ideas. This means that every person in the organization should have an opportunity to get into the act of being creative. This is achieved in four ways:

    a. Share information and techniques for being creative, like some of those mentioned above, with everyone in the organization.

    b. Support those who come up with ideas at the very beginning, cultivating a climate of creativity.

    c. Always give people credit for innovative ideas.

    d. Don't be jealous of a great idea. There are always millions of other ideas just waiting to be revealed.

These are the eight basic ways to free organization members to be creative. Review these ideas regularly and add some of your own. You'll be amazed at how they enhance the creativity of both employees and managers.

Everyone Has a Million-Dollar Idea

A multimillionaire stood in front of a group of management students. He looked over the young audience and said, "Everyone in this room has a million-dollar idea, but statistically no one in this room will become a millionaire." The tumult arose. "Why not?" shouted the somewhat irritated students. The millionaire's reply was, "Because you won't bother about implementing your million-dollar idea." He continued to explain that the real joy of creating novel ideas is in finding creative ways to put them into practice.

You should help your employees to find ways to implement the ideas by asking those involved these five questions:

1. Who could help implement the idea?

2. What resources would it take to implement the idea?

3. What permissions would be required to move ahead on the idea?

4. Is there a best time to try out the idea?

5. What would be the simplest action to take to start implementing the idea?

These five questions serve as a framework for moving ideas from being creative thoughts to being innovative actions. The real task of identifying innovations may require outside assistance.

Three Alternatives for Identifying Innovations

Several years ago, Koprowski, a business professor, argued that business, industry, and government organizations were losing the major battle for creative talent, since these types (creative people) seek careers with organizations and groups whose goals and values are more compatible with their own. As a result, the academic world, the arts, and the professions end up with the lion's share of innovative leaders. Koprowski suggested three alternatives for identifying innovations for use in business environments, while allowing creative individuals to maintain their personal identities outside business organizations.

1. Bring an innovative, creative person from a university to work with specific organization members as a catalyst and a sounding board for new ideas.

2. Provide inhouse committees with an outside resource person of acknowledged creative ability from a totally different professional area to assist in solving some specific organizational problems.

3. Use a team of individuals from the arts to guide technical projects and infuse the process with new ideas to bring about changes in the organization.

We know that creativity and fun can flourish only in a climate that supports and encourages it. Regretfully, most businesses are organized around principles that deter creativity and discourage innovation. Specific actions are usually necessary to counter the noncreative set of organizations. Creative wackiness and fun cannot come about by proclamation or administrative fiat. They must come from the careful use of methods of social change that encourage creativity, innovativeness, and enjoyment in the workplace.

Stimulating Creativity in the Workplace

A great way to enhance creativeness in the workplace is to introduce brainstorming to all organization members. The idea of brainstorming has been around for years and has a continuing place in the toolbox of ways to think up new ideas. When any problem-solving group assembles, the tendency for certain individuals to dominate discussions and for impulsive and premature criticisms to be made still occurs. Brainstorming allows every member of the group to offer suggestions without criticism. In fact, brainstorming may be used through network connections on the intranet, without bringing individuals together in a face-to-face meeting.

Alex Osborn, the inventor of brainstorming, referred to the overall process as applied imagination or the application of imagination to problem solving in an organization. Osborn was looking for a way to get ideas moving in an organization in order to surface new perspectives on a difficulty. He formulated four fundamental guidelines:

- **Criticism is ruled out**. The criticism of any idea, in your own head or out loud to someone else, must be reserved until after all ideas are on the table.

- **Freewheeling is welcomed**. Every idea that comes to one's mind must be listed, a concept called "freewheeling." The wilder the idea, the better; ideas can always be tamed down later.

- **Quantity is wanted**. The more ideas, the better; quantity is the goal. In fact, the *Guinness Book of Records* indicates that a team of 10 managers and business professors in England set the record of 464 ideas generated in 8 minutes for ways to improve the British economy. We have already suggested setting a minimum number of 25 ideas (Rule 25) for each problem to be solved before proceeding to evaluate the ideas.

- **Combination and improvement are sought**. Seeking to build on the ideas of others is called "hitchhiking," a way of combining old ideas to create new ideas. Hitchhiking allows interesting ideas to be turned into truly innovative ones.

Osborn has also offered nine questions that might be used to spur new ideas:

1. Can whatever you are talking about be put to other uses as is, or can it be modified in some way?

2. What other ideas does this suggest, or what else is it like?

3. How can changing the meaning, color, motion, sound, odor, taste, form, or shape modify it?

4. How can it be magnified by adding something to it, by using it more frequently, by making it stronger or larger, or by adding another ingredient or multiplying it in some way?

5. What can be subtracted, eliminated, lightened, slowed, split up, or made less frequent to minify the idea?

6. What can be done to make the idea a substitute for something, such as who else can use it, what else can be used to make it, where else can it be used, and when can it be used?

7. How can the idea be rearranged by another layout, another sequence, or a change in rate or speed?

8. How can using an opposite process—by turning it backwards, upside down, or inside out—reverse the idea?

9. How can an object be combined with something else to produce a blend of something or an assortment that serves a new purpose?

This checklist of questions has been used by a wide range of professionals when they have felt that their idea-well has run dry. Use these questions whenever you feel that you have a great idea and seek to find additional creative and innovative ways to solve problems. Your first twenty-five ideas may not be the most creative, since they were the easiest to think up.

Buying a Hotel in 15 Minutes!

We were asked to introduce creative thinking techniques and processes to a group of about 100 public land management employees. To loosen up their thinking, we asked them to write down one way that they could get $100. In less than 10 seconds, each person had figured out a way to obtain $100. We congratulated them on being so quick to acquire a total of $10,000. Then we asked the participants to take a few more seconds and write down one way that each person could get $1,000. Again, they responded rather quickly. Some of the suggestions included using bankcards, selling something, borrowing from a friend or family member, withdrawing money from a savings account, being an escort for a night or two, renting out a room, giving blood, and a few unmentionables.

What was surprising to the assembled group was the rapidity with which they could figure out how to get some money. Several of their wild and crazy ideas may have raised some ethical eyebrows a bit. As they became more vocal and humorous in their comments, we decided to go for broke in raising money. We announced that it was well within the ability of the group to obtain $10,000 each. There happened to be a small hotel in town that was for sale, so we suggested that if we could get $10,000 each, we could buy the hotel, giving us a rather substantial equity and an income for quite a long time.

This time, people started to write down ideas and talk to each other. Within just a few minutes, every person had figured out how to put their hands on $10,000. Now the surprise registered on their faces rather than on ours. In a little less than 15 minutes total, this group of typical employees had discovered a way to obtain a *million dollars!*

Needless to say, after this experience, the remainder of the session went quite well because everyone was having fun and felt that they could solve almost any problem. Where they were initially a bit restricted in their thinking, they were now ready to move mountains and conquer the world.

Many efforts to encourage creative thinking fail because the entire creative process is not followed. In summary, the critical steps in the process are:

1. Make a clear statement of the goal to be achieved, the problem to be solved, or the opportunity to be gained by the new ideas.

2. Engage in individual or group brainstorming to get as many exotic, interesting, wacky, useful, and creative ideas as possible.

Record the ideas, and then let your subconscious mind work on them; as new insights and inspirations occur, record those also and add them to the list.

3. Engage in an evaluation process in which you combine, reduce, expand, and select ideas that may be helpful in achieving your goals.

4. Put the ideas to work. Try some of the most innovative ideas. If you stick to routine ideas, you will not stretch your imagination, nor will you feel that you have been engaged in a creative process. The results should be something a little wacky. In that way, you will also experience the feeling of fun associated with a new idea.

The creative process involves seeing things from another point of view *and* coming up with new ways to make positive changes in a situation.

Each person can become more creative by applying a few simple principles and rules. The most important principle is to prepare yourself to become more creative in specific situations by understanding the characteristics of the objects, context, and processes to be changed. Without a detailed understanding of what things are made of and how they work, it is difficult to come up with new ideas.

Rules 23 and 24

Although we have referred to Rule 25 (always think up 25 ideas before evaluating any ideas) and Rule 26 (use checklists), there are two other rules that are important to enhancing creativity: rules 23 and 24.

Rule 23. Set aside a specified period of time, like one hour a day, to work on ideas for achieving a goal. Twenty-four hours in a day minus one equals Rule 23.

Rule 24. Be creative 24 hours a day. Have a pencil and paper at hand and when ideas come to you, make a note of them. Some of your best ideas may come at night or when you least expect them. Be ready 24 hours a day—Rule 24.

As a summary, we repeat rules 25 and 26 in their concise forms.

Rule 25. Increase your effort and avoid being critical. Free yourself from all fear of thinking up wacky ideas, and don't stop until you have come up with at least 25 ideas for achieving a goal.

Rule 26. Organize your mind and imagination by using a checklist to prime the pump for getting ideas. For example, the 26 letters of the alphabet might serve as a checklist. Gillette, they say, got to the letter *R* before he came up with something that could be used once and thrown away: a razorblade.

Toyota's Approach to Creativity

Toyota's approach to creativity is the quickest way known to achieve cost effectiveness in the world today. Toyota has saved a ton of money by asking their employees a simple question: What are eight ways that we can cut costs?

You might be surprised at the dozens and dozens of ways that money can be saved by modifying the way things are done to develop products and deliver services. Although this is a bit more elaborate than Toyota's question, have your employees think of answers to the following questions.

How can we lower the cost of parts?

How can we reduce the time of labor?

How can we substitute less expensive materials?

How can we increase the function?

How can we improve the salability of the product or service?

How can the product be made more easily?

How can the product be made safer?

How can we use fewer parts?

How can things be arranged for quicker assembly?

How can we outsource some of the processes?

How can we redesign the product or the process of creating it?

Can you imagine how many ways costs could be cut and processes improved if each employee were to make only one suggestion a day for two weeks? Our consulting friends say that if you take an idea that saves the company as little as $100 per day, over a year's time the company could realize a savings of a third of a million dollars! Many employee-generated ideas will save the organization much more than a million dollars in a year. No small amounts! Oh yes, be sure to reward the creators of ideas. Many companies recognize ideas by giving the thinker-uppers U.S. Savings Bonds, dinners on the town, or even a backrub. Regardless of the way in which you confirm creative thinking, make the recognition fun and enjoyable for the employee.

Two Magical Questions

You can be much more creative if you take a moment to separate yourself from the task and look at what you are doing. Psychologists call this "stepping outside of yourself." Stop your work for a moment and ask yourself two questions:

1. Why am I doing this?

2. Why am I doing it this way?

Let's begin with the first question and consider it from three perspectives by focusing on different parts of the question:

- *Why* am I doing this? In considering an answer, focus on the value of what is being done. Is it important? What impact will it have on the success you are trying to achieve? Make sure you know why it is being done.

- Why am *I* doing this? In considering who is to do it, should it really be you, or should it be someone else? Who else could do it? Could someone else do it more effectively? What are the costs of your doing it versus their doing it?

- Why am I doing *this*? Now, focus on what is being done. Is this the most important thing to do now? Are there other things that are not being done because of this activity?

Let us now consider the second question: *Why am I doing it this way?* Ask the following questions to reveal alternatives for doing the task this way.

- Is there a *better way* of doing it?

- Is there a *faster way* of doing it?

- Is there a way of producing *better results*?

- Is there *another creative way* of doing it?

Questions can stimulate you to think up new ideas and novel ways of doing things. You may even be able to decide whether or not something is worth doing. At any rate, you should assist all of your workers in understanding that there is always a better way of doing something. Simpler, easier, more cost-effective ways of accomplishing things can be found. Asking the two questions is a quick and efficient way to increase creativity at work as well as at home or in the community.

We have been encouraging managers across the world to teach their cohorts to take "crazy breaks"—not passive time-outs but creative time-outs. Explain to your employees that there is always a simpler and more fun way to do things that may also save time and money. Show them how to use the two magical questions to come up with ideas during the crazy break. They will appreciate the break and thank you for a little more freedom to design the way they do their work.

Left Brain, Right Brain, Broccoli Brain

For a long time, longer than we would like to remember, managers have been educated and trained to develop a corporate-management brain. Unfortunately, most managers tutored under this system have become half-brained managers. That is, they have been taught to use the left hemisphere of their brains, the part that does rational, logical, quantitative thinking, at the exclusion of the right hemisphere of the brain, which does the visual, sensing, creative, and emotional thinking. Actually, the right hemisphere engages itself in what is better called "nonthinking," often referred to as a form of intuiting.

If you manage from the left brain, you will find yourself improving performance through controlling and rationalizing. And you will probably focus too heavily on financial performance and quick gains rather than on innovating, growing, customer needs, and long-term performance.

To encourage right-brain activity, you will need to take the time to relax, free your mind from worry and anxiety, and try to disconnect from the world a little bit. In the Far East this is called meditating: Quieting the chatter in your left hemisphere so that you can hear the "thinking in the right hemisphere." Take the opportunity to find a quiet place where you will not be interrupted for a few minutes. Close your eyes, relax your facial muscles, breathe slowly, and place a problem or a concern lightly upon your mind. Don't think about it; just let it be there ready to connect with any impression or image that presents itself in your relaxed state.

With a little practice, you will be absolutely amazed at how you can come up with interesting ideas, solutions, and decisions through the better use of your right hemisphere. Sometimes, as great artists and scientists have done, you can go to sleep with the problem placed in the back of your mind and a solution will pop into your mind in the night or in the morning when you are in the process of waking.

With all of this explanation of brain hemisphere functioning, don't forget that the brain is also the great integrator of ideas. To be exceptionally innovative and creative, you must learn to use both hemispheres of the brain. Think about the problem cognitively (left hemisphere) and then think about the problem intuitively (right hemisphere). This is called "whole-brain thinking." This process represents the ultimate in developing creative and innovative thinking in yourself and everyone else. Once again, as you become better and better at whole-brain thinking, try to figure out how to encourage everyone around you to be whole-brain thinkers. The payoff will be enormous.

Test Your Creativity

Although there are different tests of creative abilities, the best one measures how many ideas you can think up. Have someone time your efforts as you do the following. Each task should take one minute.

1. List all of the things that are wrong with the ordinary telephone (a good score is 10):

2. List all of the things that are wrong with our national elections (a good score is 7):

3. List all of the words you can think of beginning with the letter E (a good score is 15):

4. List all of the synonyms for the word "dark" (a good score is 7):

5. List as many uses as you can think of for a brick (a good score is 15):

6. Now, really loosen yourself up. List all of the titles for the following plot of a short story (a good score is 5):

   Cannibals in Africa have captured a missionary. He is in the pot and about to be boiled when a princess of the tribe obtains a promise for his release if he will become her spouse. He refuses and is boiled to death.

Examples:

Friar Accepts Boiling Proposal!

To Bed or To Pot? That is the Question!

You have just completed a personal assessment of the general status of ideational creativity; that is, the extent to which you tend to think up ideas. If you tended to score below the middle scores indicated, you may want to exercise your creativity by engaging in more ideational activities. Practice improves the fluency with which you think up new ideas.

Improving Overall Organizational Creativity

Most of the research on innovation in organizations concludes that the discovery of new ways of doing things is a function of serendipitous events—a fortunate accident and the sagacity of someone who is present and recognizes the relationship between the accident and what needs to be done. Clearly, quotas for ideas, threats, and any form of coercive attempt to generate new ideas do not work. It is critical that the organization be changed to take advantage of the accidents and creative opportunities that occur naturally in work settings. The most important imperative is to give ideas many chances to be seen by many people. Thus, rotating people among a number of jobs provides the opportunity for diverse stimuli to show themselves and be interpreted by a variety of people until the serendipitous combination of people and events come together.

Russell Ackoff, one of the most interesting organizational philosophers of this era, asserts that there are five properties of good management: competence, communicativeness, concern, courage, and creativity. Ackoff declares that creativity is the greatest of them all. He says that without creativity, a manager may do a good job, but cannot do an outstanding one.

Fostering a Creative Climate

Managers must use their power and influence to develop a creative climate at work. Use the following checklist to see how you are doing. Ask yourself if you

1. Encourage open expression.

2. Discourage criticism and aggressive reactions between team members.

3. Confirm successes and avoid punishing mistakes.

4. Delegate authority and responsibility.

5. Listen to and believe another person's ideas until proven wrong.

6. Stimulate fun and wild ideas by thinking-up.

7. Create diverse problem-solving groups.

8. Ask people to be creative.

Truly innovative leaders set goals and directions in partnership with other organization members; they provide resources so that innovative people have the time and equipment for resolving problems; they reduce time pressures for arriving at the successful completion of a project, but decide on realistic checkpoints to help everyone stay on track; they find ways to confirm successes and enhance positive feelings that show employees that they are valued and empowered.

Using Creativity in Business Processes

Notice how creativity and innovation fit naturally into the functioning of a business.

- Since a successful strategy is imperative for being effective in business, this is a great opportunity to be creative in designing a strategy that is unique, competitive, and future-looking. You may have to move to an off-site location to loosen people up and free them from any restriction in their thinking. Sometimes, the reengineering process of "starting over" on a new piece of paper as though the company doesn't exist may help to free people up to think in new and unique ways.

- Stimulate your people to be constantly innovative and creative when they are trying to invent new products and services. This is probably the most frequent opportunity to think creatively, as everyone in the organization is in a position to think about what other goods and services the company could offer its customers.

- Encourage all people to think more innovatively when a problem occurs or when starting up a new project. Nothing is more helpful than solving a problem permanently by changing the process or the way something is done. A large sporting goods and firearms corporation was having problems designing new products that were manufacturable, that were desired by the customer, and profitable. Each division was screaming and yelling at the other because of lack of competence. We suggested that each unit send its manager to a meeting. In came the R&D person, a manufacturing person, a financial person, a salesperson, and a customer. It was amazing what was accomplished when we broke down all the walls between departments and all barriers to contributing their wildest ideas. Everyone left much happier, and we believe that the company was on the track to "do it right the first time."

- Many businesses try to come up with one great and mighty competitive strategy to beat everyone else into the ground. That is the single worst mistake you could make as a manager. Any advantage in terms of new products or services or processes that your organization can dream up can be quickly lost, because your competitors can copy anything new. In fact, you may just have given them an advantage to beat you, because you have already tested and redesigned the product, service, or process and possibly spent thousands of dollars in doing so. You will save them big bucks! The secret to success is that you must innovate continually. Everyone in your organization should be learning new ways to think and be allowed to make mistakes occasionally. If you encourage and stimulate them, employees will innovate regularly and your company will stay competitive. You can see immediately that dictating from the "top down" will not do much to encourage the kind of flexibility and improvement that are needed in today's struggle for survival and triumph in the business world.

Five Great Creativity Suggestions

Most conversations are about things that are happening, not about solutions. Initiate conversations that focus on how to be more innovative about something. Normal conversations usually fall into the category of ideal gossip, nonthinking or conditioned responses, or criticism. Usually it is easy, and in fact much more fun, to raise a question aimed at solving a problem or making something better. One question, innocently asked, can change the whole direction of a conversation. The beauty of this suggestion is that most people love to be asked a question. It shows that someone recognizes them and respects their opinion. But even more, everyone likes to provide an opinion about or possible solution to a problem. You can quite easily make the difference in whether a conversation goes nowhere or turns in the direction of creative dialogue.

Second, be aware that how you design or redesign something determines for a long time how you will use it. Sir Winston Churchill was said to observe that "we first shape our buildings to be functional and efficient, then they shape us." Organizations express their fundamental beliefs and aspirations through visual form, rhetoric about values, and behavior. Your job as a manager trying to be a powerful leader is to create symbols that are positive, enabling, and freeing so that fear is eliminated and freedom to be innovative is enhanced. Allowing time, not being overly harsh when a mistake is made, and recognizing and rewarding innovation sends a strong recognizable signal that you yourself are a symbol of innovation. If you start to shape a creative culture around your people by following some of the preceding suggestions in this section and talk about the possibility of making everything better and easier, you create positive signs and symbols that foster continuous innovation. However, when any form, symbol, or behavior starts to shape workers in any counterproductive way or restricts innovation, your mission then becomes one of removing it and replacing it with something more positive.

A third suggestion is to take advantage of the information technology available to everyone. Using the Internet is the quickest way for those with any computer literacy to be exposed to the latest knowledge in a variety of disciplines and to foster new combinations of ideas. Not only must you become acquainted with professionals and peers in your areas of expertise, but you also need to see what other artists and innovators are doing. Plus, you need to be exposed to other parts of your business and to your various "publics" so that you can innovatively pursue greater business potential.

Our fourth suggestion is to involve more than one person to bring a creative idea into fruition. Someone may come up with a valuable, innovative idea, but may need another person to help sponsor the idea and provide resources and encouragement to continue to develop it. An additional or third person may be required to rally cross-functional support or further direction from top management. Sometimes, it takes even another person to promote the development and use of the product outside of traditional organizational processes. The creation of 3M's Post-It notes frequently serves as an example of how one person discovered the "glue that wouldn't stick." Two other people then helped to develop a use for the unique properties of the product, found additional resources, and gave encouragement to the original founder. A fourth person brought together manufacturing people to develop a machine to create the product, and generated enthusiasm and excitement for producing the Post-It notes. Others then began marketing the product within 3M and giving away free samples outside the organization until the company finally saw the profit possibilities and used their great marketing power to sell the product.

As a manager, you must not only spot people with innovative ideas, but provide them with other resources and identify other people who can help develop the ideas and bring them into the marketplace. If you do this well, you will become known as a champion of ideas and a more powerful leader in your organization.

Our fifth and final suggestion is to teach your people how to be more innovative by holding a practice session. Organize a meeting of your people or have a professional consultant help you facilitate one. Let your employees identify problems that are impeding their performance or that customers have complained about. Then, list those problems on a whiteboard. Vote on those that are most important to solve. Divide your people into small groups of five and assign each group to come up with some creative solutions to the problems or challenges they have identified. Encourage them to be as creative as possible and try to relax, have fun, and think "out of the box." Tell them to reserve judgment of anyone's ideas until they have had sufficient time to laugh, talk, and think in an unrestricted way. After a sufficient period of time, ask each group to report their three best ideas or a combination of their best ideas. Either make a decision about which ideas should be implemented or promise the various groups that you will take their best ideas and seek upper-management support. If you have enough time, you could have each group try to improve another group's ideas and thus get additional great ideas for making something better. You are the manager. You are the main person who can help your employees be more innovative and creative.

Unlocking Your Own Creativity

Throughout this section, we have stressed the importance of stimulating creative thinking in your workers and taking innovative actions to put ideas into practice. We would now like to focus for a few moments on your own creativity at work. Few experiences you'll have as a manager exceed the exhilaration and enjoyment that you'll receive from having your creative efforts recognized at work or in the marketplace. With your personal success and enthusiasm in mind, we would like to recommend Jeanne Baer's suggestions, from the McGraw-Hill *Training and Performance Sourcebook,* for helping you become more creative:

1. Ask crazy questions that help you get out of the box, such as, Why have we always done it that way?

2. Exercise your mind before beginning a challenging mental task by taking some time to think of wild and crazy ideas about anything that interests you and letting in some creative thoughts.

3. Adapt other people's ideas for your own use, like from the dry cleaners, a fast-food drive-in, a bank, or a competitor.

4. Try some new methods to generate ideas, such as mind mapping or using a metaphor to describe the goal.

5. Invent little ideas, not just big ones, because large improvements are often made through small ideas.

6. Vary your viewpoint by taking a new route to work, browsing through different magazines, and trying new hobbies.

7. Recognize flashes of inspiration that occur in the shower or when you are jogging, and record them for future reference.

8. Eliminate the fear of failure by looking at mistakes in a positive way as a learning moment.

One Final Word about Creative Thinking

This may come as a shock to you, but after years of research and experience, we now know that (1) every normal person can generate hundreds and thousands of worthwhile, useful, and personally satisfying ideas, and (2) there are methods and techniques that you can use to find ideas to accomplish your goals and solve any problem! Your potential and that of your colleagues with regards to creativity is truly unlimited.

Not so startling, but equally important, is the realization that the creative person is not just the outstanding writer, inventor, or artist; rather, creative people are those who use their imaginations on a daily basis to find effective, exciting, and unique solutions that move them toward accomplishing their goals. Innovative people are more likely to adjust to new situations, avoid boredom, and laugh at the foibles of life than those who avoid finding creative solutions. Being innovative is a great way to develop self-confidence, satisfying relationships, and financial freedom, while at the same time having a lot more fun at work.

Promoting innovation and creativity in your organization, and particularly among the people who look to you as their leader, allows everyone in the company to contribute and to get involved. You can help them think of ideas they have never thought of before and to be taken seriously, even listened to. Being freed in this manner saves you the concern of trying to come up with new ideas to satisfy your customers and keep your division competitive.

This calls for a new form of managing. We call it *powerful leadership*. Not managing by objectives and checking off predetermined accomplishments. No! What you need to do is promote more flexibility among your workers so that they can adapt and react to a fast-changing world and marketplace. If you want to manage by objectives, then make your objectives read like this: Innovate, innovate, and innovate some more!

A Look Ahead

In this chapter we described the second essential change you need to make to take your management style to a level that further unleashes the power of employees in your organization. Promoting creativity and innovation in the workplace enhances everyone's freedom to use their minds as well as their hands, to contribute valuable ideas that promote organizational effectiveness, and to enjoy themselves at work.

The next issue that we discuss concerns the relationship between managers and employees. Most workers see their manager as a "boss," generally don't trust the manager, and feel that they are on the low side of a superior–subordinate relationship. The question is, can a more cohesive, determined, focused workforce be developed by changing the relationship between managers and subordinates?

4

THE THIRD ESSENTIAL CHANGE: SWITCH FROM BOSS TO COHORT

We are born for cooperation, as are the feet, the hands, the eyelids, and the upper and lower jaws.

—Marcus Aurelius Antonius

A recent newspaper headline proudly proclaimed that Lance Armstrong and the U.S. Postal Service bikers appear ready for the upcoming Tour de France. "The defending Tour de France champions demonstrated their fitness in Tuesday's prologue stage of the Tour of Switzerland at Rust, Germany, where Armstrong won the 5-mile time trial and his cohorts were third, fourth, seventh, and thirteenth."

Everyone a champion? No one the boss, but everyone a cohort? Become a cohort and treat others as cohorts? You may be asking yourself how these concepts got into a book about management and leadership.

Aren't managing and leading concerned with influencing others through authority and with various forms of directives and initiatives? You're right! We usually think of leadership in terms of influencing others through direction, control, and authority. The leader is usually thought of as the most influential person in a group. Leading, in a popular sense, means to be out in front with others behind. Great leaders are those who take charge and motivate people to follow them. They are the solitary souls who set the goals and direct people toward them, who boss, command, guide, blaze trails, wheel, deal, and handle the reins. Notice this dictionary definition of boss:

> ***Boss.*** n. 1. one who exercises control or authority. 2. one who directs or supervises workers. v. 3. to give arbitrary orders.

Leading implies being the head—supreme, great, preeminent, unrivaled, unparalleled, stellar, and topmost. Slang phrases indicate the popular perception of the leader: bigwig, kingpin, magnate, mogul, tycoon, godfather, and master.

This concept of managing and leading is especially prevalent in America, where organizations tend to be highly structured; much direction comes down the pipeline, and precious little communication goes upward. Too often, we distinguish between a manager and an employee by advertising "careers" in management and "jobs" for everyone else. Universities talk about education for managers and training opportunities for workers.

The ways in which a manager should manage and relate to employees has been one of the most thoroughly researched areas in the history of organizations. The plethora of conclusions reached by various investigators has been disappointing at best and devastating at worst. We mentioned our own research earlier in which a surprising number of employees saw their manager as a boss and a "jerk." They saw the manager as a person who gets in the way of their best performance, satisfaction, and opportunity to grow and develop.

One management consultant told us that there must always be a clear line drawn between the manager and the employees. And neither side should ever cross that line. When we asked about how to draw the line, we were confronted with a lengthy list of things that you can and can't do. We left that particular conversation wondering if there wasn't an easier and more natural way to lead and a much simpler way to relate to fellow workers.

Stay with us for a few minutes as we go back to Lance Armstrong, everyone being champions, and the notion of becoming a cohort. We believe that the solution to the dilemma of relating to employees effectively and leading in the simplest and most natural way is right before our very eyes!

A Cohort

The word *cohort* is of Latin derivation. In the Roman armies, a cohort was a band of 300 to 600 soldiers, constituting one tenth of a legion. The conceptual definition of a cohort is a group of individuals who are similar in some trait or situation and move forward as a unit. Similar in some trait or situation would be a group of warriors, an athletic group, or a group of workers. In each situation, everyone is trying to progress as a cooperative unit.

The early Roman legion quickly abandoned the Greek phalanx, the most popular way of fighting at that time. Something more flexible was needed to combat foes than the unwieldy, slow-moving, phalanx. The development of the early legion consisted of three lines of soldiers, one of which would engage the enemy. If things got too hot they could fall back through the lines of the heavy infantry and regroup. The second line of troops would suddenly emerge, shocking the enemy and usually winning the battle. If all else failed, the third line of troops was the last defense. If the battle was lost, the third line of troops would close ranks and the army would then try to withdraw. Everyone worked and fought as a cohort.

As the notion of cohorts developed, the Roman soldiers were seen as clever men seeking to outmaneuver their foe rather than merely lining up and marching at the enemy. In victory and defeat, the Roman cohorts were constantly learning and making changes in the way they functioned together. Proper equipment and clothing were supplied by the state. Land was allotted to each legionnaire at the end of service. Everyone received equal treatment and training opportunities.

The Roman legion reached a stage of development in its organization, strength, resilience, and flexibility that had no equal. Loyalty of the soldiers was transferred from Rome itself to the local commanders. The soldiers' loyalty lay with the one man who could provide them with the loot—the victorious commander. This reminds us of an earlier comment that we made: The most influential person in a worker's life is the manager.

A Roman legion on the march learned how to rely for weeks completely on its own resources. Ultimately, the necessity for a legion to undertake quite specialized tasks, such as bridge building or engineering siege machines, required some specialization among its members. Skilled men were recruited and trained to make the cohort as independent and efficient as possible. Emperor Leo VI pointed out that the men chosen for the cavalry should be robust and courageous, and should possess sufficient means to be free from worry about their homes and possessions while serving in the military.

As time passed and circumstances changed, the cohort groups were given more flexibility. Not every group was treated the same, and there does not appear to have been a rigid, standardized system of recruiting and organizing throughout the Roman Empire. However, the receipt of citizenship and identity with a recognized group of cohorts gave everyone a major incentive to join the army and serve with great loyalty. Cohorts were given various designations. City cohorts were given responsibilities to patrol the city of Rome as a police force. Another cohort group was given firefighting equipment, including water pumps, hoses, and even catapults with fire hooks attached to climbing ropes.

New recruits were ask to recite an oath, promising to follow the consuls to whatever wars they may be called, and neither desert the colors nor do anything contrary to law. Everyone was bound together with a determination to help each other, realizing that their whole unit acting in tandem could achieve much more than individuals working separately.

The final point and most enlightening insight to be gained for the necessity of changing from a boss to a cohort is that by acting and thinking as a cohort, the citizen-soldier's individual initiative was never blunted. Everyone seemed to understand that independent-minded soldiers who worked together as a unit posed a significantly greater threat to the enemy than blindly obedient men who did only what they were told. In any case, the changes and development of cohort relationships brought about more self-confident armies, which were more likely to revolt if an old-fashioned disciplinarian took command!

Cohorts in Education

Numerous college graduate programs are moving toward a cohort structure. One such program states, "As a member of a cohort, you will be among a small group of students enrolled in the same program, who all started at the same time. All of you will progress through the program as a group, taking the same classes together, and finishing your course of study together." The announcement continues to explain that cohorts give you an ongoing fellowship with other students who are experiencing the same academic and personal challenges and rewards at the same time that you are. You can support and work with each other as a unit as well as individually.

Cohort members find that they create stronger and more lasting professional relationships and friendships from within a cohort group then they would in a different arrangement. At the same time, the leader—faculty member, staff coordinator, supervisor, or manager—also becomes a cohort and an important part of the group. Though the original meaning of *cohort* referred to one of 10 divisions of a Roman legion, colleges are eagerly accepting the second and contemporary definition of cohort: companion, colleague.

Arthur E. Imperatore, chairman of the board of APA Transport Corporation, said, "Working people have a greatness. Given reasonable leadership, they are all too willing to follow, do what is asked of them, and give their best to their employers. They are people. They are complex. They are not willing to be treated like indentured servants. Good business leadership can create and generate the work spirit, the wish to cooperate."

The wish to cooperate is at the heart of changing from boss to cohort. Managers can look for other ways to persuade and induce employees to cooperate and give their best at work, but to do so ignores the most effective, fundamental approach.

Gordon Selfridge, who simply calls himself a merchant, caught the spirit of a cohort leadership approach when he said, "The boss drives his men; the leader coaches them. The boss depends upon authority, the leader on good will. The boss inspires fear; the leader inspires enthusiasm. The boss says 'I'; the leader 'we.' The boss fixes the blame for the breakdown; the leader fixes the breakdown. The boss says, 'go'; the leader says 'let's go!'"

User-Friendly Managers

Treating others as cohorts is a better way to lead, and in addition, it is a concept that turns the more traditional views of leadership on their heads. It opens the door for more organizational power. Hostility between managers and followers is much too prevalent in the workplace. Informed and knowledgeable workers usually view traditional leaders and managers negatively. Workers consider traditional leadership behaviors as demeaning to their abilities. Under run-of-the-mill managers and leaders, workers become alienated and passive. They withhold their insights and observations and play political games. Everyone suffers, and the organization itself loses strength and vitality.

The third essential change for becoming a powerful leader, however, asserts that leadership is *the creation of cohorts*. The challenge of powerful leadership is to cultivate a cohort relationship. People follow those whom they like; they like their cohorts and go along with them. Developing a cohort relationship with others creates a willingness in them to follow.

> *Cohort.* n. 1. one who is an ally. 2. one who is seen as a helper.
> 3. a colleague. 4. someone who helps to coordinate.
> *Ally.* n. 1. a nation, group, or person united with another for
> a common purpose. v.t., v.i. 2. to unite or become united
> formally.
> *Collegiality.* n. cooperative interaction among colleagues.

You can be a leader without being a cohort or having allies, but you will have chosen the more difficult route. Being a cohort is the simpler, easier, more effective way to achieve your goals. Being a cohort opens the door to more exciting, moving, powerful leadership without the use of complex, lengthy strategies for winning and influencing people. Many so-called leaders today are like chameleons and change their hues and views to fit the situation. Frequently heralded *situational leadership* or *contingency leadership* approaches tend to confuse associates and followers who cannot be certain about their relationship with the boss. One day, the boss may be very direct and impersonal, whereas the next day the boss may be participatory and kindly. On another day, however, he may dump responsibility in an effort to be delegatory or sell you on his ideas, creating an ambiguous and potentially threatening relationship. The truth is that no boss or leader can spend time trying to identify which situations are the most favorable for particular styles of leadership. Nor can leaders switch styles of leadership without causing considerable stress to themselves and confusing those with whom they work. By treating others as cohorts and being treated as a cohort, you have the basis for a great leadership relationship.

We learn much about the concept of cohort as we think of the many labels we use to describe those that we think of as cohorts. Helper, equal, friend, and partner come quickly to mind. A cohort is also considered a comrade, a companion, a confidant, a sidekick, a consort; a cohort may also be described as a supporter, a backer, a benefactor, a well-wisher, an encourager, an advocate, a defender, a partisan, an adherent, an ally, a colleague, an associate, a brother, and a follower.

We add to those labels some powerful characteristics when we think of a friendly person and use terms such as helpful, kind, devoted, and warm. Cohorts are also well-disposed to each other. They are ardent, generous, companionable, convivial, accessible, and affable.

What a contrast the meaning of cohort makes with the popular meaning of leader. Cohorts develop a long and abiding loyalty for one another. They sacrifice for one another. They do for one another what each would do for the other. One is not superior and the other subordinate. One is not boss and the other follower. They are true and authentic equals in each other's sight. Cohorts are generous and hospitable with one another. They are devoted and genial to each other and happy to be in the other's presence. They are willing to place the needs of the other ahead of their own.

I Return to Die

One of the greatest stories of this cohort relationship ever recorded is that of Damon and Pythias. Pythias was thrown into prison for an offense against the king. Because Pythias was married and had a family, Damon offered to take his place in prison while Pythias went home to say goodbye to his family. The king was so impressed by the offer that he agreed to the arrangement, provided that Damon was to suffer death in Pythias's place if Pythias failed to return. Damon accepted the plan.

At the appointed hour Pythias had not arrived and Damon was taken to the place of execution. Just as Damon was to be put to death, Pythias returned and took his place. The king was so taken by the fact that Pythias would return to have his life taken in order to keep his promise to Damon that the king released them both.

The loyalty and commitment of Damon and Pythias to one another is characteristic of the cohort relationship. Like the Roman legion cohorts, the relationship between Damon and Pythias symbolizes powerful leadership where the relationship itself elicits a pledge, a resolution, and a decision to stand for others, to support others, and to raise them in stature and character. The opportunity and challenge of leadership is to treat those whom you are to lead as cohorts. They are to be your equals. You are to be each other's advocates.

Treating Others as Cohorts Is Natural

In one of our leadership seminars, an executive asked, "But how do you treat a cohort different from an employee?" We answered the question by asking everyone to close their eyes and imagine a long hallway. "Now imagine that one of your best colleagues has been away on a trip for two weeks. Imagine that your colleague has just come into view at the end of the hallway. See yourself and your colleague walking toward each other. Watch what you do and say."

We then asked people to explain what they said and did when they met their colleagues in the hallway. "I smiled and talked enthusiastically about where she had been and what she had been doing," one manager said. "We laughed, shook hands, and expressed how much we had missed each other," said another. "I asked if he needed any help and suggested that he come to dinner so that we could talk longer," said an executive.

The message of cohort leadership is clear: Treat others as you treat your best friends and colleagues. Say hello! Smile. Ask questions that express your interest in them. Ask what they are doing. Express appreciation for them. Be of service. Encourage them. Don't be afraid to walk, work, eat, and dream together.

Can two walk together, except they be agreed? (Amos 3:3)

Others Include Suppliers, Customers, and Your Boss!

Treating *others* as cohorts is such a powerful principle that it can be applied with much success to all those who come within your circle of influence. Vendors and suppliers should rank especially high on your list of those to be treated as cohorts. A vendor can be of immeasurable help in bringing to your attention new products and materials, discovering ways to reduce the costs of purchasing materials and shipping them, identifying materials and products that are obsolete, and recognizing what your competitors are buying.

Suppliers can tell you when to buy at discounts and when special promotions and advertising will appear. Suppliers can also warn you of new government regulations or new policies governing the manufacture, use, and distribution of certain materials. Very often, vendors and suppliers are able to tell you about the availability of "nearly new" equipment that can be acquired for a substantial reduction in price.

Major companies spend a considerable amount of time and money sending quality assurance managers to vendors to check on the workmanship and various tolerance levels of parts in order to avoid costly errors in assembling the final product. There is a tremendous cost benefit in treating suppliers as cohorts. Spending a little time together, talking, smiling, or having lunch may do much to identify potential problems.

Remember, what you are striving for is a collaborative relationship with your suppliers. Think ally, cohort, and congenial, supportive relationships, and the profit will follow.

The Customer Is Cohort

We saw a sign the other day that said "The customer is always right, misinformed, bullheaded, fickle, ignorant, and abominably stupid...but never wrong!" A hundred or more books have recently popped up on the subject of customer service. One popular paperback listed 50 ways to get and keep your customers. Another elaborated on an extensive model of factors involved in properly servicing your customers. Personally, we thought that they were all useful. However, none seemed to hit upon the simple key concept of treating customers as cohorts rather than as customers.

The manager of a video and pizza store recently received the following note from a customer. It captures the idea of adding the quality of cohort relationships to customer service:

> Sandra and Staff,
>
> Thank you for the good service and for treating me more like a friend than just a patron. I enjoy coming to Sounds Easy because of this, and when there are so many places today that do not treat their customers like this, I appreciate it even more!
>
> Kate

For Kate, being treated like an equal with considerable warmth and respect was simple and natural. Someone smiled and with a little energy in his voice said, "Hi, it's nice to see you. What can I do for you today?" After hearing the person's request, the "cohort-manager" offered the discounts of the day so that the customer received every opportunity for a low-cost meal or video rental.

Treating customers as something other than customers is simple to do and certainly easy to learn. A computer company in California, after becoming acquainted with this idea, made it part of its corporate culture. The owner said that they have decided to treat all end-users as equals and cohorts, and that includes fellow employees who may have to take someone else's partially assembled product and complete it. Actually, it takes more time and trouble to figure out how to treat others as enemies, antagonists, and foes, which are antonyms of cohort, than it does to treat them as friends.

How to Manage Your Boss

Hundreds of articles and films have been produced that give us hints about managing the boss. Suggestions for getting along with the boss include

- Find out whether the boss likes to read or listen to reports, and respond in a preferred way.

- Always keep the boss informed, with no surprises.

- Remember, the boss is human, so determine when the boss doesn't like to be interrupted, and don't delegate upward to the boss.

Although these are interesting strategies, they miss the most critical point.

In our minds, the experience of a manager in a major electronic store chain hits closer to the mark. The company was expanding and opening new stores at a rather rapid rate. Department managers were being promoted to assistant store managers. The promotion usually meant that the department manager would be transferred to another store to work with the new store manager. In one particular instance, the audio manager was given the opportunity to become an assistant manager to a store manager who had a reputation for being extremely difficult to work with. The word was out that no one really wanted that specific "promotion."

In pure desperation, the audio manager called our office for some advice. He blurted out the reputation of the store manager and wanted some suggestions about how to "take on the boss and beat him at his own game." He felt that all the other stores would be watching to see if he was successful in "meeting the boss straight on and not getting shoved around" like his predecessor. Our main suggestion was, "Don't treat him as a boss; treat him more as a friend and cohort." Then we asked the audio manager what he would do if this new manager were his best friend and cohort. "Why, the first thing I would do is go to lunch and just have a normal conversation about what was happening at the store and find out how I could be of help." In our minds, this was a truly great idea—a simple and natural approach that would be honest and unobtrusive. We encouraged the audio manager to think of making a hero out of his boss rather than making a hero out of himself. "Try to help your boss succeed rather than fail. Don't undermine him. Support him in your work efforts and in your conversation with others." Essentially, we promised him that there would be less tension and anxiety at work if he developed a strong work relationship with the new boss rather than if he figured out a way to make the boss look bad.

The audio manager's first act consisted of going out to the new store, meeting the boss as he arrived in the parking lot, and explaining that he had come to help the manager in any way that he could. His new boss was actually dumbfounded, and said that no one had ever approached him like that. The happy ending to this story is that they became cohorts who helped each other, and the store prospered. The audio manager, after only a few months of learning, and to the utter surprise of everyone else in the organization, was offered a store of his own to manage. We are told that this was the shortest period of time that anyone had ever moved from the position of assistant store manager to store manager in this company.

I Don't Want to Be Your Parent Anymore

A father noticed how well his children treated their closest friends. He noticed that they spent considerable time on the phone talking to each other even though they had just spent the day at school together. They dreamed together about what they wanted to be when they grew up. Whenever the occasion presented itself, they worked together, walked together, and played together. When one was sad, the other tried to cheer her up. If one had a problem, they usually shared it and tried to determine a productive course of action. They seemed to trust each other and feel a certain degree of loyalty to each other. Whenever the father raised questions about the behavior of one of the friends, the child closest to the friend vigorously defended her.

When the father became aware of the way his children treated their best friends, he decided that he would rather be treated as a friend by his children. To his children's surprise, he explained his observations to them and said that he didn't want to be their parent anymore. He asked them to treat him the same way they were treating their good friends. His children laughed at the notion, but agreed.

The father reported that he immediately felt a great responsibility removed from his shoulders. He said that he always felt that he needed to be a kind of hero to his children, making decisions about what they should be doing and how they should be doing it. He had apparently spent time worrying about their problems and challenges and felt responsible for solving those problems. Now, he was feeling that they could talk about things together, in a nonthreatening way, and that their ideas were often more creative than his. He also noticed that some of the anxiety and tension of being a father figure was eliminated. In fact, he mentioned that he pretty much gave up reading parenting books and instead tried to be a best friend to his children.

If You Push Hard, They Will Push Back

The above statement actually encapsulates the final result of a massive research program aimed at finding better ways to improve the relationship between parents and children. If the parents threaten, coerce, and are too authoritative with their children, the report said, the children start to rebel, threaten their parents, and become more disobedient. The whole idea for improving parent–child relationships was to mutually decide on the rules of the house, mutually try to agree on family goals, and mutually discuss family problems and challenges in order to find acceptable solutions. The children need maximum support, which means that parents also need to make friends with the friends of their children. But more important, parents should celebrate small wins and victories so that everyone feels the excitement of accomplishing good things.

The same general principle holds true for management. If you push people too hard, they will push back. On the contrary, if you demonstrate sensitivity, show empathy, and exhibit patience, your employees will be more supportive toward you. If your relationship with employees goes well, usually the work goes well. Don't try to manipulate people and impress them. Treat them as cohorts and ask them for their ideas to make things better at work.

Edward L. Moyers, CEO of Illinois Central Railroad, gave this advice to those who aspire to be successful managers:

> Take time to visit with those people at every level in your organization. The increased production, improvement in morale, and verbal support that you will receive as the result of such activities is amazing.

Spend enough time with those who report directly to you to determine what motivates them. Have a clear understanding with everyone as to his or her objectives. Spend time with your customers. Listen to the customer. Respond to their needs.

Take care of the employees who report to you—salary, recognition, awards, et cetera. After all, these are the people who have made you a success and they are the people who will insure your future success. You have a lot in common with these people. They are depending on you and you are depending on them.

A Cohort Walks Around and Inquires

One of the most successful managers we know walked the floor of a major American automobile company and spent time talking to the employees. He learned to inquire about two things: how their personal lives were going, and how their work was going. This manager didn't wait for problems to come to him; he went to where the problems existed. Also, he didn't spend much time waiting for solutions to come from employees; he went to his employees and asked them for their suggestions.

His first questions, as he met various workers and supervisors, were about how they were doing *outside of work*. What are you doing for recreation? How are your children doing? Is everyone healthy? What's happening at home? Did you go to the Grand Prix last week? After the conversation began and various comments were exchanged, the manager then switched to questions *about the job*. What's going right at work? What's not going right? How can I help? Do you have any suggestions for making the work better?

When fellow workers sense that you are working with them, that they are not working for you, that you are not out to impress them but to be helpful and make work more enjoyable for them, you will be well on your way to making the third essential change from boss to cohort. This change will help employees contribute more, grow and develop, and enjoy their work.

Cohort is a great metaphor for describing what should happen among people. Metaphors are holistic, and they structure complex experiences by highlighting some elements and obscuring others. Metaphors transport concepts of the familiar to the less familiar and articulate practices for which we may otherwise lack ways to express them. Thus, with the concept of cohorts as the quintessential essence of great leadership, the cohort metaphor chunks the characteristics of a powerful leader into a compact and coherent whole and captures some of the inexpressible attributes of great leaders in a novel, vivid, and succinct manner.

Leadership based on treating people as cohorts may be characterized by terms that describe behaviors and roles that are typical of cohort relationships. Your goal is to develop the behaviors and enact the roles so as to change from boss to cohort. Read through the two lists in Table 4–1 and identify both behaviors and roles that you need to work on and improve. Check each behavior and role that you would like to change. Then, develop a plan for implementing those changes in your relationship with your workers.

Table 4–1 Behaviors and Roles in Cohort Relationships

Behaviors	**Roles**
_____ affable	_____ advocate
_____ amicable	_____ ally
_____ convivial	_____ backer
_____ cordial	_____ benefactor
_____ devoted	_____ colleague
_____ genial	_____ companion
_____ gracious	_____ comrade
_____ hospitable	_____ defender
_____ kindhearted	_____ encourager
_____ neighborly	_____ supporter

What effect do you think these changes will have on the way in which people respond to you as a leader? Can you now see more clearly how to change your relationship from boss to cohort? All things are easier to achieve when they are done for someone we strongly like and respect— a cohort. It is easier to achieve goals when you are working with people with whom you have a cohort relationship. Leadership, in its finest form, is much more than telling people what to do and imposing one's will upon others.

A Less Complex Form of Leading People

When you first meet a stranger, you intuitively say, "Hello, friend." Such a greeting tends to establish a positive, cohort relationship almost instantly. Even the popular Marc Anthony greeted a potentially hostile gathering of people in Rome by saying, "Friends, Romans, countrymen, lend me your ears." Dale Carnegie became famous for his widely read book called *How to Win Friends and Influence People*. Notice that the cohort approach leads to the most effective influence of people. The concept of *cohort* is almost universally understood to represent an egalitarian, helpful relationship.

Today, the world is desperately in need of selfless, powerful leadership. Exemplary leadership in business, industry, and government is sought after and generously rewarded. Daily we see leaders attempting to influence others in a variety of ways without regard to the relationship they have developed with their associates. The most powerful leadership is a cohort-to-cohort bond warranted by a resolute determination to fulfill the obligations implicit in that relationship. To feel and know that someone respects us, believes in us, trusts us, and expects good things from us is inspiring. Pure, powerful, collegial relationships permit leadership to find expression and raise the significance of workers in their own eyes and in the eyes of their associates.

Powerful leadership is based on the cultivation of strong cohort relationships. Being cohorts establishes the foundation upon which leadership can be exercised. You cannot lead an enemy. You can lead cohorts. Being a cohort makes leadership more effective and much easier to achieve. It is easier to invite cohorts to be involved. It is easier to want to serve a cohort. It is easier to be committed to a cohort. We accept encouragement more easily from our cohorts.

Being a cohort is both universal and imperative for effective leadership because it applies to all aspects of living and leading. That does not mean that we should avoid all other approaches to leadership, but leadership techniques are markedly less effective when we are not working with cohorts. Almost any leadership style will be more effective when we work with cohorts and as cohorts. The number and complexity of leadership techniques can be measurably reduced when we begin with the cohort assumption.

In front of a crackling fire in Vail, Colorado, a small group of successful business leaders met to consider the subject of executive leadership. One executive introduced the idea that it might actually be possible to be allies and partners with employees and even competitors. A hearty laugh filled the room, and a rush of comments quickly followed. "Are you kidding?" one person shouted out. "You would immediately be labeled a pushover and a soft negotiator. You'd be annihilated and probably bankrupt in less than six months." Others agreed.

The thought that leading others can be more effective and easier by operating on the fundamental principle of cohorts was discussed no further that evening. It almost seemed as though the traditional approach to leadership had won out. Yet, strangely, everyone in the room was trying to be more cohort than foe to each other.

Cohort relationships are built on true concern for the other person. It is not a soft acquiescence to problems or to mediocre performance. On the contrary, a cohort tells a close companion in need, "I understand," not "I agree with what you are doing or the way you are handling the situation." A cohort does not spend much time wallowing in self-pity, but asks, "What can we do to improve the situation?"

Being a cohort does not mean that you become an "after-hours buddy" at work. That would imply that you are trying to be a soul mate or the person that provides a listening ear for every kind of concern and personal problem everyone has. As a leader, you have much more to do than assist people as their religious advisor, doctor, parent, drinking buddy, or psychiatrist. A cohort approach to leadership simply means that you work together to achieve greater productivity and satisfaction. As the Romans demonstrated, the objective is to be successful at whatever endeavor you find yourself engaged in. As cohorts, you support and help each other, but you are not able to force anyone to succeed. You may not be able to help people who are not willing to make a great effort to help themselves.

Cohort Leadership

The paradox of leadership is that the excessive use of power leads to resentment and a loss of influence with one's followers. On the other hand, as power and influence are shared, it magnifies the talents of followers and allows the leader to strengthen cohort ties.

In the scholarly literature on leadership, there is a hint of the importance and critical place of cohort relationships as the basis of effective leadership. Yukl summarizes the status of research on leadership by explaining that

> most research and theory on leadership has favored a definition of leadership that emphasizes the primary importance of unilateral influence by

a single, heroic, leader.... An alternative perspective is to view leadership in large organizations as a sequence of multidirectional, reciprocal influence processes among many individuals at different levels, in different subunits, and within executive teams. According to this view, leadership processes cannot be understood apart from the dynamics of the social system in which they are embedded.

The heroic leader is expected to be wiser and more courageous than anyone else in the organization and to know everything that is happening in it. These expectations are unrealistic, and leaders are seldom able to live up to them.... Shared responsibility for leadership functions and empowerment of subordinates is more effective than heroic leadership, but it is unlikely to occur as long as people expect the leader to take full responsibility for the fate of the organization.

Yukl concludes by observing that "viewing leadership in terms of reciprocal, recursive influence processes among multiple parties in a systems context is very different from studying unidirectional effects of a single leader on subordinates, and new research methods may be needed to describe and analyze the complex nature of leadership processes in social systems."

In more popular language, Yukl is suggesting that effective leadership in organizations consists of interactions among cohorts (reciprocal, recursive influence processes among multiple parties) rather than between a boss and some followers. Cohorts form the basis of "shared leadership." Cohort relationships are *reciprocal* (consisting or functioning as a return in kind), *recursive* (constituting a procedure that can repeat itself indefinitely or until a specified condition is met), maintain an *influence process* (an act or power of producing an effect without apparent exertion of force or direct exercise of command), and exist *among multiple parties* (consisting of or including more than one).

If you are able to fight through the technical research language, you will recognize instantly that the technical definitions simply describe the essential features of a cohort relationship. Thus, treating others as cohorts is a simpler, easier, more direct, and more effective way to exercise leadership.

How to Build Cohorts in Organizations

Cohort relationships evolve when managers help workers accomplish their goals. Goals and dreams are grounded in hope and optimism. Organization members focus their hope and optimism on the workplace and look for ways in which their dreams can be fulfilled in that setting. Their leaders are, as we have said, the single most significant influence on how their dreams are fulfilled. John Gardner, philosopher and social commentator, has observed that "everyone has noted the astonishing sources of energy that seem available to those who enjoy what they are doing or find meaning in what they are doing." Powerful leaders build cohorts when they make work meaningful for them.

Meaningful work and enjoyable work are two types of natural growth goals. Natural growth goals direct the actions of workers, and when achieved, result in more authentic interest in the organization. Natural growth goals are the conscious intentions of workers to do things that allow them to grow and expand their lives at work. Natural goals allow workers to express their human nature and enhance their lives. Natural goals have to do with furthering the happiness and well-being of workers.

Leaders who would like to facilitate the change of organization members from being subordinates and employees to living their work lives as cohorts must devise ways for them to accomplish a variety of natural growth goals. Some common natural goals are being able to work to one's highest potential, develop knowledge and skills in a variety of areas, explore new ways of doing things, discover new opportunities at work, initiate new ideas to improve one's work, contribute to the well being of others, maintain high aspirations, and feel optimistic about what can be achieved at work.

Natural goals such as altruism are associated with the very nature of people, their ability to visualize the future and to imagine things being different from what they are. Leaders who free workers to take the lead and engage in creative, innovative, and fun things at work are moving workers from being subordinates to being cohorts. Leaders who encourage organization members to express themselves in painting, sculpting, playing classical music, or playing on a company golf team are helping create a culture in which organization members see themselves as cohorts engaged in the mutual accomplishment of organizational goals.

Through the accomplishment of natural growth goals, cohorts become stronger, more dependable, more accomplished, more competent, more autonomous, more influential, more emotionally stable, more adaptive, and happier. All of life's aspirations are shaped by goals that lead us to progressively higher levels of achievement. The cohort relationship is a superlative form of workplace achievement.

Cohort relationships evolve in an atmosphere of freedom and choice, where people believe that if they behave in particular ways, they will achieve certain goals. The argument is that people make choices as they seek to achieve goals that lead to action. When the action appears to produce positive outcomes and the outcomes appear achievable, people devote energy to bringing about the outcomes. Cohort relationships flourish when organization members are constantly making choices to achieve natural goals. Leaders must consciously aid organization members to formulate and achieve those goals in a climate where they can take the lead and engage in innovative and creative activities.

Cohort relationships are encouraged when leaders encourage goal-setting and confirm success. Confirmation is a better practice than giving rewards, because the term "reward" connotes an act of force that determines behavior. It is more important to communicate to cohorts that their work leads to the achievement of goals and that they are successful. Cohorts seek confirmation that what they are doing is acceptable and contributing to the organization's success.

Successes may be confirmed in many different ways. Letters of commendation, plaques, certificates, coupons, or cash payments are some traditional ways to confirm employee accomplishments. Powerful leaders constantly seek new ways to confirm the success of organization members in order to allow the concept of cohort to evolve. In fact, an imaginative workforce full of cohorts may very well identify innovative and creative ways to confirm their value.

Listen to David Varney, former CEO of BG Group, as he reflects on the notion of powerful leadership:

> For the purposes of this dialogue, let us begin with a basic question.
> Why do organizations need leaders? Leadership exists to create a collective effort to achieve sustained superior performance. To create a collective effort. But leaders themselves can't create that effort.
> Leaders create the conditions that enable people to achieve. Leaders foster a growth climate and a culture that enhances the ability and the willingness of the people within it to achieve.

Not only do effective leaders create a climate where growth goals are achieved, but also they become as familiar with their people as possible. David Varney explains one of his most instructive experiences in learning how to lead.

> I remember working in an electronics company, in the department that oversaw progress chasing. Part of my job was to accompany the boss around the site twice a day to update the progress against the plan data.

This little tour took about two hours. I was impressed with this man. He knew every nook and cranny of the site, every piece of equipment and how it worked. But even more impressive was the fact that he knew all the human beings that operated the equipment, by name.

I soon found out one reason for his familiarity with all those people. He doubled as a bookie's runner. As he made his inspection rounds, he collected bets and distributed winnings. What I learned about leadership from tagging along with this man was that conversations he had with his employees were mostly not about electronics. They were about their outside interests, their hobbies, their families, and of course—since the love of gossip is inherent in all human beings—about their fellow workers' exploits.

This successful CEO concluded, "One of the biggest challenges facing us in this age of acquisitions and mergers and demergers, of upgrading and downsizing and restructuring and job-hopping, is how to forge an enduring bond between employer and employee."

We too believe that there is something extremely valuable in the durable bond between the bosses and their employees. If there is any hope of creating a kind of paternalism that helps people to feel more secure, let it start with the powerful shadow and example of the boss. Your employees can hardly expect the company to care for them if the boss doesn't. If you want to create a sustainable connection with your employees, changing from a boss to cohort is the quickest and simplest approach.

Cohort Relationships Are Adult to Adult

Cohorts must be treated as adults. That is, leaders must avoid reacting in ways that are condescending and demeaning to others. In working with cohorts, it is important that leaders recognize and acknowledge their adult characteristics.

1. Adults learn and develop best when they see a need for what they are to do or learn. They resist being herded into situations just to please the leader. Adults will grow and learn more quickly to be cohorts if they can apply this relationship immediately in a productive and satisfying way. An adult will be much more involved in the learning if she or he sees a direct personal benefit. Adults see personal growth and applications as the reward for whatever effort it takes to make the transition from workers to cohorts.

2. Adults develop skills through meaningful practice in which they can see the results of doing and learning. Hands-on practice of new behaviors, active participation, and a little personal investigation and problem solving are important for adults to achieve a behavior change. Your employees will watch you and model themselves after you as you become a cohort. Your job is to give them every opportunity to practice a new way of relating with you and with each other.

3. Adults resist judgment and criticism and prefer information that points them in a positive direction so that they can develop and achieve goals. Positive feedback and the redirection of their perceptions so as to focus on how to achieve goals is the preferred form of correction. The most influential form of feedback will come from the experience itself. If employees find that what they are doing is "functionally efficient," they will have their reward. They will have internalized something that feels good and is effective. External praise and recognition from peers and from you as the manager are always useful, but not as long-lasting as the feedback that comes from within the person.

4. Finally, adults like to see how new learning and actions can be integrated into what they already know and applied to problems and situations that they are facing now. Speculation and philosophizing is less important in solving pressing issues at work than information and knowledge that leads to direct application. The greatest efficiency in learning cohort relationships at work is that no one has to leave the work site to learn, and the practice can take place at work and can be applied immediately.

Giving up the role of boss and adopting a cohort relationship can do more to increase productivity and achieve organization goals than almost any other change. However, coupled with the other essential changes, cohort relationships bring sustained strength to the workplace and provide collaborative support for the leader. This mutual reinforcement coalesces to reinforce the positive effect of powerful leadership.

From Boss to Cohort

To finalize your view of the difference between a cohort leadership model and a traditional management model, please carefully review Table 4–2.

Table 4–2 Comparison of Traditional Management and Cohort Leadership Models

Traditional Style: Controller	Cohort Style: Coordinator
Focuses on tasks	Focuses on people achieving results
Views workers as employees	Views workers as potential partners
Makes decisions without suggestions	Listens to workers' suggestions
Uses power forcefully	Enables people
Protects position	Works with people
Strictly adheres to rules and regulations	Fosters a vision

Clearly, if you intend to switch from boss to cohort, you will need to shift away from the behaviors in the left column and toward the behaviors in the right column. Most successful organizations are trying in various ways to move closer to the right side list. If you believe in the self-actualizing potential of your workers and you truly want to unburden yourself from a lot of unnecessary worry and concern about their performance at work, make this important change as quickly as you can.

A Look Ahead

So far you have been introduced to three important changes that you should make to fire up your people and unleash the power of your organization. First, we suggested that you should examine everything in the organization that keeps people from taking the lead and contributing more to the achievement of organizational goals. Anything in the way of rules, procedures, management practices, or ways that people are told to do their work that hinders employee performance needs to be eliminated. Right at a time when organizations must respond rapidly to sudden and unexpected changes in the economy, we have too much organizational pressure forcing workers to protect their jobs and not rock the boat. Lead a rebellion if you have to, but in every way possible, *free your people to take the lead.*

Second, we argued that managers should stimulate more creative action and innovation within organizations. Creative thinking that leads to creative action is a great vitalizing force for workers that keep the organization on the leading edge with customers. As soon as you start freeing up your people, provoke them and serve as a model in performing more creative and innovative actions. Everyone has insights and great ideas, but they need your help bringing them to the surface and implementing them in the face of organizational resistance.

Now, as you free up your people and promote an increase in innovative activities, begin treating employees, your boss, customers, suppliers, and others as cohorts. Be understanding and supportive of employees and their ideas. Form cohort relationships. One thoughtless word can ruin a good relationship. Give your workers more trust and loyalty, and they will begin to return the favor.

These three changes, which every manager should make, release organizational power and go a long way toward reducing the amount of resentment, dislike, and even antagonism that workers often have toward their managers and their places of work. We promise you that the use of these fundamental elements of powerful leadership significantly reduce the discouragement and anxieties that creep into the lives of members of the workforce.

You may have noticed that our list of seven changes that need to be made now does not include a section on "motivation," nor does it treat the concept of "empowerment." We believe that it is too difficult, if not impossible, to motivate someone else to do something. Most people should size up their situation and decide what they need at work and in life. The notion of empowerment also seems better replaced with what we called "enabling." Thus, it is imperative to understand, and indeed master, the 4E's talked about in the next chapter.

5

The Fourth Essential Change: Master the 4E's of Involvement

He who has great power should use it lightly.

—Seneca

In the 1950s, Harley-Davidson motorcycles were known as the greatest "hogs" on the road. They inspired countless movies and clubs of travelers. By the 1980s, however, the company was staggering and was almost out for the count. Honda had leveled some blows by producing motorcycles that were styled better and held their oil. Harley-Davidson was on its way to the junkyard in the sky.

Vaughn Beals, Harley's CEO at the time, looked in the mirror one day and concluded that the problem with Harley-Davidson was its management. Managers held tight reins and Harley-hogged the workers. As Beals reflected on what to do, he realized that he had to take Harley by the handlebars and restore that deep-throated, mesmerizing sound of Harley by introducing a new view of management.

He involved employees by creating teams that had responsibility for scheduling work, improving quality, and adjusting the assembly line. He moved supervisors out of the way of workers so they could take the lead. He introduced a "just-in-time" inventory system and got out of the way himself. The change was incredible. Harley-Davidsons surged into the lead once again.

Harley-Davidson illustrates the 4E's of involvement and how they are used to capture the heart of powerful leadership. The 4E's constitute the critical actions for focusing the efforts of your cohorts to take the lead in making your organization a standard-bearer for outstanding achievement. You might think of the 4E's as the focusing mechanism of leadership that centers the efforts of employees on what it takes to have a great organization.

The 4E's insist that workers take the lead and managers stop directing, controlling, and demanding. The 4E's set a new standard that inspires employees to higher levels of performance. The 4E's are summarized by four key terms:

1. *Envisioning*—to create an attractive picture of what can be achieved.

2. *Enabling*—to equip, make able, and capacitate.

3. *Energizing*—to enliven, stimulate, and charge up.

4. *Ensuring*—to confirm, guarantee, and substantiate.

Why Master the 4E's of Involvement?

Leaders free workers to take the lead. Regretfully and humbly, we admit that some workers have been subdued for so long that they have forgotten how to be good self-starters. They need a little nudge and a lot of support, or they don't get moving and thus fail to accomplish very much. Anyone can accomplish small tasks, but it takes a free person with the right stimulation to achieve great things.

In fact, the lives of leaders and their fellow cohorts are a jumble of the mundane and depressing details of routine jobs. The necessary tasks of day-to-day living press us to succumb to distraction and to defer to a gigantic slug that deters us from accomplishing more than the common denominator of existence and that completely alienates us from taking advantage of any high-leverage opportunity that surfaces on the horizon.

To help your cohorts achieve bigger things, or truly outstanding goals, requires your careful attention to the 4E's of involvement. As you think about transforming yourself from a manager into a leader, try to remember that your primary responsibility is to encourage and enable people in the organization *to perform at their highest levels.*

The Meaning of Performance

The two most common outcomes of performance are productivity and quality. Performance, however, has more outcomes than just those two. Productivity generally refers to the number of things that can be created at the lowest cost. Quality has to do with adding value to the low-cost items so that most items are produced with zero defects.

Performance achieves much more than productivity and quality. Performance involves working to increase production, paying attention to quality, and managing technology in creative and innovative ways; it also means helping others when they fall behind or need a little encouragement, coming in an hour early or staying a little late to make improvements in the way something is being done. It also means noticing how costs can be cut and telling someone about a disaster that is about to occur in a machine or process. Performance behaviors are a broad set of activities that leaders encourage and expect from employees as well as from themselves.

Firms Spend Billions to Fire Up Workers—With Little Luck

Companies have purchased billions of dollars of rewards to boost employee performance. However, exhaustive academic research has turned up little evidence that gimmicks make any difference in a person's sustained performance. On the other hand, many managers still try to motivate their workers the old-fashioned way: They give orders and use KITA (kick in the a—). Workers just do not respond well to such forms of semi-military motivation. Bright and capable people want more than coercion to trigger their interests. They want opportunities to use their talents and expand their abilities rather than be ordered around by a boss.

Using carrots to motivate people seems a bit childish. Worse than that, those not rewarded feel they worked just as hard as those rewarded, but came away empty; they feel slighted and resentful. Whyte, acclaimed author of *The Heart Aroused*, hates the idea of trying to motivate people "because it feels like you are having something done to you." The best way to elicit defensive responses in people is to make them feel like you are devious and strategic in distributing favors.

Someday, people may come to work inspired by a higher purpose in life, or because they have found a new spirituality in their lives. That may not occur for a while. In the meantime, leaders are stuck with whole hosts of workers who are not going to dance their way into work each day. For most employees, every day is a new day, and any help you can give as a leader to get them started and focused may fire them up and ignite a swoosh that will be of great value to the whole organization. Involvement of workers is the quickest and sturdiest way to enhance performance and get products and services to customers with immediacy and directness. Enthusiastic employees care for the company and make customers feel that they are special. Involvement is the best way to sustain competitiveness and let employees take the lead.

The Involvement Formula

Getting people to come to their places of employment regularly and on time, work hard and smart, and make positive contributions to the organization are not easy goals to achieve. Nevertheless, in all of its difficulty, you can't find a simpler and more powerful way to help people arrive on time and work harder and smarter than by learning how to use the involvement formula. Acquiring the skills associated with the processes of involvement can make your job as a leader easier and more fulfilling.

Involvement is achieved by implementing the skills described by this formula:

$$I = f(E\,1 + E\,2 + E\,3 + E\,4)$$

in which I = involvement, f = the function of, E 1 = envisioning, E 2 = enabling, E 3 = energizing, and E 4 = ensuring. The formula means that the degree to which your cohorts are involved in a project is a function of how well you (1) help them to envision the goals of the organization and your work unit, 2) provide your employees with the resources necessary to achieve the goals, (3) stimulate and encourage your employees, and (4) get your employees to assume responsibility for achieving the goals.

For your cohorts or direct reports to reach high levels of involvement, you must first help them *envision* exciting possibilities and goals. Workers contribute their time and energy when they seek to achieve things that are challenging and of great value to the organization. Second, you must *enable* them by making sure they have the understanding and the resources to accomplish the goals. Enabling workers allows them to get things done efficiently and quickly. Third, you must *energize* your cohorts by applauding when they succeed—even giving hardworking cohorts a standing ovation at times—so that they feel motivated and encouraged. Fourth, you must *ensure* that the work is getting done in the most effective way through a system of return-and-report meetings. Reporting procedures ensure accountability and provide opportunities to celebrate employee successes. Now, let us look at each of these elements in more depth.

E 1 = Envisioning

If you were to ask a group of company chief executives what their most important assets are, they would give you the same answer: their employees. If you probed further, they would say that their employees are seriously underutilized. The most common reason for underuse is that employees just don't understand what the company is trying to accomplish. It is imperative that employees know what the company is about and how it intends to succeed so that they can contribute their ideas and efforts to making the organization successful.

Most organizational communication studies reveal, ironically, that stockholders know more about the organization's mission, vision, and values than do the employees. In addition, many managers have considerable difficulty trying to understand what the company's strategic vision is so that they can share it with employees.

We had a recent consulting experience that quickly verified the absolute necessity of employees having a clear and attractive picture of the direction their organization is going and how it plans to get there. A large local steel mill was experiencing some difficulties, so the manager asked to meet with us to discuss the problems. Seven representatives of the company filed one-by-one into a conference room. A quick glance at the faces of these supervisors indicated that they were not happy people. After they had shuffled around and seated themselves, the leader explained that morale was extremely low in their organization, profits were down, and "running lean and mean" had simply made work more boring and people more irritated.

This organization was no different from many others that were trying to operate successfully without each strategic unit having a clear picture of its mission, goals, and direction. Actually, most organizations are not even able to articulate what distinguishes them from their competitors, much less describe their core competencies and how these are used to move the company ahead in some efficient and exciting way!

Not wanting to prejudge this company as another failing company, we asked the golden question: Can anyone share with us the company's vision or mission statement? The silence was deafening. No one even moved. We thought that we had better give it another try. What are you trying to accomplish over at the mill? A similar silence followed.

In his book called *Up the Organization*, Robert Townsend, president of Avis car rentals, explains how Avis needed a better sense of direction when he took over. Avis owned motels, hotels, airlines, travel agencies, and limousine and sightseeing companies. He went on to formulate some long-range objectives. "It took us six months," he wrote, "to define one objective: We want to become the fastest growing company with the highest profit margins in the business of renting and leasing vehicles without drivers." Within 3 years, Avis had reversed its losses and become number two, as its famous advertisements indicated, in its field. With a clear sense of direction, you too can do better.

Americans seem to have been brought up on the idea that the future will always be better and brighter than the present. Although our work lives have been a little frustrating, organizations have been outrageously naive about their future success. In fact, few organizations have been willing to step back and take responsibility for creating a clear direction and course of action for ensuring that things will improve in the future, that things will get better, that there is great value in having employees come to work each day.

The observation in Proverbs correctly reflects this concept when it says, "Where there is no vision, the people perish." Abraham Maslow, prominent psychologist, asserted that there must be more to life than meeting physiological needs. At the top of his hierarchy of needs is the necessity to grow, develop, and actualize our potential. Dreams and visions and excitement about possibilities seem to tap into our sources of energy and bring out an enthusiasm and commitment that nothing else in this universe can reach.

Shriberg and his colleagues, writing about practical leadership, assert, "A stimulating vision of the future binds employees together as a group." Harrison, management consultant and author, claims, "An inspiring and worthy vision can unite hundreds of people and move them forward with considerable energy even though they may face almost insurmountable difficulties." Great causes produce great effort. The Revolutionary War had "a free country" as its vision. Martin Luther King had a dream. Political campaigns, couched in images like a "thousand points of light" and a "bridge into the next century," provide a vision of the future that's better than what we have right now. Eric Hoffer says that when the causes are really great and powerfully described, people are willing to give their lives to achieve the victory. We don't need people to give their lives for an organizational cause or vision, but we do need people who are willing to give more effort and thought to making conditions better at work.

Visions and missions need to sound lofty and idealistic, or they are not going to be very energizing to anyone. Notice McDonald's vision: "To satisfy the world's appetite for good food, well-served, at a price people can afford." Get the picture? The world's appetite is part of its vision. Every McDonald's employee is asked to think about how to satisfy the world's appetite, serve food that is hot and fresh in the most comfortable environment, and do everything at a price that people can afford. Remember the conclusion of William Faulkner's brilliant acceptance speech when he received the Nobel prize in literature: "Man will not only endure but triumph!" We were not created to endure work but to find joy in working and creating something better than it was when we arrived.

Visions and missions that challenge the status quo and provoke us to think greater thoughts need to be developed and shared at every level of the organization. Top-level managers usually develop company visions, missions, and goals. Various units in the organization then contribute to those goals and visions with their input. However, individual employees should be encouraged and assisted in giving their insight into what and how goals can be achieved.

Pam Walsh, founder of Courage, Inc, a corporate coaching company, writing in *Utah Business*, observed that "managers who inspire a belief in something bigger than their group, something that rings true and stirs hearts, have the edge over managers who simply apply basic management tools, techniques, and goals."

We are acquainted with an organization in which the management team spent hundreds of hours developing a vision and mission statement for its people. When it was finally formalized, written in artistic gold letters on a velvety black background, and presented to the members of the organization, absolutely nothing happened. There was no clapping and no applauding, just a stony silence that spelled total disaster. Why? Several reasons seem apparent. For one, the mission statement contained pretty ordinary language. No superlatives were included that drove the imagination toward what could be. But the worst part about the whole thing was that it represented the vision of only a few top managers. The workers cared less about the top boys' visions. They weren't their visions. Their attitude was "you have probably created a great vision and plan for yourselves. Good luck!"

Although some outspoken consultants contend that top management has to sell the vision to the workers, we think that is the flat-out wrong approach to take. Selling takes months to get a vision up and down the line, and without any guarantee that it will ever be accepted by anyone but the original inventors of the vision. Most research and our own experience suggest that when people have a hand in creating the vision, they commit to it. When people invest a little time and effort putting together a vision, they darn well make sure it works. It's quite easy for employees to go to top management and say, "Guess what—*your* vision didn't work." The workers are off the hook and feel little responsibility for the success or failure of the vision and mission because it wasn't theirs. But when it becomes the worker's vision that they created, the shoe is on the other foot. Now they become responsible, so that if it doesn't work, they can't blame it on top management.

Make sure that your workers individually and collectively have a way of giving their input on the direction and future of the organization. This can be done by asking each unit to develop its own vision and mission, after which you can meld the unit visions into an organizational statement. Whichever approach you use, try to reach consensus at every level of the organization. The time it takes to get ideas, merge them together, and achieve agreement pays off handsomely in the long run.

A vision without a way to implement it is nothing but daydreaming. Conversely, effort without an exciting vision or goal is drudgery. As quickly as individuals and groups get a picture of what they want to accomplish and how they want to accomplish it, you as a leader must support them and help them in every possible way to move ahead.

Most influential leaders always start with a dream or vision. Martin Luther King is frequently cited as someone who had a dream. King was able to speak in such a way that others bought into his dream. Powerful leaders must be able to articulate the vision in a compelling way that attracts others. Leaders use a tone of voice that exudes confidence and body language that exhibits a positive attitude. When a powerful leader speaks of a goal and a way to achieve it, people are attracted to it and want to follow.

A vision is a clear goal and a way to achieve the goal. When explained clearly and simply to another person, especially when they see the benefits of achieving the goal or task, you will have their support, and they will frequently determine the best way they can help. Your job is simply to point the way or articulate a goal that needs to be accomplished. Do whatever you can to get cohorts started, and then let them be accountable.

Bain & Company, a consulting firm, reported that hot management ideas of our turbulent economy are souring with unusual speed. Many companies have given up on customer relations management (CRM). Tools of the past, like total quality management and reengineering, have lost popularity over the course of the past few years. Now here is the most interesting news: The most popular approaches are the old standbys, like mission statements and planning how to achieve those goals and visions articulated in the mission statements. The survey findings of Bain & Company are right. To move ahead, organizations must have a simply stated vision, with goals, tasks, and responsibilities spelled out. The vision must be as rewarding and attractive as possible. The possibility of achieving the mission must always be inherent in the statement. Employees do not want to engage in a guessing game about what is to be done to be successful.

Visions and goals are critical, but taking actions to implement the vision or goal is even more important. You don't need to do other people's work for them, but you do need to make it easier for them to do their own work. This important concept is called *enabling*.

E 2 = Enabling

Your job as a powerful leader is to help others enjoy the sweet taste of success. If you're leading effectively, others accomplish something far greater than they had ever imagined possible. You stand by them and support them all the way. You provide them with the resources to succeed and make sure that they know how to use those resources efficiently.

Empowerment Is Out, Enabling Is In

One extremely popular buzzword in organizations today is "empowerment." Empowerment means to authorize, commission, license, warrant, entitle, and permit. Managers empower employees by just giving them the authority or the license to do something that doesn't help get the work done in any enthusiastic, quick, or even efficient manner. Nahovendi contends that whether the goal is an important short-term or a rather elaborate longer-term one, to simply permit employees to try and get something accomplished in an organizational setting can be absolutely disastrous.

Leaders Enable Workers, Managers Empower Them

Conger and Kanungo explain that "empowerment is the process of allowing workers to set their own work goals, make decisions, and solve problems within their sphere of responsibility and authority." This definition of empowerment suffers from the "permitting" deficiency, as do many other explanations of empowerment. A worker can be permitted to make decisions and set work goals, but nothing much will happen if the worker doesn't have the resources to implement the decisions made. Workers must be enabled, not just allowed or authorized, to do their work in the most effective manner possible.

Another thing wrong with the notion of empowerment is that it suggests that someone else has power, and that they are going to give it to you so that you'll then have power. Rather than helping employees develop their own power, managers simply give employees a big stick that they think they can swing around and hit things with. Empowering employees by giving them clubs is a temporary and demeaning approach to helping them accomplish their goals. A colleague of ours often suggests that giving someone power is like giving them the opportunity to "hit a pig in the butt with a baseball bat." It doesn't work on pigs and it certainly will not work very well on humans. In addition, since someone else gave the power to you, there is always the possibility that they may decide to take it back.

Notice the various meanings associated with the concept of enabling: capacitate, equip, facilitate, outfit, provide, supply, assist, expedite, ease, simplify, hasten, and quicken. Enabling goes way beyond simply empowering people or giving them the permission and authority to do something.

John Humphrey, former CEO of The Forum Corporation, notes that most people do not see themselves as leaders. "They may feel confident in their abilities, but have a hard time taking on the sense of ownership that leadership demands." Clearly, involving individuals in company processes takes much more than just authorizing people to take the lead—it requires that they be enabled.

Leaders share as much information as possible about how others have previously tried to accomplish a particular task, which avoids wasteful duplication and even total failure. Information about costs, past productivity, and the general attitudes of other workers who have successfully completed a project may be useful. Some companies are moving toward open-book management, in which John Case asserts that key workers and others should find out about the financial condition of the company directly from organizational records.

Another good way to enable workers is to have the person who is assigned to solve a problem turn right around and ask coworkers what they would suggest doing to resolve the problem. Workers feel more confident about solving problems when they receive support and ideas from their colleagues about how to proceed.

The last goal of leaders in enabling workers is to let them know what the expectations are with regards to the problem. They need to know what direction to take to improve things. Is the problem cost overruns? Do they need to address the issue of declining revenues? Is the company out of line with marketing strategies or meeting customer expectations? In solving problems, workers will be more effective if they understand the bigger picture and the stark realities of the real world.

Providing insights, background history, and expectations help people perform at their highest levels, provided they have the resources to assist them in doing the work. Workers often simply need a little extra time to make an amazing contribution to the success of the organization. The 3M Company has been credited with legalizing the "bootlegging-of-time" principle when employees have an idea that may help the company come up with an innovative product. No one questions an employee who leaves a regular assignment for a short period of time to work on the new project. In another company a worker may need equipment or a little money to spend on a relevant activity. Frequently, just supplying a little space or access to other personnel enables a worker to complete an important task quickly and efficiently.

There is an old saying that goes like this: Success breeds success. We have all experienced the power of this simple statement. When we succeed in doing something, and doing it well, we seem enthusiastic and stimulated to try something else. Enabling people frees them up for success. Most important to remember is that enabling people may require a little training, possibly another workspace, or opening up some channels of communication with other knowledge workers. Whatever it takes will be worth it for you as a manager. Your people will develop a sense of self-efficacy and begin to take more control over their work lives. Once that begins to happen, you will truly be able to minimize your input to them and extract yourself from some of the traditional managerial traps that take so much of your time and energy.

An Old Oriental Parable

A wise martial arts master was ready to pass the mantle of authority for his organization to his number one student. The master prepared a final test. He asked the student to move a large granite rock from one location to another before sunset. He told the student to use all of his power to accomplish the feat.

The student tried and tried, but couldn't budge the rock. Just as he was about to give up, the master said, "Use all your power. Have you considered using a lever?"

In near contempt the student responded, "I didn't know I could use a lever." The student hurried and found a strong pole and began moving the rock. However, time was running out and he realized he couldn't accomplish the feat in time. In near despair he sat down.

The master quietly asked, "Have you used *all* of your power?"

The student cried, "Yes, I'm physically drained, mentally perplexed, and spiritually empty. I have no more power."

"Oh no," said the master, "you have more power than that."

The student looked up at the smiling master and sighed, "Where?"

At which the master's smile broadened. Then the master said, "Right here," as he pointed to himself. "Did you ask for my help? You have the power to ask for my help. Use all of your power."

"Will you help me?" asked the humbled student.

"Yes," said the master. Then, retrieving a golden whistle from his tunic, he signaled his other students, who had been hiding in the hills, to join them. They quickly moved the rock to the appointed place.

You should take from this parable the point that as a powerful leader, you are responsible for alertly identifying the multiple sources of power that workers may have to achieve their goals. You are to enable them to be successful.

E 3 = Energizing

After the goals of a task have been clarified (E 1), and the widest range of resources have been identified and made available (E 2), powerful leaders then encourage workers to begin to achieve the goals. At this point, powerful leaders must be able to energize workers through continuous demonstrations of personal excitement, personal confidence, and unswerving support. Not only must such leaders be excited about what can be accomplished, but they must get others excited and committed also. If you lack the enthusiasm and excitement necessary to inspire your cohorts, they are not likely to follow you.

Horst Schulze, president of the Ritz-Carlton Hotel Company, exclaims that the essence of leadership is having a constant focus on the company's vision. "In fact," he says, "only leadership can pull you through the tough times. You can have a vision, be committed to the vision, and do things to get there. That's easy. But to keep focused on it, to keep people motivated behind it, and to not be sidetracked by excuses and by superficial effects is hard." There lies the argument for energizing your cohorts. Employees must be inspired and invigorated to achieve the noble cause expressed in the mission statement.

What picture or feeling do you get when you read the synonyms for the concept of energizing from a computerized thesaurus?

Activating:	Enlivening
Invigorating:	Vitalizing
Exciting:	Inspiring
Boosting:	Elevating
Championing:	Encouraging
Fostering:	Stimulating

This cluster of terms captures the essence of the energizing dimension of involvement. Energizing requires leaders to feel and demonstrate excitement, inspiration, and action. Leaders energize average employees to be high-performance cohorts. Energizing is a critical skill for raising performance levels in the workplace.

Jack Welch, chairman and CEO of General Electric Company, cited self-confidence as the "absolutely indispensable ingredient in a high-performance business culture. Self-confident people are open to good ideas regardless of their source and are willing to share them.... We began to cultivate self-confidence among our leaders by turning them loose, giving them independence and resources, and encouraging them to take big swings."

Leaders build excitement in others by expressing confidence in them and their abilities to do the job. They share stories with them of the successes of others and show the workers that their successes are valued and rewarded. To be an energizing influence on your workers, you need to lead with *commitment, compassion,* and *encouragement.* Moorhead and Griffin, management specialists, claim that if you can learn to magnify these three attributes in yourself, they will constitute an inner force that is, indeed, the very soul of powerful leadership.

Leading with Commitment

Leaders who energize others commit themselves to a cause. But that is not enough; powerful leaders commit themselves to a good cause, a purpose beyond the everyday activities of daily work, a noble cause. Powerful leaders are also committed to *great causes* that become the focus of their constant and patient devotion. As Hoffer claims, great causes impel action on the part of true believers. Powerful leaders commit themselves to the mission of the organization and the unit in which they work. They see the mission as a cause to be pursued and accomplished. The challenge to accomplish the mission is important and worthwhile. As a potential powerful leader, you must likewise understand and commit yourself to the mission of your organization, which is another reason why you need to be involved in the development of the mission statement. You must be ready to advocate the organization's cause, including the programs and people involved, through thick and thin. You must feel strongly about achieving the goals of your unit as they contribute to the forward motion of the total organization. You must feel that your unit is a significant and critical part of the overall plan in accomplishing the grand mission.

You can tell when you are truly committed to the organizational mission and vision when you enlarge upon and magnify the mission to include everything that is happening around you and your unit. You sense a greater purpose in your daily work activities. You see more possibilities for your work unit than are apparent in the usual interpretation of the mission. You find yourself promoting the organization and your unit. You seek out ways to achieve goals and become the cocreator of the mission statement. The mission of the organization and your unit become personalized and intimate. When the organization fails, you fail; when the organization succeeds, you succeed.

Implementing the vision requires leaders and cohorts alike to persist under adverse circumstances. Irving Shapiro, former chairman of the board of DuPont, observed, "any fool can do it [persist] when things are going well. But how do you stay with it and keep things right when you're really in trouble? I've seen fellows who look like the greatest guys in the world and yet, when the crunch comes, they fold."

We suggest that you begin by asking yourself these key questions: Am I going to be a run-of-the-mill manager or a powerful leader of people? Am I going to commit myself to both the mission of the organization and the goals of my unit? Am I going to make all of the major decisions and tell people what to do, or am I going to encourage and enable cohorts to take the lead, make decisions, and recommend changes in the way things should be done? If you ever dream of doing anything great as a leader, you must consciously decide to commit to doing more than engaging in the routine necessities of managing.

There is a management saying that goes like this: confirm or replace. When someone is not doing well in a position and does not want to learn how to do the job better, the only alternative is to replace the person. This applies to you as a leader. If you are not committed to making certain that goals are being achieved in the very best way, your followers will soon detect that something is awry. The very fact that you are in a leadership position gives you more opportunity for personal growth and development and provides you with more ways to help your employees grow and develop. When others see that you are intensely loyal and committed to the company, to the customers, and most of all, to your employees, you will be an extremely powerful, positive force and influence in your organization.

Leading with Compassion

The boldness and directness of powerful leaders should always be tempered by a genuine concern for the feelings and needs of others. Since all of us make mistakes, it is rather easy to be critical of one another. As a leader, you need to keep your eye on preserving the confidence workers have in their own abilities. This is called *self-confidence or self-efficacy*. If something goes awry, you must focus on maintaining the self-confidence, significance, and value of employees. This often entails evaluating situations in terms of a greater goal.

Colman Mockler, CEO of Gillette, resisted three takeover attempts, but was a gracious person with a gentle manner. Phil Collins describes Mockler as a leader who experienced epic battles with corporate raiders and who never lost his shy, courteous style. "He chose to fight for the future greatness of Gillette even though he could have pocketed millions by flipping his stock." Nevertheless, "his placid persona hid an inner intensity, a dedication to making anything he touched the best—not just because of what he would get but because he couldn't imagine doing it any other way."

The idea of leading with compassion is illustrated by a conversation overheard in our university faculty health facilities. Two professional basketball officials were sitting in a hot steam room discussing their different approaches to refereeing. Apparently, the younger official had been to a refresher seminar and was acquainted with some new rule changes and interpretations. During the discussion, questions were raised about when contact fouls should be called, when moving screens should be penalized, and when a variety of other rule violations should be enforced. The younger referee displayed his seemingly infinite knowledge of the rules of the game. The older referee then said something that quite surprised his younger colleague: "If I called a rule infraction every time I was aware of one, I would be stopping the game every three to five seconds. The goal of refereeing is having a fair game, not calling fouls." Compassion calls for ignoring most of the trivial mistakes employees make, although significant violations should be handled with great care and consideration and dispatched as quickly as possible.

Workers need to be valued and feel significant. You fail to show compassion when you use tactless and offensive ways of saying things that diminish their importance. Verbal abuse must be guarded against every hour of the day if you want to become an energizing leader. Compassion is revealed by the amount of consideration you give to the basic needs of others. Maslow identified five categories of needs—physiological, safety, esteem, ego, and actualization—to which you must give constant attention.

Many workers need to rest and be relieved of tedious jobs. A worker's self-confidence is eroded by personal problems that should be resolved by assistance from resources both in and out of the company. You can be more compassionate by speaking kindly to people, by indicating that you value them as individuals, and by being supportive during times of need. Compassion is also demonstrated when you show sensitivity to workers' needs to be free from organizational constraints, to be creative and use their imaginations, and to be respected. Another way to energize workers is to be encouraging.

Leading with Encouragement

Martin Seligman, professor, researcher, and author of *Learned Optimism,* has shown that the simplest way to encourage others is to use expressions of optimism. Jesus, who is recognized by Christians as the greatest leader of all time, constantly encouraged his followers with a simple optimistic declaration: "Be of good cheer." You can lead in the same manner, giving encouragement to your associates and lifting them with words and actions that cheer them up.

Lou Holtz, a prominent university football coach with one of the best winning records, does everything in his power to encourage his players.

He teaches them the fundamentals of the game: blocking, tackling, and teamwork. Then he uses a barrage of positive comments to energize his players to perform at their highest levels: "You can do it, son." "They can't knock you down." "You're the best." He does not dwell on the players' faults or their weaknesses, but focuses on their strengths.

The whole idea is to make weaknesses insignificant. Each year, the team's objective is to play in a major bowl game. In practice, the players see how positive the coach is and how totally committed he is to his players. They in turn respond optimistically by doing things on the playing field that other coaches say border on the superhuman. More often than not, team members perform well enough to receive an invitation to play in a college bowl game.

Ken Melrose, chairman and CEO of the Toro Company, articulates the importance of this view when he asserts, "You have it within your power to help your company develop a new culture—with a climate of trust defined by a set of values that stresses the dignity and importance of every employee. This is the service you can best offer your company as a leader."

Many times we are energized by the rewards we see accruing as a result of the successful accomplishment of a task. This step in the involvement process is an excellent opportunity to visualize the contribution, money, or opportunities that are associated with the completion of a task or goal. Individuals frequently try to keep themselves going toward a goal by making a list, mentally or on paper, of all the wonderful things that will happen if they can just achieve their goal. People trying to get out of debt visualize the debt-free life. People who try to complete classes in an educational institution focus on the beneficial outcomes of a degree or certificate of completion to provide the energy to keep going. Often, people who are contributing regularly to a savings and investment program are highly involved because they visualize the good life of retirement without financial worry. You can more effectively lead your people by helping them visualize the benefits that will accrue both intrinsically and extrinsically if they complete the task or achieve the goal that you have articulated.

A sage once said, "The best way to change people is to treat them as if they had already changed." In other words, respecting a person's talents and potential encourages positive change and tends to enhance performance. Nevertheless, sustained change and performance only occur when you ensure results.

E 4 = Ensuring Results

The final E has to do with ensuring that things are going ahead as they should. Even after the first three E's have been used properly, something may still go amiss and not get done. To ensure that everything is going, as it should, you need to devise, as Moorhead and Griffin suggest, a "return and report" process to keep workers energized and to keep you informed about their progress. Adults respond positively to feedback, provided that it is not judgmental. This means that workers like information about how they are doing, but they don't like to be criticized. This philosophy is reflected in Deming's observation, "What gets measured gets done."

The most common leadership weakness is the lack of willingness or the inability to clearly focus on employees' goals, to provide support and feedback, and to create a climate of celebration and rejoicing when goals are achieved. The return and report process provides a way to strengthen each of the above weaknesses.

Ensuring results can be accomplished only if workers understand clearly what is required, how it might be accomplished, the timeframe in which it needs to be done, the importance of the task, and how the results will be reviewed. Initially, the process begins with a face-to-face meeting in which each element that needs to be understood is reviewed and agreed upon. Such an encounter fosters greater understanding between you and your employee of what needs to be done. For example, if a worker needs to show more respect to his or her colleagues, a clear statement of what the employee should do to show respect should be set forth during the initial meeting. The employee's goal might be stated like this:

> I will show respect to my coworkers by asking them, in a personal conversation with each of them, what they suggest as ways to complete our work in a simpler and easier way.

Although it may be difficult to ascertain in a return and report meeting whether respect has been given to coworkers, the number of conversations held and the number of suggestions received can be easily measured and documented.

The Return and Report Meeting

A number of steps are involved in a return and report meeting. The following list summarizes the essential steps of such a meeting, although the fine points of conducting the meeting depend on the nature of the relationship between the two parties involved.

1. Establish a positive, optimistic climate. Greet the person like you would a cohort. Sit down, face one another, and smile. Open the meeting with some small talk about the person's family and personal background. Try to make the other person comfortable and willing to talk to you.

2. Briefly review the assignment or what the person was going to accomplish. Everyone needs to be reminded about what they were to do, especially if the task to be done was discussed some time ago.

3. Ask the employee what he or she did in relation to the task or goal; especially ask about how the results were to be measured. That is, in terms of the goal cited above—to show more respect—you should expect a report on the number of personal conversations that the worker participated in, how they went, and how many ideas were derived from the conversations.

4. As the person explains what he or she accomplished, respond to the person with both verbal comments and nonverbal reactions that are supportive and positive. Assure the person that he or she has done many things appropriately and that you are pleased with the results.

5. Where parts of the task were not accomplished as planned, give responses that indicate you understand what happened, but mention that you would like to talk about what else needs to be done. Ask the person what needs to be done to complete the task. As the person explains what needs to be done, rephrase his or her comments into the form of a new goal to be achieved after the meeting. Ask the person reporting about the resources he or she needs to move ahead with the new goal. Volunteer any assistance you can to help the person get started. End the meeting by expressing appreciation for the contributions of the person, by indicating that he or she is a valuable employee, and by explaining that what the person is doing is important and useful to the organization.

Powerful leaders do not just invite employees to complete tasks. They are more encouraging and exciting. If subordinates look a little bored, they can be assigned research projects to stimulate interest.

Integrating the Four E's of Involvement

If you want to involve workers in a way that energizes them to accomplish unusually superior results, you should integrate the use of the 4E's into the following simple process. This process integrates envisioning, enabling, energizing, and ensuring into a comprehensive, coherent whole that allows you to master the 4E's in the simplest and easiest way possible. We shall assume that you have an employee whom you would like to involve in accomplishing a goal. You should extend an invitation to that person to participate in achieving the goal and to meet with you to review what needs to be done.

1. **Give the Whole Picture.** The first step is to explain what the goal is and the circumstances under which the goal is to be achieved. For example, you could say, "Our goal is to facilitate an exceptional meeting on the importance of quality in the company. The meeting consists of three parts. At the beginning of the meeting we would like to have three reports on employee suggestions about how to cut costs and make our operation more profitable. We will then separate into small groups for a discussion of the reports. After that, we plan to reassemble and integrate the ideas from the group discussions into a working plan."

2. **Describe the Need.** The second step is to explain that we already have a presenter from housekeeping and another from food and beverages. What we really need in order to complete the initial part of our quality meeting is a representative from sales and marketing to share something that his or her group is doing or could be doing to cut costs.

3. **Share the Decision.** Ask the individual this question: "As a manager in sales and marketing, do you think that you could gather some data and make one of the presentations?" If the person agrees to make the presentation, take a few moments and review the specific ways that he or she might get information for the presentation. Some ideas might be to solicit input from subordinates by making "two-on-the-town" tickets available for a dinner and play to everyone who submits five or more cost-saving ideas. Ask whether the person needs something signed by you or a higher authority to invite the subordinates to participate.

4. **Emphasize the Importance.** Be sure to stress the importance of what you are asking the person to do. Say, "Our directing

officers are concerned about shrinking profit margins. But at this point, they are more interested in the employees' suggestions than they are in trying to make the decisions themselves. You will be representing your people in marketing and sales, and you will be giving them a great opportunity to be heard by our top-level managers."

5. **Establish a Trigger Point.** Set a time, usually a few days before the assignment is to be completed, when the individual can be called, reminded, and encouraged to complete the assignment. Set a time that is convenient for the individual. If you are a busy person, you could assign an assistant to make the call. Inquire by asking, "How is that presentation coming for Thursday in our quality meeting? Is there anything further that you need to know about the meeting? Is there anything we can help you with?"

6. **Follow Up.** Either you or an assistant should make special note of how the presentation goes. Establish a specific time when the person can return and report on the presentation and the meeting.

7. **Give Recognition.** No matter how many times a person is involved in working to achieve a goal, take the time to acknowledge the efforts of the individual. You should give special recognition to and make a little fuss over the person completing the assignment. You should remember that every time someone else assists you in completing a project, they make you look good and often relieve you from doing the job yourself. You should be grateful to those who assist you and confirm in words and deeds that you appreciate what each person has done for you and the organization.

Why Inviting People to Be Involved Is Important

Inviting others to complete projects, assignments, and tasks demonstrates the trust and confidence you have in your followers. Sharing projects and important work assignments gives individuals and groups the opportunity to develop their capabilities and increase their knowledge. Most important, inviting and enabling others to complete tasks improves the morale of cohorts and increases their commitment because it allows them to decide how to do their work.

You may have noticed that we did emphasize the notion of inviting and enabling rather than telling and empowering. And you may have also noticed that we have avoided trying to explain a dozen or two theories of motivation. The reason is simple: It is much more human and ennobling to ask and invite people to do things than it is to tell them. Japanese managers feel that they have failed if they have to tell or command someone to do something. We believe they are right. All of us need to reexamine our language usage when involving others. Perhaps we would all be more effective if we used words like "could you?" "would you?" and "can you?" rather than "do this" and "do that."

Listening to the conversations about assignments in a productive company called Chemical & Mineralogical Services was more than interesting. Each time the owner/manager needed to have something done, he walked up to an employee and said, "Could you analyze these ore samples first this evening?" Or he asked, "On your way back from lunch would you be able to stop past the chemical supply house and pick up another couple of bottles of acid?" It was amazing the respect that was demonstrated for employees by inviting them to do things rather than giving orders.

The whole point of using the involvement formula is that leaders need to keep people moving and contributing. Once cohorts feel a lack of forward motion, they quickly become bored and less productive. Leaders cannot afford to wait around until workers energize themselves. They must use every means possible to keep cohorts involved, on fire, and performing. Don't forget to ensure that the work is moving forward by having a return and report session. You or an assistant need to follow up to make sure that you know at all times how workers are performing. That final step of ensuring also gives you a chance to celebrate achievements with workers and rejoice in their successes.

A Look Ahead

Because criticizing and reprimanding are considered such negative and abusive behaviors in the workplace, we make a special point in the next chapter about how essential it is to avoid criticizing others and giving demeaning responses, and instead to provide positive support and encouragement to the efforts of successful cohorts. The greatness of leaders may be measured by the extent to which they bring about this essential change in their own thinking and personal behavior.

6

THE FIFTH
ESSENTIAL CHANGE:
STOP CRITICIZING
AND START APPLAUDING

The beatings will continue until morale improves.

—Sign on an executive's desk

"Bosses from Hell" is the heading of one section of *Time* magazine's special issue on builders and titans of the 20th century. Leona Helmsley was characterized as the "Queen of Mean," and when Dick Snyder was president of Simon & Schuster, a recommended piece of equipment for executives was earplugs to lessen the intensity of Snyder's verbal assaults. George Steinbrenner, owner of the New York Yankees baseball team, was described as a paradigm of "impetuous power (throwing tantrums, bad-mouthing employees in the press, and hiring a spy to dig up dirt on Dave

Winfield)." Joel Stein, the author, asked, "What good is having power if you can't abuse it?"

All of us have memories of being criticized by a parent, teacher, or boss. Inevitably, those confrontations struck terror into our souls and left us feeling defensive, angry, and more than a little bitter. Bosses from hell elicit intense emotions that come on quickly and last for what seem like ages. Brutal criticism provokes negative feelings that cannot be easily allayed. We lose confidence in our ability to work productively and successfully.

A person's self-concept and self-esteem are terribly fragile entities and require a considerable amount of nurturing and gentle development. Most of us feel degraded, rejected, and incapable of coping when our behaviors are criticized. Negative emotional outbursts from a manager may severely damage the natural capacity people have to work productively. Malicious, critical attacks on the intimate and sensitive network of a person's self-perceptions produce equally destructive reactions of repugnance, incompetence, and impotence. Criticism tends to confirm bad images and wipe away feelings of self-reliance and confidence that are central to effective work. Even well-intentioned criticism is destructive and generates a kind of contemporary tragedy in which "you always hurt the one you love," as expressed in a popular old song.

Some days, pressures and concerns will make you particularly vulnerable to the temptation to lash out at someone. When managers threaten, punish, and criticize workers, about the only thing that happens is that employees become hostile and hurt, and they look for ways to "get even." Practically every business has experienced this form of employee response. Every day we become aware of employees undermining the boss because they have been harshly criticized for something that they were doing at work. Vandalism, theft, and various forms of slowdown are common in an organizational environment where a manager is trying to overdirect and overcorrect the actions of the employees. One-on-one criticism is bad enough; reprimanding a whole group of employees is usually always an open invitation for rebellion. But the whole failing of criticizing and threatening people is that it does absolutely nothing to redirect anyone to a more preferred behavior.

Let's examine a form of criticism that is couched in a standard organizational practice called reprimanding. We recently met with an expert in human resource management and told him that criticizing was out and applauding was in. He laughed, but when he saw that we were serious, a look of horror and concern set itself upon his face. "But I teach about reprimanding and do consulting with organizations about the proper way to reprimand," he said. Even though many management books have a section on reprimanding and criticizing, we were happy to inform this human resource expert that we were in the process of arranging an appropriate funeral service for the culprit. We hoped to bury the corpse of criticism deep enough that it would have little chance of resurfacing for at least a thousand years.

> *Animals are such agreeable friends—*
> *They ask no questions, they pass no criticisms.*

> —George Eliot

Because of its awful negative connotations, the word reprimanding needs to be scrubbed from our vocabulary. Can you imagine the feelings of a fellow employee who is going to receive a reprimand, or what usually turns into an unpleasant time of criticism? A reprimand, according to a standard dictionary, means "a severe rebuke, especially an official one." Synonyms for reprimand are admonish, censure, chastise, reproach, scold, and chide. Clearly, these are all negative actions that a leader wants to avoid because they fail to uplift people and give them control over their own lives.

The gist of a reprimand involves judging people by identifying violations of behavior and then strongly rebuking them for the violations. Winston Churchill may have expressed it best when he said, "Nothing in life is so exhilarating as to be shot at without result." We think that the most exciting thing about a reprimand is that it may miss its mark.

A traditional reprimand fails in four critical ways:

1. It fails to discover causes or reasons underlying behaviors. The tendency is to judge rather than discover why a person violated a norm of behavior or did something unacceptable. Circumstances drive managers to look at a situation that displeases them and to react in a critical manner. Too often, managers seek to disparage, disapprove, reprove, denounce, censure, nag, fuss, carp, and nitpick before they understand what has been happening.

2. It fails to focus on the effects, results, or consequences of behaviors. Employees seldom have the opportunity to visualize the results of their behavior. The tendency, again, is to judge before the employee has grasped the consequences of what has happened. The result is that employees turn their energies outside

the organization, at the least, or look for ways to sabotage organizational operations, at the most.

3. It fails to free people to discover ways to change their own behaviors. Because of the directive nature of judge-and-reprimand-processes, employees seldom have an opportunity to choose to make appropriate changes in their behavior. The hope is that the reprimand will bring about conformity to expected behaviors, but the usual result is to simply take away the agency of employees and provoke them to anger. Employees should be given the opportunity to understand what is happening and decide what to do to improve circumstances.

4. It fails to identify behaviors to applaud. A judge-and-reprimand approach to changing behavior ignores the basic understanding that goals are the visions that mobilize human behavior. Hope is weakened, leaving a void about what can and should be accomplished in the future. Criticism fails to help people set goals for future achievements.

We must acquire the ability to handle situations that displease us without being critical of others. Criticism must stop. A new way of handling bad situations is required. Let's set the stage for a transformation in responding to situations in which you have an overwhelming urge to shout, curse, or voice expletives to show your displeasure. Is it possible to be confronted with incompetent people and not express criticism of their behavior? We think so.

The Process of Redirection

The way to perform as a leader, when a colleague or cohort displays lack of competence, is to move through the steps of redirection, a simple but powerful technique. Redirection is based on the fundamental principle that people will correct deviations in their behavior when they recognize a better way to perform and are supported in making changes.

You may have felt surges of energy and the desire to do well when your efforts were acknowledged and excitement was expressed when you did something well. Just a word of thanks or praise or a pat on the back can lighten a task and make living worthwhile. People who are applauded for their efforts not only continue working in a more energetic manner, but they are also more likely to help cohorts and coworkers make things better in the workplace.

Leaders tend to fall into the criticism trap when they try to correct the mistakes of workers. Because leaders play such an important role in the happiness, vitality, and confidence of followers, adopting a way to correct mistakes without criticism is very important. Redirecting the efforts of a worker represents a skill of the highest order for powerful leaders. People become better focused and energized when deviations in their work are redirected. In addition, they have greater confidence in your leadership abilities and support you more in achieving organizational goals.

When you're on the firing line, you might assume that it is not easy to change people without criticism. In fact, you may not be able to immediately avoid every bit of criticism of others. If you slip now and then while learning not to criticize, you will want to do something to soften the blow to the person you criticized. The research of Johnson, Gibb, and Thibaut & Coules indicates that when you criticize others, you must immediately show an increase in warmth toward them or they will interpret your criticism as hostility towards them and consider you an enemy rather than a cohort.

The safest route to take in correcting others is to use the skill called *redirection*. The process of redirecting people involves getting them to acknowledge that they have deviated from acceptable performance and then to help them understand how a change might be made to get back on the right track. The basic principles of redirecting others in a positive way, without the use of criticism, can be found in this story of our turbulent teens, related in first person.

When Do You Think You Can Have It Fixed?

Sixteen isn't an age of great responsibility, as I recall, but it is an age of great exhilaration. In fact, we may have had more "pure" fun than at almost any other age. If we could retain some of the excitement we felt at age 16, our lives would be adventurous. On the other hand, it is somewhat of a miracle that we actually survived to be 17—another very good year.

Where I grew up, a young person could get a driver's license at age 16. Around that age, young people began to date seriously. My cousin and I were in the same class and often double-dated with the same girls, although he had a favorite and began to stick to her quite regularly. On Saturday evenings the small towns in the area sponsored dances. My cousin and I asked a couple of high-school girls to go to a dance in a town about 10 miles to the south of where we lived.

We had a great time at the dance, frolicking with our dates and all the other girls during every musical number. The dance ended at about midnight. The four of us piled into the car. I was driving with my date in the front seat; my cousin was in the back seat with his date. We drove out of the parking lot of the dance hall, turned north, and slithered through the small town, passing a popular cafe and the homes of several of our relatives. On the outskirts of town, I speeded up a bit. We were laughing and talking about the good time we had had at the dance, resolving to go to all of the up coming dances.

The road was narrow, as were nearly all roads in those days, and it wound around a bit, crossing irrigation canals, traversing railroad overpasses, and wandering up and down small hills, all named after local residents. One particular curve was situated immediately after a railroad overpass. The road rose up to the overpass, crossed over the railroad tracks below, immediately curved to the left, straightened out, and passed over a large culvert through which water ran in an irrigation canal. If the driver didn't keep focused attention and make a hard left, a car could easily run into the bank of the canal and capsize in the water.

We rolled along the country road, passing over a bridge spanning a local creek, a favorite fishing spot for many, steered to the right, and approached the rise for the overpass and the railroad tracks beneath. Flashing across the overpass, I turned the steering wheel slightly to the left but followed the road straight ahead rather than taking a hard left. We were looking at one another, not particularly paying any attention to the road, since all of us had driven along that stretch dozens of times.

Suddenly, the car lurched and shot into the air, catapulting us into the roof of "Old Yeller," as we called the 1932 Chevrolet. We had missed the turn in the road, banged into the culvert channeling water under the road for the irrigation canal, and landed with a jolt on the other side. We sat stunned for several minutes before we were able to shove the car doors open and stumble along the embankment.

We discovered that the right side of the car had passed over the open waters of the canal and the driver's side of the car had banged into the metal culvert. In a case like that, one would normally expect the right side of the car to dip into the canal and roll over onto its top. We, however, landed with all four wheels flat on the ground on the other side of the canal. The result was that the front axle of the car was bent, forcing the tires to literally sit at an angle to the ground.

After inspecting all sides of the car, we decided that it was possible to drive the vehicle. We climbed back into the car, started it up, pulled onto the highway, and began driving down the road. The splayed-out front tires scraped and wobbled as they tried to rotate. It took approximately 5 miles of driving before the tread on the tires was worn completely off. We were only 2 miles from my cousin's home, so we let him off to walk the 2 miles to borrow his parents' car. He met us a mile or so down the road, where we were wobbling and scraping along, and he loaded the girls into his car for the trip to their homes.

I arrived home around two in the morning, parked the car in the driveway of my dad's service station, and slipped into our house next door. Because of the late hour, my parents were awake and waiting for me. "Where have you been?" they asked. "At the dance," I said. "Why are you late?" my mother queried. "We hit a bump in the road and did something to the car," I explained. "We'll look at it in the morning," my dad said. "Are you okay?" he asked. I said we were all just fine. I went off to bed.

Early the next morning, my dad started the car and drove it into the garage on the north end of the station where he was waiting for me when I arrived to inspect the car in the light. My dad was not known for his gentle acceptance of his children's irresponsible behavior. I was more than apprehensive about facing him after an accident in which I may have been totally at fault and after having had my driver's license for only a few months.

He looked at the car as I stood there and asked, "What does the car look like?"

"What do you think?"

I replied, "It looks like the tires are all worn out and the axle is bent."

"I think so," he said. "Do you want to drive the car some other time?"

"Well, yes," I said.

"When do you think you can have it fixed?" he asked.

I was stunned. He never said, "How stupid can you be, to run off the road like that?" Or, "I'm going to fix your cart. You're grounded for five years." Or, "You could have killed everyone and even hurt yourself. What were you thinking?" No, he didn't say anything like that. He simply asked, "When do you think you can have it fixed?" and walked away.

I did fix it, with his help, of course. He helped identify what needed to be done and how it should be done, but he left me to do it. He simply redirected my thinking away from the problem toward solutions. To this day, I have been continually impressed with the manner in which my father handled this difficult situation without controlling, dominating, and reprimanding. The end result was a repaired car, albeit with a lot of perspiration and work, a closer relationship between father and son, and a great deal of applause when the job was finished.

The applause of a single human being is of great consequence.

—Samuel Johnson

Stop Punishing People

We all make mistakes, and we make a lot of them. When we criticize people, we are engaging in a form of verbal and emotional abuse. Punishment is a lose-lose situation and doesn't do very much to reduce the unacceptable in behavior. In reality, we ought to learn how to turn a mistake into an opportunity for applauding. In that way, the worker, staff members, you as a manager, and the organization will all benefit.

The approach to redirecting people's behavior discussed in this chapter focuses on the more salient process of *applauding rather than criticizing* and guides individuals away from less relevant ways of thinking and acting toward more positive capabilities. The principles and processes are the same for individuals who fail to meet our expectations, whether the failures seriously affect organizational functioning or involve poor performance. In fact, this entire book may be considered an effort to transform run-of-the-mill thinking and acting into exceptional thinking and acting.

Nothing so soon the drooping spirits raise
As praises from the men, whom all men praise.

—Abraham Cowley
Ode upon a Copy of Verses of My Lord Broghill's

The process of *applauding employees* begins by eliciting from them the goals to be achieved for exceptional levels of performance and relationships, then giving them the freedom to achieve the goals in creative and innovative ways. The applause naturally follows celebrations of achievement.

Will Someone Please Authenticate Me!

A corollary principle is: *legitimize, don't reward.* To legitimize means to make something lawful, real or genuine, or conform to recognized practices; to authorize or justify. Rewards are frequently viewed as prizes that offend and belittle people rather than elevate them. The goal of an authentic leader is to help people feel legitimate.

I remember a story my mother used to tell about a family who went out for dinner at a restaurant. After they were seated, the waitress took the order from the adults present, then turned to the young boy.

"What will you have, young man?" she asked.

The boy said, somewhat tentatively, "I'll have a hot dog."

The mother immediately interrupted the boy and said, "He's not going to have a hot dog. Bring him a hamburger with potatoes and carrots."

The waitress, however, ignored the mother and continued speaking to the boy. "Would you like ketchup and mustard on the hot dog?"

"I'd like ketchup," the boy replied with a smile on his face.

"Coming up," said the waitress.

The mother sat in stunned silence.

Finally, the boy turned to his parents and said, "You know what? She thinks I'm real!"

This story is a great example of the effect of *legitimization*. It makes people real.

When employees' thinking and actions are legitimized, few external rewards, beyond routine salary advances and typical monetary disbursements, are necessary. The legitimization is its own reward. What is critical, essential, appropriate, and most effective is a variety of forms of legitimization.

From Redirecting to Applause in Four Easy Steps

The replacement of criticism with redirection and applauding can be implemented by using four simple actions, as illustrated by the car incident:

1. Directly address the problem. My dad asked, "What happened? What does the car look like? Do you see a difficulty there?"

2. Recognize what the person would like to achieve. My dad asked, "Do you want to drive the car again?" He was getting at my long-range goal and was simply helping me maintain the proper focus.

3. Identify what changes need to take place. Dad asked, "When do you think you can have it fixed?" He knew we would have to talk about the specifics of how the car was to be repaired, but I

had the general idea as a result of looking at the state of the car and what appeared to be the difficulties.

4. Applaud efforts to correct the difficulties. Of course, dad guided the work. I did repair the car, and my dad encouraged and supported me in doing the work. I learned a great deal about car repair and what kind of effort was involved in straightening an axle. My efforts were applauded.

Reality Therapy

William Glasser, a famous psychologist, uses a similar four-step approach in helping people confront their problems and change their behaviors. His method may give you some additional ideas about how to help people make constructive changes in a positive way.

1. **Awareness.** Help individuals recognize what they are doing that is causing problems. Ask them simple questions in a friendly way. If necessary, give them information you have received about the problem behavior, and ask them if they are aware of what is happening. Don't make any judgments; just ask questions.

2. **Consequences.** Ask them what they are trying to achieve in the particular situation under discussion. If necessary, clarify with them what will probably happen if the behavior continues.

3. **Decision to Change.** Ask the individuals if there is anything they would like to change in their current behavior to make things better or to avoid some of the eventual consequences. If it seems appropriate, or if an individual asks about various options, offer examples of what others have done. The important thing here is to let the individual decide how to make things better. When you jump in with all your great wisdom, your suggestions tend to fit no one but you. Each of us is different. What works for one may not work for another. Also, we seldom know the unique strengths and capabilities of other people, especially those with whom we work. Let them play to their own strengths, and they will probably succeed.

4. **Support the Decision.** This step is a lot like the enabling, energizing, and ensuring steps in the 4E's formula discussed earlier. Once the person has made a decision to change for the better,

offer your help in every way possible to facilitate the change and to reinforce the desired behavior. Encourage and energize the individual by pointing out the benefits of the change. Then, express personal confidence in the person's ability to move ahead in the decision. Don't forget to provide an opportunity for the person to return and report on successful progress so you can celebrate together.

Avoid Undermining Employees and Cohorts

Whenever you attempt to redirect a person, keep in mind some fundamental do's and don'ts:

Don't try to help people when you are upset and angry. Others will see your anger and feel that you are out of control and in no condition to listen to their points of view.

Do attend to the mistake quickly. Talk to the person as early as possible before the problem gets worse or the behavior repeats itself. Never draw attention to a person's difficulty in public, of course. Find a private place and speak to the individual in a relaxed atmosphere.

Be clear and specific, and focus on behavior. Never attack individual personalities; always look at what is being done. Support individuals while you assess the extent to which their behavior should change. If the person is unaware of his or her troublesome behavior, you may need to provide supportive explanations with specific data that show the undesirable effects.

Do not redirect and give praise at the same time. A famous entrepreneur said, "We stack every bit of criticism between two layers of praise." Although that sounds good, *don't do it.* A "sandwich" approach tends to create confusion. Any perceptive employee knows that you are only trying to ease the pain of criticism. If you have grasped the concept of applauding and redirecting, you have little need to squeeze a criticism between unnecessary compliments.

This chapter tries to move you from criticizing to applauding. Most of us have difficulty giving "constructive criticisms" to others anyway, primarily because all such actions are offensive. All parties are uncomfortable with the process and the consequences of poorly handled confrontations with people. Most attempts at reproving and criticizing others end up with both the employee and the manager feeling more discouraged than encouraged. You may find, for example, that what was said and done could be subject to appeal and review, and could even result in arbitration. You might be carrying out the reprimand and discipline for the wrong reasons, and those reasons may be unlawful. Judgments made when you are highly emotional may be difficult to justify later.

Personality clashes between managers and employees may be somewhat inevitable, but the definition of effective leadership includes the ability to tolerate and deal with different personality types. In addition, when different cultural backgrounds are involved, a question may arise concerning whether the reprimand was precipitated by work difficulties, personality differences, or cultural and ethnic differences.

The four steps leading to applause are a positive force that give the employee the necessary direction to avoid future troubles and that lead to better relationships in the organization.

Confrontational Anticipation Scares the Heck Out of People

Let us consider for a moment the most irritating aspect of moving toward applause: the general attitude of the people who are about to be redirected in their thinking and actions. They tend to have one of three attitudes as they anticipate being confronted. They are defensive; they rationalize or try to justify their actions. They are withdrawing; they are noncommunicative and attempt to avoid involvement in the process. They are aggressive; they overcommunicate because any criticism is considered a threat. The assumption is that those being criticized are wrong, and few people want to appear foolish and wrong. No one wants his or her ego and self-concept to be attacked.

Applause counteracts each of these attitudinal problems and paves the way for more constructive relationships with less pain for everyone involved. Coupled with the basic premise that you should treat others as cohorts, applause is the simplest, most effective way to redirect the thinking and actions of those with whom you work. The four-step approach to reaching the stage of applause allows you to bring about changes in the thinking and actions of others in a way that they understand and accept. They will then engage in supportive and more positive contributions to the organization.

There is a story about one of the leaders of a developing business organization. The leader used stickpins on a big map to show where every representative of the organization was located. One of the reps in the northern sector wasn't doing as well as the leader thought he should be. He was invited to the office of the leader for some redirection. "I'm not saying that you're in imminent danger of being replaced," explained the leader, "but, if you look closely at the map, you'll see that your pin has been loosened."

The applause process may loosen a few pins while at the same time reestablish them even firmer on behalf of the company. Since leaders are some of the most important people in the lives of employees, you should take every opportunity to help your colleagues perform well at work. If you sense that an employee is struggling, like the leader of this organization did, don't wait for the difficulty to escalate. Invite the employee in and figure out a way you can help redirect and energize the individual so that when the cohort leaves your presence, both of you will have a reason for celebrating and being happy.

So little, so little, did you say? Why, if there's nothing else—there's applause. I've listened, from backstage, to people applaud. It's like— like waves of love coming over the footlights and wrapping you up. Imagine. To know, every night, that different hundreds of people love you. They smile. Their eyes shine. You've pleased them. They want you. You belong. Just that is worth anything.

—Anne Baxter indicating what makes her tick.
From Joseph L. Mankiewicz's *All About Eve*

Praising Is Good, but Applauding Is Better

These two word columns illustrate key differences between praising and applauding:

Praise	Applause
Words	Feelings
Comment	Demonstration
Downward	Across
Congratulate	Celebrate
Pat-on-the-back	Embrace
Lips-to-ear	Heart-to-heart
Short-lived	Enduring

Applause is a richer and fuller concept than praise. To applaud means to give your whole self to the process rather than just a smile and a comment. Praise wears thin, especially when repeated over and over again. What is worse, if everyone knows that they are in a contest "to catch people doing something right," praise turns into a game with winners and losers, and an awful lot of resentment. It is considerably better to do what a number of leaders are doing. When their people are working hard and need a little boost, the manager walks up to them, hands each of them a couple of two-on-the-town tickets for a dinner and a show, and gives them a warm hug. No big fuss is made and the leader says, "Thanks for working here. We appreciate you."

Applauding, rejoicing, and celebrating are different from praise. With applause, we feel something inside that comes out in the tone of our voice and the expression on our face. We are truly excited about the success of another. We treat the other person's achievement as a victory and a triumph. There probably isn't a parent alive who doesn't spend a considerable amount of time coaching their children to use the potty. Do you remember the way you celebrated and applauded the first success of one of your children, even to the point of describing in detail the size of the success?

> For the first time in my life, people cheering for *me*. Were you deaf?
> Didn't you hear 'em? We're not Hitchhiking any more. We're riding.
>
> —Kirk Douglas hallucinates about his first flush of prizefighting fame.
> From Mark Robson's *Champion*

Applauding is like that! You shouldn't speak down to the employee from a position of leader. You shouldn't just communicate words, but you should express your feelings of happiness because a fellow human being has accomplished a good effort. Remember the third essential change: Switch from boss to cohort! Imagine that the succeeding employee is a cohort who has accomplished something that is good in his or her life, or who has completed a task well. Would you simply offer a compliment? Or would you find yourself elated and excited that things went well? No question about it, you would let the cohort know that you truly appreciate his or her work.

We saw a sign the other day that said, "Life is Short, Eat Your Dessert First!" Applause is the dessert of the workplace. You need to serve a lot more of it, and not just at the end of a meal. A colleague of ours raised the question, "If life is so short, why do we spend so much time beating up on one another?" Maybe we think that putting people down lifts us up! Nothing could be further from the truth. We get what we give. If we start applauding and stop criticizing, the odds are pretty good that others will also start applauding and stop criticizing.

What Is the Most Powerful Workplace Motivator?

Recognition programs clearly move in the right direction, but they are often a bland and uninspiring form of praise. Praise is, of course, a good thing, but as we have noted, applause is better. Technically, applause has to do with clapping, and we enjoin you to use physical clapping to engender the kind of spirit implied by applause. On the other hand, plaudits are considered to be verbal clapping. Plaudits add to applause by providing a verbal supportive dimension. Thus, although we like the idea of applause, technically speaking, you should give both applause and plaudits.

Applause means that you should do everything in your power as a leader to indicate your approval of, acclaim for, praise of, and appreciation for the contributions of every employee within your scope of authority. Physical and verbal clapping is the generic way in which your approval is indicated, but there may be many other ways to reveal and demonstrate your support of your employees.

Although Caudron, writing in *Industry Week*, considers such actions as congratulating an employee in private for doing a good job, sending a handwritten note of appreciation, keyboarding an email message of congratulations, recognizing employee accomplishments in public meetings, and celebrating both individual and team accomplishments as top ways to motivate employees, they fail to meet the high standards of applauding. They are much too routine.

When you applaud people, do it with enthusiasm, feeling, and excitement in the presence of the person. Praise is at the lowest level of applause. Applauding, in its ultimate form, comes from the soul and the heart and is exhibited spontaneously. All parties are to applaud one another, to celebrate together. Applauding is a mini-carnival. It is the spirit of two people communicating together. It goes beyond just a mouth-to-ear experience, and it involves feeling joy together. Congratulations are okay, but they lack the fundamental emotional dimension of applause. One can hardly applaud with an email message or a plaque in a public meeting. Applause is heart-to-heart, mind-to-mind, soul-to-soul. You must feel applause as a visceral, free, uninhibited dance, where jumping up and down is encouraged and the joy of accomplishment is acclaimed.

A standing ovation involves cheering performance, clapping your hands, stretching your bodies and minds, and loving every minute of it. As a member of the audience, you are alive, expressing your appreciation by means of a total experience. Praise pales in comparison to applause. The emotion of applause leaves an enduring memory of the pleasant, the positive, and the personal creative expression of support. The strong feeling in one's heart is unmistakable when applause occurs. Applaud more, avoid criticism, show emotional support, fly with eagles, sing praises, and enjoy the moment. Stop criticizing. Start applauding!

> At night, she goes to sleep with the music of applause in her ears.
> And, Danny, she can't see you and she can't hear you because she's
> blinded by those lights and deafened by that applause.
>
> —Arthur Kennedy telling James Cagney about Ann Sheridan's true love.
> From Anatole Litvak's *City for Conquest*

The stop-criticizing-and-start-applauding philosophy has broader applications to leadership in all types of organizations. For example, Tobia and Johnson have documented the fall and rise of the Chrysler plant at New Castle, Indiana. The plant manufactured shock absorbers and steering knuckles for rear-wheel-drive cars. When Chrysler moved to building front-wheel-drive vehicles, the parts became obsolete and consideration was given to closing the plant.

Awful relationships between workers and management, deteriorating physical condition of the plant, and excessive costs of production provided additional support for closing. Relationships between union and management were openly hostile, with employees filing as many as 85 grievances a month. Rubble littered the floors, and the outside walls were revolting. The same parts manufactured by the plant could be purchased on the open market for less than it cost to produce them. Employees had been let go so that only 500 out of 3,500 were still employed. Everyone expected Chrysler to whack them off and eliminate the operations.

Corporate executives decided, however, to see if someone could turn the plant around. They selected a new plant manager who introduced a Modern Operating Agreement (MOA) that proposed some new ways for management and the union to work together. The MOA changed the hierarchical structure of the plant by consolidating 50 work classifications into 4 and reduced 22 trade classifications to 8. The agreement eliminated some management levels and brought self-managed teams into the plant. Seventy-two teams were created and each assigned 20 duties.

The agreement was vague about what workers and teams were to do, making it necessary for employees to make decisions about the details of production. The MOA created two new job classifications: team coordinator and facilitator. Each team elected the coordinator, who served as liaison between the team and the facilitators, who were the liaisons between team coordinators, leaders in management, and the union.

Teams met weekly to discuss everything from employee suggestions to quality reports, making information-sharing a high priority. Team coordinators met with facilitators to discuss issues arising from team meetings; they also discussed scrap reports and productivity figures. Team coordinators then reported back to their teams, and the facilitators met with management and union leaders. Eventually, meetings became part of the culture of the plant so that quarterly townhall meetings were held and a video network was developed to keep workers informed about the company's financial position, production costs, performance levels, and projected changes in labor.

Before this entire process was implemented, the plant was running a deficit of $5 million a year. After the MOA and teams, the plant began making a profit and saved $1.5 million a year. Defects in materials shipped dropped by 70 percent, morale took a sharp rise, and employees reported taking pride in the plant. The New Castle plant was awarded the U.S. Senate Productivity Award for the organization that improved its production the most.

This case illustrates a key point about leadership: Leadership skills are interrelated and integrated. Embedded in the new MOA was the assumption that workers were capable of self-management and that positive relationships among all organization members were critical to effective operation of the plant. Workers were given some respect and enabled to carry out production plans. Managers got out of the way and let workers take the lead.

Implicit in the MOA was the clear mandate that workers were not to be criticized. Workers responded by feeling more positive about the plant and its leadership. Improvements in workflow and productivity were applauded. Bosses from hell were moved elsewhere. Creativity and inno-
va   workers were considered to be cohorts
in   ective. Everyone, including the U.S.
S   aying the foundation for even greater
in

End the Everyday Put-down

When trying to be an effective leader, you may find that you are involved in helping people to change more than you ever suspected. In doing so you may find yourself falling into some poor communication habits. Indeed, many of our interpersonal problems begin when we misuse our communication skills. For instance, if you say such things as

"Why didn't you ......?"

"You should have......."

"You ought to....."

"You must never...."

"If you had only...."

"Don't you understand that...?"

you will immediately put people on the defensive. The words themselves do not present a problem. The difficulty arises with the listener. Most people perceive these phrases as criticisms. Notice that each phrase implies a judgment. Nobody likes to be judged or criticized. When we feel criticized in some way, we get defensive. We get angry and want to fight back.

A fundamental premise that comes out of research on human relationships is that the primary vehicle for all human interaction is communication. That is, we spend most of our time interacting with each other through some form of communication. At work, we use communication from morning until evening. At home, the same thing happens. We spend much of our time just talking to each other in order to socialize, improve relationships, and accomplish tasks.

A corollary principle is that if the communication goes well, usually the relationship goes well. When communication between people proceeds in an understanding, informative, and friendly way, relationships are strengthened and people feel supported. Especially important to you as a leader is to know what kind of messages you send to your employees when you communicate with them. Do you communicate support and appreciation or do you more frequently communicate judgment and criticism?

Check up on your communication skills by responding to the following questions:

1. I know when I am failing to acknowledge someone's message to me. I am quite aware of how passively I respond and when I ignore them entirely.

   Yes.

   Sometimes.

   No, Sally. Oh, George could you come over here? I have something I'd like to talk to you about.

2. I know when I cut people's messages short and interrupt them.

   Yes.

   Sometimes.

   No, are you joking with me? I never jump in on a conversation and turn myself into the speaker forcing the other person to become a captive listener. Have you heard the story about the new Barbie dolls?

3. I know when I make irrelevant and tangential responses to someone who is talking to me. I am always aware of when I respond to someone's problem by saying that "I had a similar situation last year when...on and on and on."

   Yes.

   Sometimes.

   No, if someone were telling me about a difficulty in manufacturing, I would never in a million years ask them how they liked the new high-tech robotic welding machines.

4. I definitely know when I fall into formal, stilted, or boring responses when a person is talking to me. I know when pat-formula answers aren't solving any problems.

   Yes.

   Sometimes.

   No, we all have those problems, but we moved into a red house last year. I have some home movies of it.

5. And finally, I always make sure my verbal and nonverbal messages are not contradicting each other. I know when my mouth is saying "I am vitally interested in what you are saying," but my face is looking frowny and tired.

Yes.

Sometimes.

No, I just learned four ways to improve your looks. I can hardly wait to explain them to you the next time we talk! I have more important things to do than listen to what you're saying.

You may have smiled a little at the wording of the "no" answers, but this issue of communicating in a facilitative way is crucial to building and maintaining good relations with all the people within your range of influence as a manager and leader. When changing from boss to cohort, we don't know of many steps to turn employees into cohorts that are more important than making sure you don't make disparaging comments to them or about them in your frequent conversations at work.

> *Only if we can restrain ourselves is conversation possible.*
> *Good talk rises upon much discipline.*

> —John Erskine

Since most lists of leadership and management failures put ineffective communication and interpersonal skills at the very top of the list, let's explore some ways to become more supportive and effective communicators.

First, when talking with your cohorts at work, do you tend to dominate conversations? Do you speak more than they do? The question here is whether you can discipline yourself to truly hear the other person out. Most communicologists tell us to consider our first attempt at communication a failure. When we ask a question, the first response will usually be what is known as a conditioned response. If we ask someone, "How are you?" the likely answer is "fine." The person may not be well at all, but just responds that she is fine without even thinking.

We are reminded of a segment of theater called "avant-garde" that pokes fun at how we fail to be genuine in our communication with each other and fail to get past the first efforts of understanding each other. In a play by Beckett, a woman knocks on the door of an apartment. A man answers the door and says, "Come in. Take off your clothes and stay awhile." Dialogue in the play shows how cliché responses dominate many of our conversations, making much of what we say trivial and subject to misunderstanding.

I don't understand this conversation at all. How drunk am I?

—Paul Douglas missing the intrigues going on around him.
In Joseph L. Mankiewicz's *A Letter to Three Wives*

The solution to this communication breakdown is to ask more than one question about an issue. For example, if you asked someone how their work is going and they answer "fine," you may want to follow that question with another. "What specifically is going fine?" Or you may want to ask about things that are not going well at work. Or ask about the most recent difficulty the person has run into when trying to do their job well.

Keep helping the other person talk about his or her situation by raising simple journalistic type questions like, When? Why? Who was there? How did you feel about that? Can you tell me more about that? Where did this occur? And then, when you are ready to bring closure to an issue, you might ask the person what they think would be an effective action to take with regards to the issue being discussed. Try to help them explain themselves. Be a good listener. And then at the end of the discussion, be prepared to support any solution that might help resolve the issue discussed.

*One of the best ways to persuade others is with your ears—
by listening to them.*

—Dean Rusk

Second, when conversing, you fare much better if you avoid speaking down to another person who has less authority or information than you. This is not an easy thing to do, especially when you are the recognized leader and privy to information unavailable to the other person. The goal is to engage in a form of "egalitarian" communication. This is accomplished when both parties feel equal. Allowing the other person to be heard and giving that person at least an equal share of the speaking time are good first steps. Asking questions is another way to show respect for the person's point of view, and it shows your willingness to engage in joint problem solving.

He's the only man I know who can strut sitting down.

—Gene Kelly puncturing Fredric March's pomposity.
In Stanley Kramer's *Inherit the Wind*

The whole idea is to convey to the other person that regardless of your position, you are not a "know-it-all" and the keeper of superior insights. When you present an idea, try to couch it in words that communicate a point of view rather than an inflexible position. Try not to turn your opinions into facts by stating them with great articulation of each syllable and with loudness. Be calm and understanding, adult to adult. Avoid all indications of a parent speaking down to a child. Eliminate pointing a finger at others while judging and indicating the error. You are working with adults who seek understanding, feedback, and applause, and who try to avoid the pain of criticism, judgment, and punishment.

Speak when you are angry and you will make the best speech that you will ever regret.

—Ambrose Bierce

Third and finally, find an opportunity to visit regularly one-on-one with the people that work with you. We know that many managerial books recommend having formal interviews with each employee and a whole array of private meetings. If you want to do this on a continual basis, keep records of decisions made and action steps to be taken, and institutionalize the program. Read several management technique books on the subject. On the other hand, what we are talking about in terms of leadership says that you should be walking around among your cohorts and finding opportunities to applaud them and cheer them on, and of course, solving urgent problems without waiting for a formally scheduled meeting.

Leaving your office and walking around among the workers easily accomplishes this. Ask people personal questions about how their family is doing. What's happening with the children? Did they see the football game last night? Be complimentary and supportive about what people tell you. Cheer and applaud their successes. Continue to inquire about their personal lives and social activities. Ask how their work is coming. What snags are they running into with their work? How have they thought we could improve the way we are doing things around here?

This is the most important communication activity you can carry on with your work associates. This takes place on the floor during work, not at a special hour of a set day in a particular room. This kind of communication is spontaneous and real. Your job is to make it happen by walking among the workers, asking simple questions.

Some communication research also shows that leaders often fail to look pleasant when they try to communicate with others. Men are particularly guilty of not smiling when they speak to other men. Of course, the frequency of smiling goes up considerably when men talk to women. Since so much research shows that smiling is a great addition to being an influential communicator, be sure to make that change first, especially if you are predominantly a nonsmiler. If you are on the receiving end of a critical comment, you might try saying, "Thank you for telling me," and be sure to say it with a smile!

You know, it takes two to get one in trouble.

—Mae West advising Rochelle Hudson.
In Lowell Sherman's *She Done Him Wrong*

Gary Baughman, retired president and CEO of Fisher-Price, Inc., adds a final idea to the importance of communicating in an influential way. After leading his company through a turnaround and return to profitability, Baughman said, "I have also learned the hard way that the real foundation of successful communication is not a huge vocabulary nor a silver tongue, but good listening skills. The higher you rise in organizations, and the further removed you are from your areas of so-called technical expertise, the more important listening skills become."

Baughman further explained that several times he joined a company as the president with little knowledge of the business or the industry and was expected to turn the company around. He said, "I would spend the first several weeks doing almost nothing but listening. Over time I learned to listen between the lines, notice subtle changes in emotions or body language, and pick up on patterns and recurring themes. Ultimately, I would take all that I heard, summarize it, prioritize it, develop a strategic plan, and finally work hard to get everyone to support the plan. But listening came first."

Talk low, talk slow, and don't say too much.

—John Wayne

A Look Ahead

So far we have discovered five essential changes that characterize powerful leadership: freeing people to take the lead; promoting creativity, innovation, and fun at work; switching from boss to cohort; mastering the

4E's of involvement; and stopping the iniquitous practice of criticizing by substituting applause for criticism. Now, we add to those the significant idea of taking the high road, which involves not only ethical, honest actions, but also consideration and gentleness.

7

THE SIXTH ESSENTIAL CHANGE: TAKE THE HIGH ROAD

Honesty is One of the Better Policies.

Charles David Saxon
New Yorker Cartoonist

Hardly a day goes by without a report in a national publication about some scandal. The history of American business and government is riddled with stories about how unscrupulous leaders resort to lying, cheating, and misrepresentation to achieve their goals.

Practices such as insider trading, considered illegal and unethical, brought down one of the world's renowned brokerage firms. Charges of unethical practices in the auto-repair business have certainly altered the image of Sears. Charges of investment fraud and improper fund-raising

141

activities have even been leveled at the office of the President of the United States.

Some elected officials pad their expense accounts; occasionally lawyers who know the rules knowingly avoid payments of social security taxes for their household help; reports have appeared of employees in various companies covering up defective military weapons; and an increasing number of people appear to lie to avoid embarrassment and prosecution for various misdeeds.

Our courts of law are filled with cases dealing with dishonesty and abuse. Deceit has become so prevalent that some business leaders have posed the question, "Is it possible to succeed in business and still be honest?"

In one of Saxon's World of Business cartoons in the *New Yorker* magazine, a group of business executives are sitting around a conference table talking about business policies and one says, "Of course, honesty is one of the better policies." Have we lost the significance of the adage that honesty is the *best* policy?

What Are Best Policies?

Taking the high road has to do with the *best policies*. A policy is defined as a definite course of action selected to guide and determine present and future decisions. In an organization, policies define what are "right," "wrong," "good," and "bad" decisions and behaviors for the organization and its employees. Most dictionaries define *best* as that which produces the greatest good, advantage, utility, or satisfaction. In an organization, the *best* policy is one that creates the greatest good for the organization. Since employees are part of the organization, the implication is that the best policies are those that produce the greatest good for members of the organization as well as for the technical or business part of the organization.

Most people agree that the best policies are those that produce the greatest good, but the problem for leaders and managers in organizations is to tell what is meant by "the greatest good." With some fondness, we turn to a standard dictionary to ferret out the meaning of *good*. The diversity of definitions, however, boggles the mind. Good is characterized as something

of favorable character or tendency; amusing, clever.

well-founded, cogent; deserving of respect.

true, honorable; conforming to a standard.

virtuous, just, commendable; handsome, attractive.

of the highest worth or reliability; commercially sound.

bountiful, fertile; salutary, wholesome.

suitable, fit to eat; certain to pay or contribute something conforming to the moral order of the universe.

The most profound synonym is the one dealing with the moral order of the universe. What tends to trouble most of us is deciding what "conforms to the moral order" of something, or what is of "highest worth," or what is most "deserving of respect," or what is "just and commendable," or what "standard" something should conform to. If we understand the moral order, highest worth, and justice, then we can frequently, although not always, determine what is "good."

Ethics is concerned with understanding what constitutes good people and right actions. Thus, ethics in organizations is about what constitutes good and bad human conduct and right and wrong decisions in organizations. Since leaders are the central figures in organizations, they are often the focus of ethical questions; that is, are they good people who make the right decisions?

Ethics should be distinguished from fashion, etiquette, and artistry. Fashion, etiquette, and artistry have to do with prevailing customs, styles, and tastes, which we often call fads, rages, or crazes, and are assumed to reflect temporary, transient, and more personal uses of things. Ethics, on the other hand, concern decisions, thinking, and actions that can have serious consequences for the welfare of human beings in general. For example, conventional ethical norms against lying, stealing, and murder protect us from actions that can bring serious injury to us. The ethical guidelines that argue for treating people with dignity and respect uplift human beings in general and promote supportive relationships.

Where Do Ethical Standards and Guidelines Come From?

William Shaw and Vincent Barry, professors of business management, discuss ethics and morality in organizations and provide a plausible explanation for the source of ethical standards. They suggest that fashions may be set by designers, that language usage may be set by grammarians, and that artistic standards may be set by art critics; the validity of fashions, usage, and artistry may be legitimized by authoritative bodies such as legislators, licensing boards, and consumers. On the other hand, ethical standards depend not on authoritative fiat, but on "the adequacy of the reasons that justify them."

The justification for ethical standards is, of course, the stumbling block of ethical behavior. For example, let's assume that you shop at a large supermarket on a fairly regular basis. One afternoon, you pay for your groceries with a twenty-dollar bill and receive change for a fifty-dollar bill. The basic question is, would you keep the extra $30? Would you be more likely to keep the extra dollars if you thought no one would notice the mistake? Would you be more likely to keep the extra dollars if you felt the store regularly overcharged its customers? Thus, the fundamental issue is one of ethics. Is keeping the extra money ethical? The answer depends on the strength of your justification for returning or keeping the extra money. How would you justify your decision to return the over-payment? How would you justify your decision to keep the overpayment?

Here is another instance that may allow you to assess the soundness of your justifications. You've gone down to that same supermarket to do some more shopping. When you finish, you back out of your parking stall and your front bumper scratches the paint on a brand new car parked next to you. You can see that the scratch is relatively small, but it is noticeable. You guess that a dealer would charge $200 to $250 to repair it. Would you drive away without contacting the driver, who is probably also shopping? Would you be more likely to drive away if you thought no one saw your contact with the other car? Would you be more likely to drive away if the damage were more extensive and might cost $1,000 to $1,500? Do you think that driving away is unethical? Why? How would you justify either decision?

Require Everyone to Violate the Principle

A simple way to test whether a decision is ethical or not is to apply the decision universally; that is, to find out whether a decision, a way of thinking, or an act is ethical, all you have to do is assume that it is required of everyone. Take the paint-scratching incident, for example. What would be the effect on social relations if everyone were required to go to a parking lot each day and scratch someone's car and get away without telling them? What kind of society would develop if everyone were required to do some scratching every day? We can see more easily, using this approach, why the Ten Commandments have stood the test of time as ethical guidelines. What would happen if we were all required to kill someone once a month or even once a year? What kind of society would evolve where the opposite of each of the Ten Commandments was required of each of us? If you think stealing even small things is ethical, just ponder the consequences of requiring everyone to steal something every day. How could a social system survive with a systematic and widespread violation of each of the fundamental guidelines expressed in the Ten Commandments?

Why Have Explicit Ethical Principles?

Mitt Romney, president of the Salt Lake Olympic Committee and founder and CEO of Bain Capital, Inc., explains the connection between your own personal success and living with integrity.

> Some years ago, the firm I founded seemed to be coming apart at the seams. Our five partners were at each other's throats. It seemed we all wanted different things from our lives and from our business. One was consumed with making money; he was obsessed with becoming a member of the Forbes 400. Another wanted power and control. I was of two minds, trying to balance the goals of my faith with the money I was earning. We met with a team-building consultant-psychologist. At the last of our week-long session, he led us to something transforming.
>
> He said that if we lived our lives in conflict with our core values, we would experience stress, ill health, and deep regret. How, we asked, could we know what our core values were? He proceeded to ask us to think of the five or six people we most admired and respected, people currently living or who had ever lived. I chose the Master, Joseph Smith, Abraham Lincoln, and my mother, father, and wife. Then he asked us to write down next to each of those names the five or six attributes we thought of when we thought of that person. The attributes that we had then listed most frequently, he explained, represented our core values. Simply, if we lived in concert with those values, we lived with integrity. We would be happy and fulfilled. And, in contrast, if we lived in a way that was not consistent with those core values, we would ultimately be unfulfilled and unhappy.
>
> To my surprise, all five of my partners revealed the same or similar values: love, family, service, and devotion. While we each may

have pushed them aside to a different degree in our daily pursuits, they were at each of our centers.

Now, some twenty years later, I have discovered something else about these core values, about living with integrity, about these fundamental measures of successful living: With these at our center, chance does not come into play in determining our success or failure. The ability to live with integrity with the core of our values of love, family, service, and devotion is entirely up to us. Fundamentally, this is the business of successful living.

The most critical point is that you must have a clear set of ethical principles to guide your decision-making and the actions you take. We call this *taking the high road*. By this we mean that you should state explicitly, clearly, specifically, precisely, distinctly, candidly, and frankly the ethical principles that you use to make decisions and take actions in your leadership role. For example, you may decide that one of the ethical principles you'll use is "to be fair to all concerned." Then, you need to write out your justification for each of the principles. This is the only way you will determine what ethical foundation you are using to take the high road, or even if you are trying to take the high road. For example, your justification may be that being fair allows everyone to benefit from the resources available.

Be sure to test each principle by reflecting on what would happen if we were all required to violate the principle on a regular basis. If negative consequences come from the violations, then you may feel somewhat secure in assuming that you have identified a reasonably valid ethical principle. For example, if everyone were to violate the principle of fairness, would there be any negative consequences? If so, you have identified a good ethical principle.

In order for you to develop your own personal code of ethics, you must state and justify each principle. When you have done this, you will be more strongly motivated toward making decisions and acting consistently with your ethical code of conduct. You will attempt to avoid decisions and behaviors that conflict with your personal code of ethics.

A personal code of ethics, nevertheless, may be a drawback to making money and looking successful in business. For example, John E. Pepper, former CEO of Proctor & Gamble explained, "Integrity is paramount when deciding on product safety. If you know a product is unsafe for some reason, you pull it off the market. No decision could be easier. But what if you can't be sure that your product is unsafe?" He explained that you now have to depend on your judgment and do what you believe is the right thing.

Procter & Gamble withdrew its Rely Feminine Protection product in the 1970s because science did not allow the company to categorically separate the disease of toxic shock syndrome from product attributes in that category. No evidence ever appeared connecting the product with toxic shock, but the product was withdrawn because Proctor & Gamble wanted to treat consumers with the utmost integrity. That decision cost the company hundreds of millions of dollars in lost revenues.

Another ethical decision had to be made when a senior executive from one of Proctor & Gamble's advertising agencies got into a cab in New York and found a computer disk lying on the floorboard. The disk included the marketing plans of one of Proctor & Gamble's toughest competitors. The senior executive returned the disk to the chairman of the competitive company, assured him that no one at Proctor or the advertising agency had looked at the contents of the disk, and added that, "We always compete with commitment and intensity, but we'll never compromise our ethics to win."

You will tend to feel guilty when your conduct violates ethical principles; you may also tend to disapprove of people whose decisions and actions conflict with your code. But you will also tend to esteem those whose actions and decisions are consistent with your personal code of ethics. Once you have identified your code of ethics, you may never be able to return to your former status as a nonethical leader—that is, a leader without a code of ethics. You will want to follow your code and its principles for their own sake. You may feel guilty for even thinking of violating the code. At that point you will, in fact, be taking the high road.

On a practical note, with the amount of publicity being given to unethical and illegal activities, the increase in government and special interest group audits, and the amount of whistleblowing that is going on in many businesses, no company or its employees can afford to be unethical and dishonest in their dealings with other employees, suppliers, and customers. Covering up one lie with another is a horrible way to live life. Running the risk of costing the company millions of dollars in fines and lawsuits plus a lengthy jail sentence for oneself just isn't worth it.

Manipulation Is Unethical

Before we proceed further with our discussion, we would like to point out that whether you mean to or not, you influence those around you. The question is whether you are influencing them for good or manipulating them for personal gain. Notice the differences between manipulation and influence. Manipulation is measured by the act, generally uses formal authority, works for the advantage of the manipulator, pushes and pulls, and is a negative force. On the other hand, influence is measured by effect, works for the advantage of both parties, doesn't use formal authority, and is a positive process.

In brief, manipulation is dishonest, whereas influence is honest. Those who manipulate usually end up being resented by the people who have been manipulated. They feel undermined and hurt and may even seek revenge. Also, if a higher authority learns of the manipulation, there may be strong sanctions taken against the manipulator.

Ideally, strong leaders are those who consider their own motives and avoid selfishness. People who are examples of integrity and do not compromise their values continue to grow and develop from a foundation of correct principles and values. Truly powerful leaders with lasting influence always inspire and invite, never manipulate or coerce.

What Ethical Principles Should Be Included in Your Code?

A rash of unethical behaviors has encouraged many companies to adopt codes of ethics that are distributed to their employees. Sanford N. McDonnell, as chairman and CEO of McDonnell Douglas Corporation, said,

> At McDonnell Douglas we adopted a Code of Ethics, which incidentally, was based upon the Scout Oath and Law; and we did not just hang it on the wall. We realized that we had to teach our employees what we mean by these values, so we initiated a training program in 1984, which began with me, the chairman of the board.... We take every opportunity to underline the basic philosophy that we want our employees to always take the high road. Other companies throughout the country are ahead of us and many more are following us. This same approach must be taken by the news media and the entertainment media—especially television, the most influential educator of our times—and it must certainly be followed by those people in our government.

The McDonnell Douglas' Code states, "In order for integrity and ethics to be characteristic of McDonnell Douglas, we who make up the Corporation must strive to be:

Honest and trustworthy in all our relationships.

Reliable in carrying out assignments and responsibilities.

Truthful and accurate in what we say and write.

Cooperative and constructive in all work undertaken.

Fair and considerate in our treatment of fellow employees, customers, and all other persons.

Law abiding in all our activities.

Committed to accomplishing all tasks in a superior way.

Economical in utilizing company resources.

Dedicated in service to our company and to improvement of the quality of life in the world in which we live."

The key principles included in this code are service to company, improvement of quality of life, economy in resource use, completing tasks in a superior way, abiding by the law, and being fair, considerate, truthful, accurate, honest, trustworthy, and reliable. As Sanford McDonnell realized, the Scout Law is part of a code of ethics that could appropriately be adopted by leaders in any organization. The Scout code of ethics is divided into two parts: the Scout Oath and the Scout Law.

The Scout Oath expresses ethics in this way:

On my honor, I will do my best to do my duty to God and my country, to obey the Scout Law, to help other people at all times, to keep myself physically strong, mentally awake, and morally straight.

The Scout Law articulates 12 fundamental ethical principles:

1. **Trustworthy.** A Scout tells the truth. He keeps his promises. Honesty is part of his code of conduct. People can depend on him.

2. **Loyal.** A Scout is true to his family, Scout leaders, friends, school, and nation.

3. **Helpful.** A Scout is concerned about people. He does things willingly for others without pay or reward.

4. **Friendly.** A Scout is a friend to all. He is a brother to other Scouts. He seeks to understand others. He respects those with ideas and customs other than his own.

5. **Courteous.** A Scout is polite to everyone regardless of age or position. He knows good manners make it easier for people to get along together.

6. **Kind.** A Scout understands there is strength in being gentle. He treats others as he wants to be treated. He does not hurt or kill harmless things without reason.

7. **Obedient.** A Scout follows the rules of his family, school, and troop. He obeys the laws of his community and country. If he thinks these rules and laws are unfair, he tries to have them changed in an orderly manner rather than disobey them.

8. **Cheerful.** A Scout looks for the bright side of things. He cheerfully does tasks that come his way. He tries to make others happy.

9. **Thrifty.** A Scout works to pay his way and to help others. He saves for unforeseen needs. He protects and conserves natural resources. He carefully uses time and property.

10. **Brave.** A Scout can face danger even if he is afraid. He has the courage to stand for what he thinks is right, even if others laugh at or threaten him.

11. **Clean.** A Scout keeps his body and mind fit and clean. He goes around with those who believe in living by these same ideals. He helps keep his home and community clean.

12. **Reverent.** A Scout is reverent toward God. He is faithful in his religious duties. He respects the beliefs of others.

The selection of these 12 principles for inclusion in a code of ethics for young men around the world implies that they may have general applicability in many areas outside of Scouting. Through years of refinement, they have stood the test of application. They summarize the "good" in people and represent standards of thought and behavior that epitomize that which is most worthy in human relationships. They do grasp the salient features of ethical behavior as expressed by one great man:

> In a general sense, ethics is the name we give to our concern for good behavior. We feel an obligation to consider not only our own personal well-being, but also that of others and of human society as a whole.
>
> —Dr. Albert Schweitzer

As a result of articulating an ethics code, McDonnell Douglas coaches its employees in several key areas: how to represent the company in an honest and understanding way to various stakeholders and publics such as the customers, contractors and suppliers, local and state governments, and fellow employees; how to handle all transmissions of data, reports, and communications in an honest and accurate way; how to perform assigned work in a responsible and cooperative manner; and how to refrain from abusing physical property and proprietary information and protect the same from theft and misuse. In general, employees are asked to avoid any activity that might involve a conflict of interest, including acceptance of favors and rewards that might be construed as improperly influencing the decisions of the recipient.

Rotary International, with a membership of over a million business and professional men and women worldwide, has made explicit a Four-Way Test for all the thoughts and actions of its members. The Four-Way Test expresses some fundamental principles of ethics in four questions:

1. Is it the TRUTH?

2. Is it FAIR to all concerned?

3. Will it build GOODWILL and better friendships?

4. Will it be BENEFICIAL to all concerned?

These are powerful ideas for men and women in the business community to apply to decision making. They are the ideas and ideals of worthiness and goodness. We support the Four-Way Test of Rotary and urge you to state your own code of ethics.

Testing Your Decisions

If any of the foregoing aren't specific enough for you, or if at this point you have not yet been able to develop your own code of ethics, consider the following questions before you decide to take a course of action:

- Ask yourself whether your decision or proposed action is legal. That is, does it conflict with the laws of the country in which you live, the industry in which you work, or the policies of the organization of which you are a part?

- Ask yourself whether your proposed action is going to be fair to all concerned. Is it a balanced transaction, and is it beneficial to others? Or, are you taking unfair advantage of someone and undermining their well-being?

- As an appeal to your own internal personal code of ethics, ask yourself how you will feel the next morning about what you are about to do. Will you have good feelings about your decision or feel pangs of regret and saddle yourself with a guilty conscience?

- Could you feel comfortable explaining your decision or behavior to your family or on public television?

Until a clear set of values is developed, or at least a checklist of questions is reviewed when an ethical dilemma occurs in our lives, our responses will be erratic at best and possibly illegal and unethical at worst. Most people spend too much time rationalizing away poor decisions by pretending that their behavior is in the best interest of the company, others, or themselves. If no one was supposed to find out, but someone did, would they support you and understand why you made that kind of a decision? Sorry to say it, but that kind of conjecture is probably not going to happen. Acting unethically puts your job in jeopardy and leaves you feeling pretty miserable. Powerful leaders need to get on the high road as quickly as possible and stay there. Then, they can teach their employees to do the same.

Ethics and the Peaceful Mind

Violations of ethical codes are inconsistent with our need for inner peace. We have had employees of both large and small businesses call and ask whether they should do something illegal because a boss asked them to.

One employee was asked to falsify a report about the amount of polluted material the company was dumping into an inland harbor. "What will happen to you," we asked, "if you don't falsify the reports?" The employee felt that he would get fired or lose a chance at a promotion. It was not easy for the employee to select the "right" thing to do in his particular work situation. He made the decision, however, on what he thought was ethically right. He refused to falsify his report. Interestingly, the boss said that he would find someone else to do it. The employee asked to be relocated in the organization to a position where such requests might not be made of him.

Another employee valued his family time above working unreasonable hours 7 days a week. Even though his initial salary was in the six-figure bracket, his family came first. The employee's circumstance illustrates what some have called *dissonance*, which involves making choices between two equally desirable alternatives. Working excessive hours may violate the value or ethic of maintaining regular family relationships. However, if you work every day of the week for 12 hours, you may keep your job, make more money, and get a promotion, but you may very well suffer dissonance. Not being able to resolve dissonance leads to unmanageable stress and anxiety. If you are experiencing such a dilemma and have not taken steps to resolve it, you may not realize that you are in direct confrontation with an ethical principle that you appear to hold but that is not clearly stated. Thus, the best move is to write out your ethical code. You will then have a list of principles against which to evaluate your actions and anxiety when they occur.

Even the most upright and morally honest people can become desensitized if they see people around them being dishonest, profiting from dishonesty, and getting away with it. All of us see ourselves as basically honest people until we feel the pressures of home, children, personal finances, and the expectation that we are supposed to get ahead, get promotions, and enjoy significant salary increases.

We had the opportunity to observe a group of salespeople. The observations led to some startling revelations showing how quickly people can become dishonest when a personal need arises. When the pressure was put on this particular group of salespeople to make more money because sales were down and personal income was decreasing, the salespeople started to make false claims for their products and services, exaggerated benefits, omitted important information and disclaimers, and essentially misled customers.

The company had said, "Make more sales. Don't spend a lot of time trying to figure out how to do it, just do it." The company failed to link ethical guidelines to the "make more sales" goal; hence, the results were disastrous, especially because the employees were inexperienced and the transactions were impersonal.

In this case, the sales effort was ultimately destructive to the company. At first, sales increased and profits went up. But then the customers started to complain about the misrepresentations that were made. They initiated several lawsuits, one of which was a class-action suit charging that the company had marketed and sold inappropriately to its clients. Costs to the firm rose, liability claims increased, and the general reputation of the company was publicly tarnished. The lesson was an expensive one to learn: Honesty with an organization is ultimately more profitable than dishonesty.

As a leader who is concerned about ethical behavior in your organization, you must do a few necessary things. First, you must specify appropriate behaviors and conduct by both word and deed. That means being a good example yourself. Most people have a general sense that right is good and wrong is bad, but they may not understand what ethical behavior means in a particular organization.

Second, you must provide the necessary resources to make the code of ethics known. "Hot lines" should make answers to ethical questions available. Booklets can raise specific ethical questions and portray scenarios that provide a clear statement of the company's ethical policies and standards.

Third, you must orient new employees, from day one, to the code of ethics; everyone needs to know that the company is going to take its ethical responsibilities seriously. Subsequently, employees should be held accountable for whatever they do. This third step should be initiated in the new employee orientation program, and in fact should become an important part of a discussion of company values and standards of behavior.

Fourth, you should make certain that everyone understands the reality of doing wrong things and getting caught. Violations of standards and policies should be stopped immediately. Appropriate action must be taken to assure that ethical violations do not occur repeatedly. If you fail to question the actions of your employees, you are the one who is irresponsible.

When you are in a position to make significant financial gains, annihilate the competition, and make strong increases in your power and position, there may be a tremendous temptation to do whatever it takes to win. A temptation is an invitation to violate one or more ethical principles. The whatever-it-takes dimension of temptation frequently consists of doing something that conflicts with an explicit, latent, or unstated principle concerning what would be the right and good thing to do. Often, the question we ask ourselves is not "Is it right?" but "Will anyone know?" Do not compromise your code of ethics, even if no one knows or cares about what you're doing.

Peter Drucker said that "There are no business ethics, there are only ethics." In our research and studies we are constantly reminded that clearly stated ethical codes articulate correct principles that can guide our decisions and actions so that they do the most good in a worthy and commendable way.

Does Ethical Behavior Pay?

A strong case can be made for engaging in ethical behavior. Ethical behavior maintains excellent relationships with coworkers. If you get caught in a lie or a misrepresentation, people won't trust you, and your chances of implementing all of the seven essential changes discussed in this book will be seriously compromised.

Ethical behavior also indicates that a person is mature and able to take responsibility. Maturity is at the heart of good business practices, relationships, and profit. Responsibility is a leadership characteristic valued at all levels in the management hierarchy.

Ethical behavior communicates to others in the organization that you are committed to high standards and have the best interests of all employees, customers, clients, and the community in mind.

Ethical misjudgments end careers more quickly and more definitively than any other kind of mistake in judgment. To err is human, but to be caught lying, cheating, stealing, and violating other widely accepted canons of ethical behaviors will not be forgotten quickly or easily.

Principles of ethics provide the broad framework in which organizational life is to be understood. Business is just part of a total life, and a full, complete, and effective life can only be sustained in a context of a total code of ethics.

Take the Highest Road

For this cogent summary of ethics, we are grateful to the Chinese community in general and to the Chinese martial arts in particular. To understand the proper relation of standards of morality, goodness, and honesty to leadership, two important points must be introduced. The first and perhaps the most important point is that *the level of achievement of the usual leader*, not just the exceptional person with exalted talents, *is directly related to his or her morality or goodness*. If leaders are unethical people, their abilities as leaders will be severely limited. Conversely, if leaders are good people, there are few limits to what they can achieve.

This idea may seem a little strange to us here in the Western world. For example, in the West, an athlete may be a drinker, take drugs, or act maliciously or immaturely, and yet we may believe that such behaviors do not reflect on the athlete's ability and potential accomplishments. Such an assumption is seriously deficient in both theory and practice. In the short run, a talented athlete may win a few games or tournaments, but in the long run, without the undergirding of ethical goodness, that athlete will find that his reputation, speed, talent, and accomplishments are like a wisp in the wind.

We believe that the same holds true for leaders. The good person's development is unlimited; the bad person's progress is fixed. Robert C. Solomon and Kristine Hanson describe the role of ethics in business.

> Business is not a scramble for profits and survival. It is way of life, an established and proven *practice* whose prosperity and survival depend on the participation of its practitioners. Business ethics is not ethics applied to business. It is the foundation of business. Business life thrives on competition, but it survives on the basis of its ethics.

They offer eight rules for good ethics in business:

1. Consider other people's well being, including the well being of non-participants.

2. Think as a member of the business community and not as an isolated individual.

3. Obey, but do not depend solely on, the law.

4. Think of yourself—and your company—as part of society.

5. Obey moral rules, because there can be no ethics and no business without them.

6. Think objectively; the rules apply equally to everyone, and being able to think for a moment from other people's perspectives is essential.

7. Ask the question, "What sort of person would do such a thing?"

8. Respect the customs of others, but not at the expense of your own ethics.

The second point derived from the Chinese martial arts is that the good person is one who always thinks properly, then speaks and acts accordingly. Morality of the mind, when contrasted with the honorableness of our actions, deals with the inward spirit or soul of the leader and consists of (1) garnishing our thoughts with virtue, (2) filling our minds with a charitable disposition and feelings of kindness, (3) exercising more patience and gentleness, and (4) developing a strong will to guide and direct our energies in truthful ways, supporting noble activities.

Some people believe that being morally good means simply to refrain from cheating, lying, and stealing. The highest view of being ethical and good, however, involves the total way in which a person thinks, speaks, and acts. It is a way of living and leading in the noblest manner possible. Leaders who aspire to reach the noblest level must cultivate a number of key attributes.

Five Traits of a Good Person

Humility should guide the way in which you speak and act. Humility leads you to understand that there is much to be learned from everyone around you and that you must keep striving for a better way to lead, manage, and live life.

Respect is related to humility. If you are humble, it is easy to give respect. Both traits recognize the goodness in everything and elevate you to a position where you learn and grow.

Loyalty involves faithfulness to the ideals of family, culture, nation, and correct leadership principles. As a good leader, you pass on correct principles associated with leadership effectiveness to others in the organization. With loyalty to correct ideas, you acquire a noble leadership style that allows you to achieve a stability that helps you to become strong and effective.

When you have a sense of *righteousness*, it means that you stand up for high ideals and honorable activities. It also means that you fight against immoral and unethical activities, whenever and wherever you can.

Having *trust* does not mean that you trust everybody but that everybody can trust you. By showing others that you are dependable and honest, you build a reputation of sterling character, and you strengthen your relationships with others.

When even one of these traits of a good person becomes a part of the leader's character, some things become immediately obvious. For example, once a leader becomes humble, the thought of showing off one's power and ability seems to disappear. The leader who is on the highest road realizes that showing off and boasting are simply disguises of pride and limited leadership ability. Perhaps we should ponder this old Chinese proverb: "The half-filled water bucket makes great splashing noises; the full bucket is silent."

To crystallize the point that great leaders have good thoughts that lead to positive actions, we would like to present a short story used by Chinese masters to teach students valuable points about the proper conduct and morality of a martial artist.

There is a Sky above a Sky, and a Talent above a Talent

During the early years of the Chin dynasty, two brothers lived near Jeou Lien Mountain of Fu Chien province. Since the time of their early youth, the older brother, who was bigger and stronger, constantly oppressed the younger, weaker brother. This situation was made worse by the death of their father.

When the father died he split his land in half and gave an equal portion to each son. But the older brother, not fearing the authority of his father anymore, decided to take away his weaker brother's rightful inheritance. To take away anyone's land was at that time a great tragedy, because a person's whole livelihood depended on the amount of land he had to cultivate. Every day the older brother took a little land away from his brother; after a few months the younger brother found that he had no more land left. Utterly discouraged, he was forced to move.

For weeks the younger brother attempted to regain his land by bargaining, asking relatives to intervene, and seeking help from authorities; all these methods failed. Finally, the younger brother concluded that he had to build up his body by learning martial arts—only violence could force his brother to give back his inheritance. To achieve this, the younger brother traveled to the greatest of all martial schools—the Shao Lin Temple.

Upon entering the temple, he sought the master of the Shao Lin monks to ask for martial training. "With your permission I will gather water, plow the land, scrub the temple walls, and cook meals in the great kitchen if you will teach me martial arts."

"But why do you wish to learn?"

"So I can get my rightful inheritance back from my brother. He has taken all the land my father left for me. I tried every peaceful path to get it back. Now, only violence is the answer."

Without hesitation, the master answered, "Yes."

Word soon spread about the younger brother and his request. Many people who heard the story wondered at the reasoning of the master; some people could not believe that a Shao Lin monk would teach someone martial arts with the intention of purposeful violence. But those who understood the ways and habit of the Shao Lin monks knew that the younger brother would get a valuable lesson from his training.

To begin training the younger brother, the master found a small young willow tree and asked the brother to jump over the tree while holding a new born calf, which was given to the young man as a present by the master. The young man was commanded to do this task everyday. As time passed, the quick-growing willow became taller and the calf grew bigger and heavier. After three years, the younger brother was able to jump the tall willow with a cow in his hands.

After the third year, the younger brother soon became impatient with this task and went to see the master. "Master, for three years I have been jumping over the willow with the cow and I still haven't learned the techniques of fighting. When will I begin to learn these things?"

The master, with a smile on his face, answered, "Young man, your training is now over. You now possess the ability to get back your rightful inheritance. Take the cow that you have been training with and go back to your land and start plowing it."

"But, what will I do when my older brother comes to force me out?" he asked.

"Pick up the cow and run toward your brother," answered the master.

The young man was utterly shocked by this statement. He pleaded with the master, but the master insisted he was now capable of his original goal. The young man left the Shao Lin Temple very disappointed. But still, he decided to do what the monk advised. He was hoping that his brother had changed in the three years since his absence.

The younger brother soon arrived home and began immediately to plow the land with the cow with which he had practiced for three years. The older brother quickly appeared and said, "Brother, do you think that you can get your land back? Never! Now get off this land before I beat you."

The younger brother immediately picked up his cow and ran towards his brother. The older brother was so amazed and shocked at this feat that he ran away and never returned. The younger brother at last regained his rightful inheritance as well as his dignity and respect.

Although the moral of this story may be more obscure than Western thinkers prefer, you may recognize that in learning to lift the cow, the younger brother was taught many of the principles of thinking and acting on the basis of ethical, good, and moral principles. For example, the younger brother was taught to shun violence, confrontation, revenge, and the general use of force to achieve his goals. In the story, these symbolize the development of a way of thinking that is a foundation for the ethical person. The younger brother was taught to focus on strengthening his talents rather than on getting even. He was taught patience and long-suffering along with respect for others and for his own abilities. Thus, we see that he nurtured the finest traits of a good person and translated them into an inner power, albeit exhibited externally by lifting the cow, which led him to regain his land nonviolently and without harm to the other person.

We conclude this essential change by commenting briefly on some of the areas in which conflict may occur between a leader's personal ethics and company practices. Six areas represent pressures to compromise individual ethical standards in order to carry out company programs. Powerful leaders must be prepared to confront situations in each of these categories. These examples of ethical principle violations appeared in the news media, including *Business Week, The Wall Street Journal, Newsweek, Fortune,* and *The Houston Post.*

1. **Honesty in Interpersonal Communication.** This is the most common problem area for taking the high road. Small deceits about organization activities, little bits of dishonesty in daily conversations, and minor distortions of details combine to create a pattern of ethical laxity. Taking the high road insists that you make every effort to engage in carefully couched honesty in communication.

2. **Gifts, Entertainment, and Kickbacks.** One prominent example is that of the leaders of the Southland Corporation, who admitted that they paid nearly $2 million in kickbacks to big buyers of its dairy products for a period of time. The strain to maintain corporate competitiveness is often the source of unethical behavior. Powerful leaders will find that they are pressured to give gifts and kickbacks to those who help them maintain competitiveness.

3. **Fairness and Discrimination.** Ethics in this category are illustrated by a situation in which a new financial analyst for a company was asked to evaluate three proposals for a portion of a construction project, one of which appeared to be clearly the best. The assistant to the analyst's boss gave the analyst an envelope with a copy of the best proposal in it, and instructed the analyst to hand-carry it to a friend of the boss who ran a contracting business. The assistant commented that this company always got a chance to look at the best bids before submitting its own. The boss was out of town for a couple of days and couldn't be contacted. What would you do in a similar situation? Powerful leaders shun questionable decisions and practices that lead to violations of ethical standards.

4. **Price Collusion and Pricing Practices.** General Dynamics established an ethics hotline after discovering numerous instances of wrongful charges to customers. The hotline received over 400 calls during the first 2 months it was in operation. Exxon was ordered by the Supreme Court to refund $2 billion for overpricing oil from a Texas field. Eighteen Fortune 500 companies, each with over $1 billion in defense contracts, were investigated by the Defense Department for cost mischarges.

5. **Executing Contracts and Agreements.** Ivan Boesky settled a Securities and Exchange Commission's claim that he engaged in insider trading by paying $100 million; he implicated other Wall Street professionals in the insider-trading scheme. E. F. Hutton charged that a customer defrauded the company of $48 million using an elaborate stock-and-commodity-trading scam. The customer alleged that Hutton's managers helped him play a float game to maintain their commissions.

6. **Firings and Layoffs.** Despite laws such as the Civil Rights Act of 1964 and the Age Discrimination Employment Act, many individuals feel systematically and unethically discriminated against in firings and layoffs. In this day of downsizing and retrenchment, cutbacks are affecting the ultimate make-up of all industries, companies, organizations, and employees. Few companies have escaped laying off employees. The hope has always been that these direct methods of cutting employees and managers will result in significant savings and benefits to the company. Much research has indicated that the actual savings is far less than expected. The sad part, however, is the vast amount of human carnage being generated and the large number of lawsuits being sparked by some rather questionable layoff tactics being used.

One popular method to identify employees who are to be laid off is to use a ranking system. Companies like Ford Motor Company, Sun Microsystems, and Cisco Systems use an approach in which employees are ranked in a top group, a middle group, and a bottom group. The 10 percent of the employees in the bottom group are generally not able to get rated into a higher group and usually are asked to leave. Such rankings have spurred lawsuits in which minority group members contend that managers favor their white friends, white employees claim that minority CEOs are discriminating against them, and various individuals contend that they are being discriminated against because of age and education. This last contention occurs when employees see that as quickly as they are fired, the company hires replacements who appear better educated and a better fit for a job.

A classic example of a questionable practice is the leveraged buy-out of Safeway Stores reported in *The Wall Street Journal*. In a leveraged buy-out, a small group of investors that usually includes senior management borrows heavily to buy a company from public shareholders and takes it private. Debts are to be repaid from the company's own cash flow or from sales of its assets. The Safeway directors were allegedly told that by selling the company to a group headed by buy-out specialists, they saved thousands of jobs and everyone associated with Safeway had a great deal for which to be thankful. Initially, the buy-out group sold 10 percent of the company back to the public at a price of $800 million, more than four times their cash investment.

Employees, on the other hand, faced the human disaster. Sixty-three thousand managers and workers were cut from Safeway. Many were rehired at lower wages, but thousands found themselves unemployed and in a horrible state of despair. The human costs and unintended side-effects of LBOs are enormous. Is it an ethical practice?

The debate rages on, but fortunately, companies like Kroger, a former rival of Safeway, took a different route. Kroger offered shareholders a good-sized dividend and gave employees significant ownership in what remained a public company. Few workers were cut and fewer assets were sold than in Safeway's case, and shortly the operating profit per employee matched that of Safeway.

An Ethical Bill of Rights

Good leaders encourage practices that treat people with respect and protect them from unfair discrimination. Workers and managers alike deserve to be treated fairly and, even more than fairly—nobly. Read carefully and slowly the following "Bill of Rights" developed by human resource management administrators and teachers. Notice how each moral principle supports the essence of the Proclamation of Leadership found in the outset of this book.

   1. All employment decisions regarding hiring, promotion, pay increases, training, and terminations should be based on objective,

performance-related criteria rather than on subjective biases or personal whims. Employment decisions should be more than just nondiscriminatory; they should be based on job-related criteria.

2. Each employee should be treated as a person of worth with dignity and respect rather than as an object that can be physically, sexually, or verbally abused. Employees should not be subjected to unwelcome or intimidating acts.

3. Disciplinary actions and criticisms should only occur for good cause, and employees should have the right to due process before any punitive actions are taken.

4. Employees should not be terminated unless their jobs are eliminated or they are unable to perform them. Personal whims and personality clashes are not valid reasons for termination.

5. Performance should be fairly and objectively evaluated against clearly defined standards; the evaluation should not be influenced by subjective biases or irrelevant personality traits.

6. Employees should be fairly and equitably paid for their work on the basis of the job's requirements, the employee's performance, and the employee's knowledge, skill, and ability. One person should not be paid less than another unless there is a legitimate, job-related reason for it.

7. Employees should be taught how to perform their jobs, and they deserve accurate and timely feedback on their performance.

8. Employees should have a safe and healthy work environment that is free from unnecessary hazards or harmful substances, and they should be informed about anything that could cause health problems.

9. An employee's personal health and family responsibilities have a higher priority than organizational responsibilities; therefore, the organization should make reasonable accommodations to help employees overcome personal problems and family emergencies.

10. Organizations should not invade employees' personal privacy. Only relevant, job-related information should be disseminated within an organization, and nothing personal should be disseminated outside the organization unless the employee authorizes it or the outside party has a legitimate need to know.

If every employer and manager followed the high road, numerous laws that regulate how employees should be treated would be unnecessary. But the best and strongest leaders look at the laws and moral principles that they try to articulate as stepping stones to finding a higher road and a more ennobling way to encourage workers to perform more efficiently and happily at work. The powerful leader is not confined or restricted by state and federal antidiscrimination laws, but realizes that each law or policy is an attempt to correct some kind of abusive situation. If an unfair or abusive situation can be corrected, then that particular rule, policy, or law is no longer necessary and ought to be discarded as quickly as possible.

A Look Ahead

So far we have examined six essential changes that a person needs to make in order to become a powerful leader. Each one builds a stronger foundation as it is added to the preceding changes. You become a powerful leader when you free your people to take the lead, when you promote creativity, innovation, and fun at work, when you switch from boss to cohort, when you master the 4 E's of involvement, when you stop criticizing and start applauding others, and when you take the high road.

Our greatest mythical leaders also engage in one additional behavioral characteristic—they stay on the peaceful path, the next essential change. James Bond; Wonder Woman; Walker, Texas Ranger; Tarzan; Charlie's Angels; and even Superman share this feature. Regardless of the circumstances, they face adversity with calmness and a personal peace of mind.

With apologies to Rudyard Kipling, we summarize the final change with this brief poem:

> If you can keep your head when all about you
>   Are losing theirs and blaming it on you,
> If you can trust yourself when all men doubt you,
>   But make allowance for their doubting too;
>   . . . .
>   If you can fill the unforgiving minute
> With sixty seconds' worth of distance run,
>   Yours is the Earth and everything that's in it,
> And—which is more—you'll be a [Leader], my son!

8

THE SEVENTH
ESSENTIAL CHANGE:
STAY ON
THE PEACEFUL PATH

*"Master, how may I walk a peaceful path
when the world is seldom peaceful?"*

*"Peace lies not in the world,
Grasshopper, but in the man who walks the path."*

—From Kung Fu

Let's face it: We live in a hectic world. Pick up a daily newspaper and you'll find a well-documented litany of stories about man's inhumanity to man, various kinds of abuses and accidents, as well as a whole array of warnings and predictions of future problems. Adversity and conflict seem to surround us on every side. In such a state, it's all too easy to reach the point of feeling stressed out beyond our ability to cope.

Unfortunately, things aren't much better in organizations. Take the case of Jim Clark. Jim left his house in a bit of a panic one morning because he overslept. He needed to drive 23 miles to work by 8:00 a.m. This particular morning he had 25 minutes to get there. As luck would have it, two fender-benders and a construction project slowed Jim's drive from warp speed to turtle crawl and triggered a whole set of stressful reactions. He became more and more anxious as the minutes turned into horrendously slow-moving chunks of time. His frustration turned to anger. Adrenaline shot into his nervous system. He started taking quicker and shorter breaths. His blood circulated faster and veins enlarged. His face started to discolor and his ears became red. Soon his feet were tapping, his hands were fidgeting, and poor Jim was twisting every which way, looking for any possible signs that the traffic would start moving again.

Jim finally arrived at work, but he was 45 minutes late. However, when he stepped out of his van, he noticed that the left rear tire was flat. Once inside, things didn't improve a whole lot. The main milling machine was malfunctioning and consequently holding up the entire production line. Several employees were standing around wondering what to do. A delivery of valves had been promised by 9:30 a.m. And then in the midst of this scene of sheer despair, one employee wanted to talk to Jim about an idea that he had been thinking about. That was all Jim could take. At the top of his voice, he screamed, "Can't you see we have a problem here? Why is everyone standing around like a bunch of idiots?" After witnessing this bit of terrorizing behavior, the employees seemed more confused than ever. Jim looked as though he was ready for a coronary attack, or at least a bad case of stomach ulcers. Finally, one employee said that he thought he knew what was causing the machine to stop intermittently but had been afraid to shut down the whole assembly to check it out.

Managers and employees who've survived the recent rash of layoffs now face the challenge of doing more with less. Many managers are being asked to tackle new job responsibilities due to corporate restructuring. Because there is less of a feeling of security in this changing economy, everyone is feeling more stress. More managers than ever before are curtailing time with family or putting off personal priorities such as vacation or sabbaticals. Gabrielle Antolovich, executive director of the San Jose, California, office of the National Council on Alcoholism and Drug Dependence, says, "We've gotten calls from people who have been using diet drugs to stay awake, and they're using them more often."

Getting Hit at Work

The point that we are trying to make is that stressors such as Jim experienced that day are not going to go away; in fact, frustrations at work may be continuous and unrelenting. If you find yourself reading a book or attending a seminar that says you can eliminate these annoyances from your life, throw the book away or leave the room and find a quiet place to sleep. You can't eliminate them from your life. They are part of your daily routine.

People at work make insensitive comments about one another and about you. Workers say things that undermine each other in order to climb the corporate ladder. How do you respond when you see and hear such negative comments? Workers with abrasive personalities are a continuing source of anxiety. The worker who has a quick temper and an even quicker tongue, though quite talented, has a habit of speaking without thinking. What do you do when you come face to face with such a person?

Abrasive personalities are not the only problem at work. You may also have a group of employees who worry about their job security, the boss, and even the demise of the organization. They tend to be suspicious of the company's motives and intentions. They are insecure about their own abilities to perform well and to be viewed as valuable workers. They lack self-confidence and self-efficacy. These worriers create imaginary tigers and lions that are about to attack them. They create stress where there is no stress. To make matters worse, they feel impelled to share their concerns with others on a regular basis. Soon they have a number of coworkers worried about things that are of little or no consequence or that do not present any real threat to anyone's job. As a result, workers' happiness and performance decline. Now you have a management problem and a possible confrontation with the person doing the damage. How do you respond to those circumstances?

Frequently, as in Jim's case, defective tools, equipment, and materials add to your woes at work and become a regular source of irritation. A noisy or crowded office may further annoy you. An open work area may leave you with little privacy for a short respite. Moorhead and Griffin, organizational behavior researchers, suggest that computer terminals that are networked together and suffer temporary overloads, downtime, and fixing right at the moment when a message needs to be sent or a calculation needs to be made can be a real test of your ability to remain cool, calm, and collected.

In such instances it is easy to become angry or discouraged. And it is not uncommon to feel like returning "an eye for an eye and a tooth for a tooth," sometimes several eyes for an eye and several teeth for a tooth!

Managers and employees alike can feel overloaded and underappreciated, and having various conflicts at work can begin to result in an astounding variety of painful symptoms. Christina Maslach, a pioneering researcher on job burnout, and Michael Leiter, dean of the faculty of pure and applied science at Acadia University in Canada, describe some of the most prominent symptoms: "One feels physically, emotionally, and spiritually exhausted. Physical symptoms such as high blood pressure, headaches, excessive muscle tension, and gastro-intestinal illness begin. Mental distress causes depression, anxiety, and sleep disturbances."

These physiological and psychological manifestations of poor management practices, coping skills, and a negative work environment cause managers to become cynical, indifferent, and increasingly ineffective at work.

Can You Survive?

Yes! Fortunately, there is hope. There is a way to navigate the sometimes unfriendly terrain of daily life and work organizations. It begins with the realization that you can't control the world around you, but you can control how you react to the world around you. Every day, you see people who are upset by what the government is doing, how a neighbor is acting, a new company policy, or something the boss said. You can become depressed because it's a cold, rainy day instead of a sunny one, or because it's winter rather than summer. When you react to people and things around you and let them dictate how you feel, you realize that you're living life on an emotional roller coaster. One hour you're up and happy, the next you're down and discouraged. To allow other people and things to irk and vex you is to give them control of your life.

How Do You Take a Hit and Feel Calm?

As a manager, you may take a number of "hits" each day. Karl Albrecht, author of numerous stress articles, asserts that the challenge is how to stay somewhat calm and in control, especially when you are already under pressure at work. Is there a way to become emotionally resilient and tougher so that when you get smashed you can avoid total devastation and can bounce back?

An approach to controlling your reactions to the world around you and finding greater joy in daily living is almost too close to see. Joy, or the thrill of acting for ourselves, thinking the thoughts we wish to ponder, and interpreting life as we see it, is the driving force inside all of us. Our approach allows you to feel joy and become a more stable, constant, peaceful, and powerful leader. We call it "staying on the peaceful path." When you are on this path, you feel in harmony with yourself, your colleagues, and your environment. Fulfillment, peace of mind, and hope increase significantly when you stay on the peaceful path. In contrast, you can tell very quickly, because of the discomfort, unrest, anxiety and loss of self-esteem that you experience, when you depart from this path.

Six Strategies for Staying on the Peaceful Path

If you slip off the peaceful path, get back on and resolve not to fall off again. To get on the peaceful path and stay on it, we suggest the following six strategies, each of which can be used separately or in conjunction with the others:

1. Start the morning peacefully.

2. Control the way you react to people.

3. Avoid allowing things to control you.

4. Choose to do only important things.

5. Strengthen yourself each day.

6. Create balance in your life.

Start the Morning Peacefully

For most people, the simplest way to reduce stress and relax into the day is to allow more time than usual to get up and get ready for work. This may mean getting out of bed 20 or 30 minutes earlier, but it will be worth it.

When was the last time you got up early enough to have a warm, soothing shower? Did you feel the water on your neck and back? Did you close your eyes and do nothing but stand quietly for a few minutes? Did you allow enough time to towel off and find something appropriate and comfortable to wear to work?

The imperative key here is to allow more time than what these tasks usually take. A peaceful path is not filled with anxiety and all the fears of being late or getting behind. You must give yourself enough time to enjoy cleaning, grooming, and getting dressed for work. By the way, most stressed people never allow themselves enough time for a shower and breakfast. These are the very things that you need most to reduce anxiety.

Unless you get up early enough to eat and shower, you will start the day in a state of tension. Morning is also a great time to pray, briefly meditate, think about the good things in life, and to listen to your own inner thoughts and directions. Some people find it helpful to read their favorite biblical passages or other positive messages. Many people play upbeat or inspirational music while they are getting ready to go to work.

Leaving early enough for work so that you don't have to rush and panic because of heavy traffic or unexpected delays is, of course, an absolute must. If you allow sufficient time to travel while listening to some beautiful music and looking at the lovely scenery, you may even enjoy the trip. Preparing your mind and your body properly in the morning greatly aids you in getting on the peaceful path and staying on it during the day.

Control the Way You React to People

The second strategy for staying on the peaceful path is to control the way you react to people. You have the power to control your mind and to chart your course. That power comes from positively interpreting outside events, learning to control the inner experience, and determining your own response to what is happening around you. You can and must determine how you will respond; you cannot afford to just react. Responding as you choose makes all the difference. Mihaly Csikszentmihalyi, currently on the faculty at the University of Chicago, made a powerful and instructive statement at the Leisure and Mental Health Conference in Salt Lake City, Utah, July 9, 1992:

> What I discovered was that happiness is not something that happens. It is not the result of good fortune or random change. It is not something that money can buy or power command. It does not depend on outside events, but, rather, on how we interpret them. Happiness, in fact, is a condition that must be prepared for, cultivated, and defended privately by each person. People who learn to control inner experience will be able to determine the quality of their lives, which is as close as any of us can come to being happy.

While we were visiting with a manager of a prominent surgical supply company in California, the manager suddenly jumped up, looked out his office window to the plant floor, and said, "See what that guy is doing, see what that guy is doing?" Being somewhat startled by the obviously irritated response of the manager, we looked at the worker and, frankly, couldn't see anything that he was doing that would cause such consternation. "What is he doing?" we asked. "He is out of his work area and bothering other workers. He is always doing that. Someday he is going to get into a lot of trouble!"

Actually, from what we could see, the worker seemed to be enjoying himself, but the manager was most certainly not. What started as a rather calm discussion with a rather peaceful individual had suddenly turned into a serious interruption of our conversation and a major disturbance in his previously calm disposition. Ironically, the worker didn't even know that he was doing anything to irritate the manager. The manager, however, was clearly off the peaceful path.

When you let others interfere with your attempt to stay on the peaceful path, you surrender control over how you feel and give it to someone else. As a leader, you may find yourself constantly in working relationships that are not always ideal and that are many times combative. In these trying situations, you may feel uncomfortable; you may have the sensation of "taking a hit" so that your emotions are aroused. This agitation pulls you off the peaceful path. If you continue to let others control the way you feel, your emotional life will be a series of peaks and valleys. One moment you may be happy, but the next moment you may feel sad and disheartened.

How many times has someone said something to you by way of judgment or rejection, or made a negative comment about what you did or an idea that you had? How did you feel? Did you feel angry or depressed? If you felt rather happy and then suddenly felt sad because of what someone else said, you just gave control of your feelings to another person. You just let someone else decide how you were going to feel.

These four suggestions should help you to stay calm and in control when you are confronted by a potentially irritating experience.

1. **Zip the lip.** This means that you shouldn't speak until you've weighed the situation very carefully. When you're feeling upset, you tend to say things that you regret at a later time. Too often you become defensive and fire back a message that only makes the other person more nervous and anxious. Remember that positive statements to your cohorts should underlie all of your interactions.

If interaction goes well, problems are solved and relationships are strengthened. If communication goes badly, you simply alienate yourself from others and build barriers that often take a long time to remove. Zipping the lip gives you time to avoid a negative conditioned response and to figure out how to respond in a more positive and useful way.

2. **Take some deep breaths and relax.** The onset of emotional disturbances causes our bodies to tense up. For many years, stress management experts have been aware of the benefits of deep breathing. A few breaths can release a considerable amount of tension and enable you to respond far more favorably to a hit. Actually, breathing slowly through your nose is even more helpful than breathing through your mouth. If you follow step one, zip your lip, you may not have a choice!

3. **Think a peaceful thought.** Think about how good it feels to be on the peaceful path, and tell yourself that you would prefer to stay on it rather than fall off. This means trying to see the great gifts, talents, and potential of others. Consider the bigger world around you with its magnificent wonders and opportunities. Recall a lovely place on the beach or in the mountains that you have enjoyed. Picture yourself in such a relaxing place. Immerse yourself in the scene: Feel it, see it, and enjoy it. If you let one person seriously irritate you, the situation will be like putting a little stone in front of your eye. The stone will be so close to your eye that you will not be able to see anything else. To stay on the peaceful path, you need to keep your focus on the bigger picture. This way, you can stay in control and relax.

4. **Decide what kind of response is necessary.** Sometimes no response is required. Simply forgive the other person and turn the other cheek. Try to be helpful rather than confrontational. Be willing to forget and leave the ill feelings behind. Most often, only a simple response is required. You might say, "I'm sorry, I didn't know this was happening. How can we do better?"

We tend to label all of a person's negative reactions to someone or something as resentment. We tend to have the most intense resentments toward people who seem to consciously or deliberately threaten us in some way. The interesting thing is that even if another person has tried to hurt you deliberately, it is your own negative feelings, not the other person's attempt to hurt you, that produces pain in your life. You pay a great price for hate, bitterness, malice, and resentment.

When you choose to resent what someone else has said or done, you are choosing to live with the emotional pain resulting from your own resentment. Giving up resentment means that you can relinquish the source of pain and choose the peaceful path. For example, Dennis was driving along a street in a west coast city. In front of him was a family in an old, battered car. A young boy leaned over the back seat and, for no apparent reason, made a vulgar gesture toward Dennis. He later reported handling the situation like this: "It was easy to see that the boy's behavior had nothing to do with me. His gesture must have come from pain created by family concerns. Instead of adding to his pain, I mustered up all the love I could and beamed it out to him in a big smile. He suddenly began to smile in return, and we waved at one another until his car was out of sight."

Waving off resentment is not a self-righteous or Pollyanna-like turning of the other cheek, showing that we condone rude behavior. Rather, it is based on an understanding of the deep pain from which hurtful actions arise. Sense the suffering of others and see beyond the negative gestures to the person who is speaking and acting.

Here is a story told by Dass and Gorman* that illustrates how giving up resentment can be used in powerful leadership.

The train clanked and rattled through the suburbs of Tokyo on a drowsy spring afternoon. Our car was comparatively empty—a few housewives with their kids in tow, some old folks going shopping. I gazed absently at the drab houses and dusty hedgerows.

At one station the doors opened, and suddenly the afternoon quiet was shattered by a man bellowing violent, incomprehensible curses. The man staggered into our car. He wore laborer's clothing, and he was big, drunk, and dirty. Screaming, he swung at a woman holding a baby. The blow sent her spinning into the laps of an elderly couple. It was a miracle that the baby was unharmed.

Terrified, the couple jumped up and scrambled toward the other end of the car. The laborer aimed a kick at the retreating back of the old woman but missed as she scuttled to safety. This so enraged the drunk that he grabbed the metal pole in the center of the car and tried to wrench it out of its stanchion.

I could see that one of his hands was cut and bleeding. The train lurched ahead, the passengers frozen with fear. I stood up.

* From HOW CAN I HELP? by Ram Dass and Paul Gorman. ©1985 by Ram Dass and Paul Gorman. Used by permission of Alfred A. Knopf, a division of Random House, Inc.

I was young then, some twenty years ago, and in pretty good shape. I'd been putting in a solid eight hours of aikido training [Japanese art of self-defense] nearly every day for the past three years. I liked to throw and grapple. I thought I was tough. The trouble was, my martial skill was untested in actual combat. As students of aikido, we were not allowed to fight.

"Aikido," my instructor had said again and again, "is the art of reconciliation. Whoever has the mind to fight has broken his connection with the universe. If you try to dominate people, you are already defeated. We study how to resolve conflict, not how to start it."

I listened to his words. I tried hard. I even went so far as to cross the street to avoid the *chimpira*, the pinball punks who lounged around the train stations. My forbearance exalted me. I felt both tough and holy. In my heart, however, I wanted an absolutely legitimate opportunity whereby I might save the innocent by destroying the guilty.

"This is it!" I said to myself as I got to my feet. "People are in danger. If I don't do something fast, somebody will probably get hurt."

Seeing me stand up, the drunk recognized a chance to focus his rage.

"Aha!" he roared. "A foreigner! You need a lesson in Japanese manners!"

I held on lightly to the commuter strap overhead and gave him a slow look of disgust and dismissal. I planned to take this turkey apart, but he had to make the first move. I wanted him mad, so I pursed my lips and blew him an insolent kiss.

"All right!" he hollered. "You're gonna get a lesson." He gathered himself for a rush at me.

A fraction of a second before he could move, someone shouted, "Hey!" It was ear splitting. I remember the joyous, lilting quality of it—as though you and a friend had been searching diligently for something and he had suddenly stumbled upon it. "Hey!" the voice repeated.

I wheeled to my left; the drunk spun to his right. We both stared down at a little old Japanese man. He must have been well into his seventies, this tiny gentleman, sitting there immaculate in his kimono. He took no notice of me, but beamed delightedly at the laborer, as though he had a most important, most welcome secret to share.

"C'mere," the old man said in an easy vernacular, beckoning to the drunk. "C'mere and talk with me." He waved his hand lightly.

The big man followed, as if on a string. He planted his feet belligerently in front of the old gentleman and roared above the clacking wheels of the train: "Why the hell should I talk to you?" The drunk now had his back to me. If his elbow moved so much as a millimeter, I'd drop him in his socks.

The old man continued to beam at the laborer. "What 'cha been drinkin'?" he asked, his eyes sparkling with interest.

"I been drinkin' sake," the laborer bellowed back, "and it's none of your business!" Flecks of spittle splattered the old man.

"Oh, that's wonderful," the old man said, "absolutely wonderful! You see, I love sake too. Every night, me and my wife (she's seventy-six, you know), we warm up a little bottle of sake and take it out into the garden, and we sit on an old wooden bench. We watch the sun go down, and we look to see how our persimmon tree is doing. My great-grandfather planted that tree, and we worry about whether it will recover from those ice storms we had last winter. Our tree has done better than I expected, though, especially when you consider the poor quality of the soil. It is gratifying to watch when we take our sake and go out to enjoy the evening—even when it rains!" He looked up at the laborer, eyes twinkling.

As he struggled to follow the old man's conversation, the drunk's face began to soften. His fists slowly unclenched. "Yeah," he said. "I love persimmons, too...." His voice trailed off.

"Yes," said the old man, smiling, "and I'm sure you have a wonderful wife."

"No," replied the laborer. "My wife died." Very gently, swaying with the motion of the train, the big man began to sob. "I don't got no wife, I don't got no home, I don't got no job. I'm so ashamed of myself." Tears rolled down his cheeks; a spasm of despair rippled through his body.

Now it was my turn. Standing there in my well-scrubbed, youthful innocence and my make-this-world-safe-for-democracy righteousness, I suddenly felt dirtier than he was.

Suddenly the train arrived at my station. As the doors opened, I heard the old man cluck sympathetically. "My, my. That is a difficult predicament, indeed. Sit down here and tell me about it," he motioned to the drunk.

I turned my head for one last look. The laborer was sprawled on the seat, his head in the old man's lap. The old gentleman was softly stroking the filthy, matted hair. As the train pulled away, I sat down on a bench. What I had wanted to do with muscle had been accomplished with kind words.

Staying on the peaceful path enlarges the strength and power of those who sustain the walk. Leadership that is grounded in the practice of a peaceful path encourages others to follow, to appreciate, to enjoy, and to respect the leader. Staying on the peaceful path isn't so difficult to do if you also appreciate, respect, and honor those with whom you work. You can stay on the peaceful path if you lighten up, exercise patience and understanding, and use your energy for doing good among your cohorts.

Avoid Allowing Things to Control You

The third strategy for staying on the peaceful path is similar to the second, but it involves articles, objects, materials, and processes used in organizations to accomplish work. Things are not people, but they try to pull you off the peaceful path. How do you respond, for example, when you have a flat tire on the way to work? Or what happens inside of you when your computer temporarily shuts down? You live in a world of things and processes. Things frequently don't function properly, even things like meetings. If you let everything that malfunctions make you angry or distressed, you have just turned over the control of your feelings to an inhuman, insensitive, nonthinking, and nonfeeling object! Getting irrational and extremely angry over something that malfunctions may not be the most positive or even sensible way to respond. You, not things, are in control, and you can determine your own responses. Happiness and peacefulness come from within.

Choose to Do Only Important Things

The fourth strategy for staying on the peaceful path concerns the kinds of decisions you make about using your time and your energy. In our human endeavors, there is far more to be done than time or energy permits. None of us can do all the things that we would like to do for our family, spouse, neighbors, profession, or ourselves. Most of us are already involved in what is called "hyperliving." Our whole goal is not to enjoy what we are doing, but to hurry to get it done so that we can move on to the next thing. We lose perspective, and personal relationships suffer. Often, the high-leverage opportunities and things of real value in our lives are neglected.

You cannot do everything. You must be selective and wise in the way you intend to use your time and energy. A helpful model for deciding what to do contains four elements: First, consider all the things that you would like to do at home, work, in the community, and for yourself. Second, pick out one thing you would especially like to do in each of these four areas. Third, make a simple plan for how you are going to get those four things done—not for everything, but only for those four things. Focus on results. Identify the steps involved in moving from where you are to where you would like to be. The steps should be a logical sequence of activities that move you from one point to another and should involve the most direct approach possible. If the plan can involve only one step, choose to get what you want done in that one step. And fourth, relax and follow your plan. Do what you decided to do, follow the steps, and stop worrying about what you have decided not to do. You may pick up on those other things at a later time. If you continue to worry over what you haven't done, you will be unlikely to do the things you planned, and that will be painful. You will be unable to stay on the peaceful path.

Keeping on the peaceful path involves making choices about your time and determining what you really want out of work and life in general. Specific answers will come if you take the time to think about and focus on important items. Joy and happiness come from taking control of your time and your life so as to move ahead and do something useful. The mind has the power to select what it will think about and act upon. The key to staying on this path, then, is to consciously decide what to think about and act upon.

While the serenity and peace of a mountain valley in the wake of the morning sun could influence the environment and encourage a walk along the peaceful path, you must recognize that it is not the external environment that makes the difference. The peaceful path is found in the mind and the heart. Walking the peaceful path is just as possible in the battlefield of organizational life as in the waning shadows of a tropical island sunset. Convictions come from the inside out, not the outside in. What you choose to think, speak, and do is all important.

Controlling the way you react to people and things and finding harmony within is not an easy task. Substituting tendencies to be egotistic, arrogant, and self-gratifying with attributes of humility, love, patience, and charity takes time and refinement. But the rewards of inner peace, mental tranquility, and greater confidence are well worth the effort.

Staying on the peaceful path may require a significant change in your heart, especially in the manner in which you respond to the people, technology, and the material things that surround you. Fortunately, once you make these changes, you will have little disposition to return to something more stressful and less fulfilling.

Strengthen Yourself Each Day

The fifth strategy for staying on the peaceful path has to do with both physical and mental hardiness. When you lose your mental energy and physical strength, you are limited in what you can do. You become weary, vulnerable, and susceptible; in fact, your resistance levels and power to manage are compromised. Your ability to take a hit and still stay on the peaceful path is weakened. You become tense and terse in your comments and less patient with others. Your ability to govern your thoughts and maintain control over how you respond is weakened. In short, a tired trooper is a sitting duck for emotional duress and disease.

Fatal error number one for most managers is that they do not take the time to strengthen themselves and reenergize themselves on a daily basis. During our last dozen management seminars, we took the time to ask, "What is the manager's number one priority—not major responsibility, but number one priority?" Though we received hundreds of sincere responses dealing with various aspects of management and leadership, no one seemed anxious to suggest that they themselves were their first priority.

After some discussion about their ability to maintain positive attitudes, enthusiastic management styles, and appropriate energy levels, day in and day out and week after week, most reconsidered their priorities. You should not feel guilty about thinking of your needs first. Flight attendants always advise parents to fix their oxygen masks first, before they tend to their children or others. When you lose your strength and energy, you don't lead nearly as well as you could, and everyone around you ultimately suffers the consequences of your tiredness and fatigue. To lead others tirelessly, patiently, and effectively, especially during periods of disappointment and fatigue, requires that you master the basic principles of physical regeneration and self-renewal.

You must not ignore opportunities to relax with friends, eat nourishing food, and sleep after a day of work. Observance of the laws of health—together with commitments to good eating habits, sleep, exercise—and positive thinking patterns are absolutely fundamental in all that you do. They are especially important to people who are trying to manage and lead effectively.

To strengthen yourself on a daily basis, consider these four fundamental ideas: you are what you eat; you are how you exercise; you are how you sleep; and you are what you think.

You Are What You Eat. No matter what your age is, a balanced, nutritious diet is essential to good health. Eating a variety of foods helps ensure that adequate amounts of vitamins and minerals are entering your body. The Food Pyramid is a good guide to daily food choices. You should follow it in choosing what to eat. The problem comes about when, as our doctor friends report, many people don't follow the recommended diet—sometimes, not even the doctors themselves or their wives do. But you can and should follow it.

Our nutritional colleagues report an additional disaster in the making. What used to be known as a wholesome dairy product called "ice cream" has now turned into a bunch of frozen desserts containing antioxidants, neutralizers, buffers, bactericides, surfactants, stabilizers, and emulsifiers. We bought a packaged sandwich from a vending machine the other day and couldn't even pronounce the names of all the additives in the scrumptious, processed-to-last, beautifully packaged chemical treat.

You probably need to cut back on what you do eat, and eat more of what you should eat. For example, ask yourself these questions about the foods you consume:

1. Do you eat starchy foods frequently?

2. Do you regularly eat sweets, sugar, syrup, jams, jellies, candy?

3. Do you eat green or yellow vegetables less than twice daily?

4. Do you frequently eat bakery products like cakes, pies, cookies, and doughnuts?

5. Do you usually avoid having regular helpings of raw fruits and vegetables?

6. Do you usually omit daily vitamin or mineral supplements?

Numerous "yes" answers indicate a less-than-optimal diet, and as most medical practitioners say, you'll have "a proneness for tiredness, loss of vitality, and illness."

Glenn Ford, famous movie star and a man who worked at a pace most stars half his age would find exhausting, was asked about his energy secrets. His comments were: "I swim in my pool every day, and I eat lots of proteins and a lot of fish. But I never eat white bread, chocolate, desserts, sweets, sugar, or any kind of junk food." Give your diet a Glenn Ford overhaul.

You Are How You Exercise. Research has demonstrated that exercise can ease tension and reduce the amount of stress that you feel. Simply put, exercise is one of the best things you can do for your health. The beautiful part about exercise is that it need not take more than 20 to 30 minutes a day, but to be beneficial, it must be regular.

We were surprised to learn that, according to exercise physiologists, the first three benefits of exercise have little to do with improving the cardiovascular system. Regular exercise tends to build a healthier self-concept. You feel better about yourself. Another benefit of regular exercise is that overall stress and anxiety levels go down. You feel less depressed and worried. A third benefit of exercise is that you experience an increase in self-confidence. You feel more self-assured and positive.

Brisk walking, jogging, cycling, dancing, swimming, and competitive sports are all useful ways of strengthening our bodies. The secret is to choose something that you enjoy doing. Set small goals to start. Try not to miss an exercise session, but if you do, make it up the following week. Exercise with a friend if it will help you stay motivated. When you feel progress, reward yourself with time to relax and enjoy your success. Remember that the exercise is for you. You are not out to prove anything to anyone. You just want to be healthy.

You Are How You Sleep. Sleep and rest are great rejuvenators. Even if you are not a top-notch athlete, you know the connection that exists between good sleep and good performance. And you probably know that sleep is basic to everything you do, whether it's at the office or on the tennis court. Most research shows that the best achievers get a good night's sleep. Early to bed and early to rise, and don't sleep longer than necessary, is still the best advice.

Better Sleep Council experts point out that the best system is to go to bed and wake up at about the same time every day—including weekends. The weekend sleep-in syndrome won't catch you up on sleep you miss during the week. Erratic sleeping habits can be a real energy drainer.

If you seem to be sleeping for an adequate amount of time, but still feel quite tired after arising in the morning, you may be short on third-stage deep sleep. Doctors of internal medicine explain that (1) if you feel cold during the night, or are awakened by sounds or an uncomfortable pillow or mattress, or (2) if deep anxieties keep returning you to levels of light sleep or awaken you, you need to make some immediate changes to increase deep sleep. If you need help in obtaining the rest that comes from deep restful sleep, consult your local physician. There are some new medical helps that can be useful for regulating sleep.

Also, be aware that exercise can help relieve problems with insomnia and erratic sleep. Mild exercise a few hours before bed, or during the day, helps many people get a restful night's sleep.

You Are What You Think. Researchers are continuing to prove that your thoughts, your emotions, and even your relationships have a great effect on your health and well-being. Your thoughts actually transform themselves into "chemical entities" like hormones and neurotransmitters that have a direct effect on how strong and healthy you feel. Meditation and relaxation techniques not only relieve the short-term stresses that you feel, but they also contribute to the strengthening of the immunization system and your ability to fight diseases and long-term stress syndromes.

Our own research in the area of biofeedback and stress management shows conclusively that as people think, so are they. When you think negatively, angrily, and with self-defeating thoughts, your breathing, heart rate, skin response, and brain waves change and put a tremendous strain on your body. When you relax and think positive thoughts, the physiological parameters also calm down and you feel better and are more hopeful. To think positively is to believe that the world is basically a friendly place, your life is not being threatened by invisible forces, and that there is reason to feel optimistic.

Relationships have a potentially powerful effect on how you feel. If you are married, you should create a warm personal relationship with your spouse. If you don't have a spouse, find some close personal friends. Most human beings crave intimacy and a sense of community. Nurture yourself socially, and the chances are that you will be a happier and healthier person.

Create Balance in Your Life

Most managers and leaders feel driven to produce and take on the additional responsibility of encouraging others to perform at their highest levels. You may seem to run out of time to be with your family, serve in your community, and do other things for your personal enjoyment. As your stress level increases, depression, discomfort, and disease creep in.

We recently asked 500 people in a stress management seminar this familiar but provocative question: "How many of you, when you are laying on your death bed, will wish that you had spent more time at work? Please raise your hands." At first, there was total silence and no movement. Then, a considerable amount of smiling and giggling erupted, but not a single hand was raised. Although no one wanted to spend more time at work, just about everyone appreciated being confronted with issues that most get in their way when trying to balance their lives.

Lee A. Daniels, President and CEO of Titus Communications, explains his approach to balanced living:

> With total immersion in the information age, it seems that we can
> never escape from the emails, voice mails, fax messages, cellular
> phones, and the Internet information overload. I am finding fewer and
> fewer executives who, in my definition, have balanced lives. The rapid

pace of change in technology, competition, globalization, liberaliza-
tion, and consolidation force executives to work longer and longer
hours to stay competitive.

Many executives justify long hours by saying they are providing
for their families. If the truth were known, most families would willingly exchange some of the material wealth for more time with their
spouses, fathers, or mothers. During my career, I have turned down
promotions, prestigious positions, and some attractive compensation
packages because I felt that the job required too much travel or would
disrupt my ability to maintain an appropriate balance in my life.

Since most of us will be required to work to provide for our families, let me share with you my philosophy of career management. All of
us are going to spend a certain amount of our lives away from our families earning a living. In order to balance my time between family,
church callings, employment, exercise, and community service, I start
by determining how many hours a day I need to dedicate to work. After
I have made that time allocation, I do everything in my power to be as
productive and successful as possible and to maximize my earnings
capability. The challenge is not to increase the amount of time we allo-
cate to work as our management responsibilities expand and our salaries
increase. It is important to safeguard the time set aside for the other
important areas in our lives. Matthew 6:19–21 is a constant reminder of
maintaining the right priorities: "Lay not up yourselves treasures upon
earth where moth and rust doth corrupt and where thieves break through
and steal: But lay up for yourselves treasures in Heaven, where neither
moth nor rust doth corrupt, and where thieves do not break through nor
steal: For where your treasure is, there will your heart be also."

Many managers spend too much time at work. When they do get
home, they often spend time doing work that they carried home from the
office or worry about work they left at the office that still needs to be
done. Though work gives people many rewards, they pay dearly by for-
feiting the joys of an intimate and healthy marriage and family relationship. Other family and community responsibilities are often ignored. The
hard labor and long hours leaders devote to work usually end up putting
their health at risk. The desire to eat properly and exercise regularly is
weakened by trying to contribute too much energy at the office. Even
obtaining a good night's sleep becomes a problem.

To stay on the peaceful path you should pay more attention to the
concept of balance in your life. You have many needs as a human being.
If you respond to those needs, you increase your feelings of wellness and
strength. Fundamentally, you should view balance as comparable
amounts of work and play, enjoying being with people and being alone,

getting an adequate amount of exercise and rest, and balancing tension and relaxation. The notion here is not to become overloaded with too many challenges or events that produce inordinate amounts of stress, and at the same time, to not deprive yourself of challenges and opportunities to grow and develop.

Although this approach to balance is worthy of your consideration, there is another philosophy of human happiness and well-being that implies that life must be lived more holistically if you are to be an effective manager and stay on the peaceful path. Though many "wheel models" have been developed to help us examine the important areas of living and working, most of them include the same general categories.

As you look at each of the five areas, remember that the well-developed and most rewarded individual is the one who gives time and attention to each category.

1. **Work and Profession.** These activities have to do with making a living, earning a livelihood, and strengthening your relationship to the organization or professional group of which you are part. You must give time and attention to this set of activities, but you must leave time for other activities as well.

2. **Social and Family.** These are the activities that cultivate relationships with your family, friends, colleagues, and others at work, in the community, at the lodge, and during recreational pursuits. Time and attention must be reserved for these activities.

3. **Intellectual and Cultural.** These activities broaden and refine your appreciation for art and scholarship. They consist of activities such as studying new ways to do your work, traveling, attending classes and seminars, and viewing plays, art exhibits, and other programs and films. You need to have time to engage in some of these activities.

4. **Physical Health and Well-Being.** These activities include things like exercise, dieting, relaxing, and personal hygiene. Be sure to consider activities that allow you to express your own unique creative self, such as hobbies, crafts, singing, dancing, building things, riding bikes, hiking, and engaging in recreational and competitive games. It also includes the development of emotional stability as well as creating a set of practices to honor the Divine within you and your relationship with a Higher Power or God. You should engage in some spiritual activities regularly, whether it be at a church, a synagogue, at home, or out in nature.

5. Financial and Material Possessions. These activities involve acquiring money, benefits, and goods, but they also involve anything that gives you a sense of temporal security, such as insurance, savings, adequate emergency supplies, a car that runs, and a full tank of gas.

The reasoning behind the balanced life is that as you reap rewards from these five areas of living, you will be happier and more enthusiastic about life. Also, if something tends to go wrong in one area, you will not succumb to unbearable amounts of stress because other areas of your life are going reasonably well.

To assess how well you are living in a balanced and holistic way, go back over each activity area and rate yourself. Ask yourself what is happening in your life in each area. Are you deriving the potential benefits in each area of your life, or are you limited in some way? Do you need to make some changes in a particular category? Go through all five areas and try to determine whether you see any deficiencies in your overall balance of activities.

If you are married, you should go through this process with your spouse. You may think you are doing well in all of the areas, but it helps to have another point of view. Your spouse may feel differently, which should give you an opportunity to talk about which activities are most critical to a balanced life. You should also observe whether you are gaining a lot of satisfaction from a specific area or just a small amount of satisfaction. Many people see themselves as well-rounded, but with only minimal benefits and happiness in every area. This means that some adjustments should be made to increase the benefits and happiness in each area. Whether you have some glaring deficiencies in a category or whether you are receiving few benefits, now is the time to set some goals and make a plan to increase the level and quality of activities in each of the five areas.

Are You on the Peaceful Path?

To get on the peaceful path and stay on it means that you must invest time, energy, and personal discipline to implement the six strategies discussed in this chapter. As you recall, the six strategies are to

1. Get on the peaceful path as early in the day as possible, preferably in the morning.

2. Control the way you feel about others with whom you come in contact during the day.

3. Don't let mindless and heartless objects decide how you will react to them.

4. Fix in your mind the reality that you will never be able to do everything—you can only do the most important things.

5. Strengthen yourself physically, spiritually, and emotionally on a daily basis so that every little adversity that comes your way will not knock you off the peaceful path.

6. Increase and decrease the number and quality of activities in the five activity areas so as to create more balance in your life.

Attending to only one or two of these six strategies weakens your ability to stay on the peaceful path. The benefits of strengthening yourself physically are reduced considerably if you allow other people to control the way you feel. If you keep worrying about not being able to do everything you would like to in do your life, you may have difficulty implementing the six strategies. The six strategies are interrelated, and they collectively give you a tremendous opportunity to stay in control, to be happy, and to continue moving ahead in your life.

Ask Yourself These Questions

In order to determine how far along the peaceful path you are, complete the following questions by answering yes or no to each one.

1.	Do you get a good night's sleep?	yes	no
2.	Have you developed close relationships that motivate you to your highest good?	yes	no
3.	Are you involved in a regular exercise program?	yes	no
4.	Do you spend most of your day on the peaceful path?	yes	no
5.	Do you eat healthy?	yes	no
6.	Have you recently enjoyed the serenity of nature?	yes	no
7.	Do you find something to cheer about each day?	yes	no
8.	Are you creating a better balance between work and play?	yes	no
9.	Are you doing anything to strengthen yourself spiritually?	yes	no
10.	Do you stay in control when people upset you?	yes	no
11.	Are you separating the important from the unimportant?	yes	no
12.	Do you allow enough time to start the day unhurried?	yes	no

A lot of "yes" answers is good. "No" answers mean that you need to make changes in the way you are living your life. Remember, the goal is not to compound problems by adding more undertakings to your already busy life. Rather, your goal is to pick out areas of concern and do something to balance activities in all areas. Unfortunately, no one is going to do these things for you. If you don't wind yourself up in the morning and get going, no one else will do it for you. You are responsible for making yourself sick or well, sad or happy.

As a manager, you really don't have a choice. To be effective, you must feel effective. Your efforts should be directed toward getting on the peaceful path first thing in the morning, leaving for work with a feeling of enthusiasm and confidence, and retaining your energy level and composure at work. All this is relatively simple if you maintain control of yourself, relax and enjoy your work, and stay balanced in your daily activities. Ultimately, your goal is to learn how to enjoy each moment of your life, both at work and at play.

> For the uncontrolled there is no wisdom,
> nor for the uncontrolled is there the power of
> concentration; and for him without concentration
> there is no peace. And for the unpeaceful,
> how can there be happiness?
>
> —Bhagavad Gita

A Look Ahead

We have introduced seven essential changes that you should make in order to become a powerful leader. In the next chapter, we ask you to make an assessment of where you stand as a powerful leader. This activity helps you identify what you need to do to make the essential changes in your leadership style. The assessment can be of great benefit to both you and your cohorts.

9

WHERE ARE YOU AS A POWERFUL LEADER?

*One day it was announced by Master Joshu that the
young monk Kyogen had reached an enlightened state.
Much impressed by this news, several of his peers went
to speak with him.
"We have heard that you are enlightened. Is this true?"
his fellow students inquired.
"It is," Kyogen answered.
"Tell us," said a friend, "how do you feel?"
"As miserable as ever," replied the enlightened Kyogen.*
—Anonymous

Kyogen's enlightened misery occurs when correct principles are understood but not practiced. You are now approaching the moment of truth.

You have read and studied seven changes that maximize worker involvement and minimize the efforts of leaders to micromanage others. Can you make the necessary changes in your leadership style to help your cohorts also make changes in their work that will keep everyone happier, more satisfied, and more productive?

In the business section of the *Salt Lake Tribune* on Sunday, June 17, 2001, Marilyn Elias of *USA Today* reported the results of a study released by two psychologists from the University of Michigan; the article was entitled "Rude Behavior Common in Workplace." Though not surprising, the results confirmed our long experience with people who work in organizations: They have a penchant for being rude. Seventy-one percent of the employees of a federal court system reported encountering rampant rudeness where they worked. When rudeness occurred, it affected the productivity and satisfaction of employees. The higher the number of rude contacts, the more anxiety and depression the employees experienced, which reduced their productivity and made the workplace less appealing. Do you think that the leaders were exempt from being harsh, discourteous, and impolite? We don't think so, and neither do most people.

It's not a pretty face, I grant you, but underneath its flabby exterior is an enormous lack of character.

—Oscar Levant introducing himself
at the outset of Vincente Minnelli's *An American in Paris*

This is the time to do a little self-inspection. Willard F. Rockwell, Jr. of space shuttle fame explained that one fact of executive life is that you can get all the flattery you want. The executive who thinks he's "the greatest" usually finds considerable support for his conviction. Rockwell further explains that recognizing weaknesses that exist is an essential ingredient of successful self-appraisal. The executive who believes himself totally lacking in weaknesses is usually the weakest of all.

We recently inquired about a new incoming manager of the local division of United Parcel Service. Previous new managers had come into the company trying to hide their ignorance of local procedures and to take strong control of the office. This new manager came in and admitted that she was new to this particular area of the company and was going to first ask for everyone's assistance in "teaching her the ropes." She interviewed key employees to ascertain the good things that were happening and some of the problems and challenges that existed in this unit of UPS. Employees reported to us that this was the first manager they had ever had who took the time to ride with the delivery people to become more personally acquainted with them and find out exactly what happens when they deliver mailed packages.

Because this new manager made such an interesting and rather humble entry into a workplace filled with people she had never met before, the employees went out of their way to support her and share ideas for making things better. Notice that she didn't use all of the seven essential changes initially, but she changed her relationship from boss to cohort, encouraged employees to contribute their ideas for making work more efficient and fun, tried to free workers to take the lead, and of course avoided criticizing employees.

If you are a manager, supervisor, or administrator, you probably achieved your position because you are willing to work hard and accept responsibility. At this point in your career you may have gained experience and a vision of what it takes to get ahead. Our point is this: Usually managers have some areas of considerable strength. However, all of us have areas of uncertainty or weakness. The ideal is to engage in a process of self-appraisal that identifies our strengths, our adequacies, and our weaknesses.

Although we have identified specific behaviors that need to be changed to tap into the full power of employees and unencumber your own life as a manager, it now becomes your responsibility to try them out, practice them, and adjust them to fit your individual personality and strengths and to enjoy the rewards of your effort.

There is absolutely no reason why you shouldn't make these seven essential changes so that you can free your cohorts to take the lead, and by doing so actually become a more powerful leader yourself. However, just as with any other skill, you do not learn to become more effective simply by reading about it. Just as you acquire a skill in piano playing, golfing, or skiing, you must rehearse, practice, and apply the changes in your own leadership relationships.

Throughout this book we have pointed toward a more natural and less complicated way to lead people than those discussed in contemporary management literature and seminars. It may be useful at this stage of our discussion to summarize those natural and easy ways found in each chapter.

Free People to Take the Lead. The most unnatural thing you can do is put people into real or imagined confinement. When people feel like they are trapped in a building or in a work system, they become fearful, frustrated, and angry. Their energy is directed toward trying to escape. They want freedom to run, think, and play. The best thing you can do as a leader is to help the people that work with you feel free, grow and develop, and use their talents and energies at work. Stop telling them what to do and how to do it. Point the way, be around to support and encourage, and then get out of the way!

Promote Creativity, Innovation, and Fun at Work. As you start to free people to take the lead, immediately encourage them to take a fresh look at what they are doing at work. See if they can make the work easier to do or more cost effective, overall better. Workers have many creative ideas that can make their work more interesting and efficient. If given the opportunity, they can innovate and change things for the better. Your role as leader is critical in releasing the creative juices of workers and supporting them as they engage in one of the most exciting and energizing thing they will ever do.

Switch from Boss to Cohort. Workers hate people who boss them around. They prefer to be treated as equals. They reject leadership that makes them feel controlled, abused, and anxious. People work better when they have a positive relationship with their leaders rather than one that fills them with fear and intimidation. When you treat your workers as cohorts, they go out of their way to do things for you. In today's world, the old time butt-kicker is going to get kicked back. If you really want to build worker loyalty, customer loyalty, and supplier loyalty, try treating them as cohorts. Who knows, you might actually like it.

Master the 4E's of Involvement. The process of involving workers in making decisions about their work and making the workplace stimulating, inspiring, exciting, and activating requires engaging in the 4E's. Lead people by pointing the way with a clear vision, enabling them to do the work and achieve the goals by having resources available, energizing them through interesting work and the freedom to improve their work, and ensuring that the goals have been met by return-and-report meetings. This is the appropriate way to lead in the new economy. Involvement may be the heart of leadership in the new economy.

When workers are invited to participate in the achievement of a goal and taste the sweet fruits of its successful implementation, you can't keep them from being involved. If they know that you are supporting them by providing them with time and resources, they voluntarily contribute even more effort. When you use the 4E's properly, you won't have to worry about 40 new ways to motivate your people. In fact, you may find that your workers are asking to be involved even more.

Stop Criticizing, Start Applauding. People everywhere hate to be criticized. Workers do not like to be criticized and berated. To do their work well, adults need to know what they are supposed to do and how well they are doing it. Feedback and positive responses are always welcome, especially when it comes from a colleague or a leader. Employees are more willing to change and try out new ways of doing things when they are applauded for what they do. Find opportunities to support, applaud, and celebrate the accomplishments of workers. When you have to, redirect people, don't reprimand them. Eliminate criticism completely from your leadership style.

Take the High Road. Honesty is still the best policy. It is easier to lead when you are honest and moral than when you are dishonest and immoral. Employees respond positively to leaders who make accurate statements, treat others fairly, say things that increase goodwill, and do things that are beneficial to everyone. Leaders who follow a simple code of ethics feel better about themselves and can relax with employees. They can avoid the pressures of government inquiries, such as internal and external audits of finances and management practices, and avoid incongruities between what is right and good for both the company and employees. Taking the high road is comfortable. You avoid the constant worry of getting caught in contradictions, in resolving double standards, and in avoiding embarrassing incidents. Even better, if workers see that you have high ethical standards and invariably maintain your integrity, they will increase their trust in you as a leader.

Stay on the Peaceful Path. Most people abhor living in a state of tension, anxiety, and anger. In such a condition they become irritated and impatient with everything around them. Leaders may be more susceptible to pressures than other people because of the responsibility they have and the number of decisions they have to make that affect colleagues and cohorts. Leaders may not realize it, but workers are among the first to know when you as a leader have "lost it" and fallen off the peaceful path. When you are tense, restless, and anxious, your actions reflect more contradictions than usual. Workers may become confused about their relationship with you and wonder what is happening in the organization. If you find yourself in such a predicament, take time to review how you can get back on the peaceful path and what you need to do to stay on it. You will not only be more productive, but you will actually enjoy going to work.

> The life you knew is over. You must live in a new way.
> Before, everything was decided. Now you must make choices.
> You may choose to hate the necessity of choosing,
> or you may value it. Each choice has consequences, so
> choose wisely.
>
> —Mary Doria Russell

How Are You Doing as a Powerful Leader?

You have already taken considerable time to study and imagine in your mind seven changes that help managers turn themselves into more powerful leaders. Take the additional time now to assess where you are in using these powerful ideas and to determine the changes that you should make to improve.

Jack Dempsey, the great boxer, once said, "In order to become a champion, one must have two characteristics. One is the ability to give a big punch, and the second is the ability to take a big punch." An opponent in the ring with Dempsey once complained to the referee that Dempsey hit him when he wasn't looking. The referee said, "No one has the right to get into the ring with Dempsey unless he pays attention." Leadership may be something like getting into the ring with Dempsey: You may have to take and give some big punches, but more than that, you must pay attention to what's happening.

A Simple Quiz

Leaders often fail to have readily available systematic ways of assessing how well they are doing. This quiz is designed to give you a quick profile of where you stand as a powerful leader. The quiz helps you pinpoint areas where you may want to make some improvements as well as identify areas where you are doing well. This is not a test in which you are graded on what you know about powerful leadership; rather, it is an inventory of what you feel you are doing well and what you think might strengthen your leadership skills. You may want to ask others at work, home, or in the community who know you well to fill this out too.

Don't ponder each item. Sit back, relax, grab a pencil, and quickly check off your response to each question. To complete the quiz, circle the answers that describe most accurately the ways in which you are presently functioning as a leader. When you have completed the quiz, analyze the scores according to the instructions.

Quiz: Where Are You as a Powerful Leader?

F = Frequently	O = Occassionally	N = Not Usually

1.	I eliminate bureaucratic restraints from my part of the company.	F	O	N
2.	I enable employees to make decisions about the company and resist "synergistic ignorance" in which managers pool their ignorance on issues and give orders to employees who know more about the situation than they do.	F	O	N
3.	I regularly eliminate one or more rules, procedures, policies, routines, or bureaucratic expectations that don't make sense to employees and that keep them from doing their best work.	F	O	N
4.	I let cohorts know that I am committed to the highest ideals of the company's mission.	F	O	N
5.	I show a genuine concern for the feelings and needs of those with whom I work.	F	O	N
6.	I show self-confidence in my dealings with coworkers and cohorts.	F	O	N
7.	I express statements to cohorts that are optimistic.	F	O	N
8.	I treat cohorts whom I would like to change as if they had changed already.	F	O	N
9.	I conduct return-and-report meetings.	F	O	N
10.	I use an approach that integrates the 4 E's of Involvement into a single, harmonious process.	F	O	N
11.	I invite rather than tell workers to complete projects, assignments, and tasks.	F	O	N
12.	I avoid criticizing other people, their ideas, and their actions.	F	O	N
13.	I applaud others when they successfully complete a job.	F	O	N
14.	I avoid giving reprimands.	F	O	N
15.	I give standing ovations for workers who do a job very well.	F	O	N
16.	I legitimize exceptional performances of workers.	F	O	N
17.	I redirect behaviors that are not on target for achieving a goal.	F	O	N
18.	I talk and act with honesty and personal integrity.	F	O	N
19.	I make decisions that are based on a personal system of ethics.	F	O	N
20.	I follow the company's code of ethics to the letter of the law.	F	O	N
21.	I test whether an act or decision is ethical by hypothetically making the opposite of the act a requirement for everyone.	F	O	N

Quiz: Where Are You as a Powerful Leader? (cont.)
F = Frequently   **O = Occassionally**   **N = Not Usually**

22.	I review my personal code of ethics for inconsistencies.	F	O	N
23.	I report my feelings about work accurately to my superiors.	F	O	N
24.	I treat customers fairly and with consideration.	F	O	N
25.	I do things that promote goodwill and better relationships with others.	F	O	N
26.	I do what is beneficial to all concerned, not just to myself.	F	O	N
27.	I inform new employees about my personal code of ethics and the company's code of ethics, and insist that they follow them.	F	O	N
28.	I do not compromise my code of ethics even if no one knows or cares what I'm doing.	F	O	N
29.	I avoid responding with rude behaviors, even if I am pressed by inconsiderate people.	F	O	N
30.	I avoid becoming angry when things do not go my way.	F	O	N
31.	I avoid becoming irritated by defective tools, noisy people, and equipment that is malfunctioning when I need it most.	F	O	N
32.	I react with emotional resilience when trouble develops.	F	O	N
33.	I begin the morning with a soothing shower and a leisurely period of getting dressed.	F	O	N
34.	I leave for work early.	F	O	N
35.	I take hits and recover in a calm and considerate manner, take deep breaths, and relax when others disturb me.	F	O	N
36.	I avoid reacting to others with bitterness and resentment.	F	O	N
37.	I focus on results rather than on distractions.	F	O	N
38.	I do what I plan to do and don't worry about other things.	F	O	N
39.	I relax with friends.	F	O	N
40.	I eat nourishing food.	F	O	N
41.	I have a good night's sleep.	F	O	N
42.	I take a brisk walk or engage in other physical activity.	F	O	N
43.	I engage in meditation or other relaxation techniques.	F	O	N
44.	I take time to be with family members.	F	O	N
45.	I attend cultural and social events.	F	O	N
46.	I engage in a hobby.	F	O	N
47.	I attend religious services.	F	O	N
48.	I share my goals and dreams with my cohorts.	F	O	N
49.	I control my emotions in my relationships with those with whom I work—my cohorts.	F	O	N

Quiz: Where Are You as a Powerful Leader? (cont.)

F = Frequently	O = Occassionally	N = Not Usually

50.	I invite cohorts to be involved in projects rather than assigning or ordering them to do so.	F	O	N
51.	I work out an agreement with coworkers about what we are trying to accomplish at work.	F	O	N
52.	I provide ways for my cohorts to indicate to me what they are achieving so we can celebrate their successes.	F	O	N
53.	I use various forms of information technology (fax, email, Post-It notes, videos) to share ideas and exchange information.	F	O	N
54.	I have email and use it to keep in touch with people inside and outside of the company.	F	O	N
55.	I have restructured my part of the company to make product delivery more direct.	F	O	N
56.	I review and accept cohorts' ideas for making their jobs safer, simpler, and more cost effective.	F	O	N
57.	I create an atmosphere for creativity and innovation among cohorts and employees.	F	O	N
58.	I meet with employees to remind me what it was like to be a worker.	F	O	N
59.	I encourage employees to lighten up and have fun at work.	F	O	N
60.	I help employees put innovative ideas into practice.	F	O	N
61.	I nurture an atmosphere of laid-back creativity.	F	O	N
62.	I listen to employees' ideas even when they seem to contradict our policies.	F	O	N
63.	I ask employees to come up with at least five ideas for making changes.	F	O	N
64.	I invite faculty from a local college to help us think up new ideas.	F	O	N
65.	I don't allow employees to criticize ideas until we have eight or more alternatives on the table.	F	O	N
66.	I implement the most innovative ideas possible.	F	O	N
67.	I encourage employees to take a "crazy break" to think up new ideas.	F	O	N
68.	I hold brainstorming sessions with employees.	F	O	N
69.	I treat the people with whom I work as cohorts rather than as subordinates.	F	O	N
70.	I find the equipment and make the money available for employees to do their work.	F	O	N

Scoring Instructions

Give each circled F a score of 3 points; each O, 2 points; and each N, 1 point. Now total the scores.

A score in the 70 to 116 range suggests that you are not doing as well as you could be as a powerful leader. You may be keeping your employees from contributing fully to the success of the company. Regardless of the reasons for a low score, give yourself credit for what *you are doing* well. Make necessary changes in the way you lead in order to encompass even more of the essential changes.

If your score falls into the 117 to 163 range, you are on the right track, but perhaps you aren't doing the right things often enough.

Scores in the 164 to 210 range indicate that you are making a strong effort to fire up your employees and release their full power to achieve organizational goals.

Regardless of your total score, review the entire quiz and pick out a "usually not" or an "occasionally" response that you would like to turn into a "frequently" response. Plan to change something for the better and celebrate your own successes.

Our contention throughout this book is that leaders have fallen into some terribly artificial ways of trying to increase productivity and profits. The natural way of working with people has been sorely neglected. Consequently, when you try to strengthen your leadership approach by making these seven essential changes, you will need to pay a great deal of attention to each of the them until you break the bad habits you may have fallen into.

The adoption of these seven essential changes opens a new, exciting way to lead people. Powerful leadership not only frees up your people to take the lead and contribute more, but it also frees you up to do your own work more efficiently. You can plan better for the future—and of course worry less about problems and go on a vacation!

How to Change

Unfortunately, no one is going to improve our lives for us. We have to do that for ourselves. A recent report researched the question, "Why don't more things happen in our lives?" Why don't we accomplish more? The answer was startling. Most things fail to happen because there is no plan to make them happen. We thought it might be a lack of motivation or commitment. But no, whether a plan exists or not makes the difference.

Making a plan is extraordinarily simple and consists of only a few key items. Constructing a plan means figuring out what you want to achieve, how you are going to achieve it, when you are going to do it, and keeping the rewards and benefits in mind that will accrue to you when you achieve your goal. Pretty simple isn't it?

Let's spend a few minutes right now talking about how you can start the process of making the seven essential changes in your leadership approach. First, we will describe a rather comprehensive way to approach behavioral change. Then, we will describe five shortcut ways to get going immediately, and finally we will offer our help as you and your organization implement these powerful leadership concepts.

Five steps are usually part of a change process that involves personal and interpersonal behaviors such as those that are part of leadership. Follow us in outlining a program for making changes in your personal behavior.

Step 1. Select a goal. This can be done, as we have suggested, by examining the quiz about where you stand as a powerful leader and selecting one or more actions that you would like to do more often. Select those actions that are important to you or those that result in some form of pain, such as embarrassment or anxiety, when you fail to do them. When you make a change in those behaviors, positive improvement will be noticeable and naturally reinforcing. Be cautious in trying to change well-entrenched actions at the beginning. It may be better to take a goal that seems important but that involves behaviors that you can change somewhat easily. Then, you will experience immediate success and feel that you can continue to have success in achieving the next goal.

> Define the change in terms of some observable acts or behaviors. An observable act is some type of overt behavior that can be seen and recognized by others. Nodding, smiling, speaking up, stepping back, and holding hands are overt behaviors. Feeling better, being more confident, and doing what's right must be translated into some type of overt behavior before we understand what is actually happening. For example, being more confident is expressed in some overt behavior. What do you do when you are confident? How about looking right into the eyes of a person who disagrees with you? At least you can tell when you are being more confident with that kind of goal. By identifying the overt behaviors clearly, you can carefully select ways to make changes.

Seek to change behaviors that can be changed readily. Sometimes we set our goals too high. The best thing to do is achieve changes that are just a little bit higher than the way you behave now. When you can regularly perform a new behavior, then raise your standards and set a higher goal. Behaviorally, we change in small increments.

The end result of a change program is to develop the presence of positive behaviors, so state what you want to achieve in a positive way. You might eliminate a large number of negative behaviors and still not produce much improvement in the area with which you are concerned. It is also easier and more motivating to recognize and experience the presence of positive behaviors than to notice the absence of negative ones.

Step 2. Record the quantity and the context of current behaviors. If you are attempting to substitute optimistic statements with critical ones, your first effort should be to get a handle on how many times you make statements that are critical of others. You also need to identify when critical statements are used. This step allows you to recognize the extent to which offending behaviors occur and the circumstances in which they take place. You might discover that you make critical statements more when someone does something that you think you could do better or when someone disagrees with you in a group. Keeping a record of the behavior to be changed sensitizes you to the progress you are making. You can make records of behavior in three different ways.

1. **Use frequency counting.** Simply, this involves tabulating the number of times a particular behavior occurs. To be counted, a behavior must be defined in terms of discrete cases. The behavior must occur over a short period of time and have an identifiable beginning and ending.

2. **Record duration of behavior.** Staring, crying, dozing, and other types of behavior do not occur in discrete segments. Such behaviors are best recorded by amount of time devoted to the activity. The simplest approach is to indicate when the behavior starts (with a stopwatch or by recording the time) and when it stops.

3. **Note results of behavior.** Rather than recording the behavior directly, you can monitor actions by keeping track of what happens as a result of the behavior. Weighing yourself, for example, can provide information about eating habits. By recording the

amount of waste in a manufacturing plant, you can tell a great deal about behaviors in the plant. Nevertheless, to make changes, you need to identify the specific behaviors that lead to gaining weight or to the creation of waste.

The very act of recording may lead to changes in behavior. When people are able to see an objective report of behaviors, they may be motivated to make a change. Identifying behaviors and maintaining a record of how frequently the specific behaviors occur may be all that you need to adopt alternative behaviors. Some, on the other hand, may need to proceed to the next step.

Step 3. Change the situation in which behavior occurs. Some behaviors are triggered by the situation in which they occur. One way to get people to adopt new actions is to change the situation that encourages the old actions. This can be done in two different ways.

1. **Avoid the situation.** Although staying away from people because they provoke an angry response in you may not eliminate your undesirable behavior entirely, it does limit the situations in which the anger occurs. Ultimately, you will need to deal with the behavior directly, but at the beginning, avoidance may help you to gain control of and start to modify such responses.

2. **Alter the situation.** If you tend to get sleepy sitting in a lounge chair, modify your behavior by sitting in a chair that seems less conducive to sleeping. If you tend to eat snacks at your desk, you might put the snacks in a sealed container and place the container in a file drawer so that you have to think about what you are doing before engaging in the undesirable behavior. You might even put a mirror on your desk so that you have to watch yourself eating. By altering the situation, you are providing yourself with supportive settings in which to control your behavior.

Step 4. Arrange reinforcing or punishing consequences. If you unnecessarily argue with people, but in the end you win arguments or receive a lot of praise and encouraging comments, you will most likely continue arguing. You may find that you receive reinforcements for arguing. You will therefore need to identify some punishing consequences for arguing. The difficulty in arranging appropriate consequences for our behaviors is that most of us have not thought about how things affect us. We are not sure how a particular act affects our behavior. Thus, you nearly always need a broad list of consequences that might be used as reinforcers or punishers. Two things might be done.

1. **Require yourself to exhibit the new, preferred behavior before participating in any reinforcing activity.** You must earn certain privileges by behaving in specific ways. If you speak to others in a critical manner, for example, speaking in a positive way should be made a condition for receiving any compliments or positive reactions. When you speak positively, the act should be reinforced as soon as possible. The principle of immediate reinforcement is so important to an effective change program that a plan for self-management might be used. Since unwanted behaviors are often reinforced naturally, individuals are authorized to administer reinforcements themselves. Because it is not entirely feasible to give direct reinforcement immediately in an organizational setting, a system of credits may be used. When you have earned five or ten credits for adopting new behaviors, you get credit toward an appropriate reinforcement, such as a standing ovation, going to a movie, or just having some quiet time.

2. **Also use punishments.** Although the idea may not seem very appealing, flipping yourself with a rubber band around your wrist or administering pain in some other way when you fail to carry out a new behavior is clearly a procedure consistent with change theory. Pain can also be administered through social disapproval by having others remind you to inflict the pain or administer the punishment when they catch you behaving in an undesirable way.

Step 5. Focus on and verbalize the consequences. One of the main problems in behavioral change is making impulsive responses. We often react before we have a chance to think about the consequences. We need to heighten our awareness so that we think about the consequences of undesirable actions before we act. One way to do this is to talk about such consequences before acting. The verbalizations must be said aloud, at least at the beginning. The sound as well as the statements heighten awareness more than does just the thought or silent verbalization of behavior. Thus, if you are attempting to extinguish critical comments, you would say out loud, just before engaging in a conversation with someone whom you might have a tendency to criticize, "If I criticize this person, I will be forced to sit in the corner of my office for ten minutes," or "If I criticize anyone, I will lose two days of vacation time."

Preparation for behavior change is often accomplished through "modeling." Research suggests that nearly all learning that results from direct experience can be acquired vicariously by observing other people's behavior and recognizing the results for the person being observed. People can develop new response patterns or intricate ways of behaving merely by observing the performances of appropriate models.

Modeling occurs by seeing a good example of what to do, having a framework for understanding the important elements of the new behavior, practicing or rehearsing the new behavior, and receiving positive feedback when you succeed in performing the new behavior. Leading involves a series of concrete behaviors that can be modeled, observed, practiced, reinforced, and integrated into the total behavior repertoire of a person.

Behavior change using models is achieved most efficiently through the preparation of a series of videotapes that individuals can view, identify with the situation, rehearse the modeled behavior under the supervision of a coach, and practice to transfer the specific behaviors back to the workplace.

James A. Winans, pioneer in the field of behavior change, observed years ago that "what holds attention governs action." Writing down and reviewing goals, for example, directs both our conscious and unconscious attention toward them. The persistent focus of attention on what you want to or need to change, in and of itself, leads the mind and body to pursue that goal. If you give full, fair, and undivided attention to a goal, you are much more likely to achieve it than if your attention is divided and diffused.

We also know that goal accomplishment is enhanced through group support. The old adage "It is easier to do anything if someone else is doing it with you" implies that change occurs more effectively when group support is given. People who feel accepted subsequently devote more energy to accomplishing a goal. Enlisting the assistance and support of others is a valid and useful approach to adopting new behaviors.

Success breeds success. With the realization that you are achieving a goal, your efforts intensify and more energy is devoted to accomplishing the goal. When you discover that you can reduce the number of critical comments made about something you do, your enthusiasm for the change effort increases. Failure to immediately make a change in behavior, however, does not necessarily deter a person from seeking change, especially if the person feels that success is possible. In fact, people tend to work harder at making changes if they are dissatisfied with their performance but still think that attaining the goal is important and possible.

Though the foregoing explanation has been comprehensive, you will do well now if you draw up a contract that includes the main elements of making changes in your leadership behavior. This is done by following these steps:

1. Write down one single change you would like to make in your leadership approach.

2. Decide and write down specifically what you are going to do.

3. Decide when, where, and with whom you will make this change.

4. Think of the possible benefits that will accrue if you make this change and write these down. If you falter a little in making the change, you will want to strengthen your commitment by revisiting these rewards of success.

5. If you want to put a little more pressure on yourself to accomplish the change, share what you are going to do with a close friend, spouse, or someone to whom you will feel an accountability.

A Short Planning Exercise

This is an interesting approach to use if you would like an additional opportunity to discover what you really want to do about your style of managing and what actions you are willing to take. It's not unusual for people like yourself who have just read a book on leadership to become a little paralyzed by the number of changes that could or should be made to enhance their leadership abilities. Not being able to follow through on good intentions often leaves people frustrated and a little discouraged. Here is a way to make some good planning decisions.

First, take a piece of paper and divide it into thirds by folding it like a letter about to be put into an envelope.

Second, open the paper, which now should contain three sections, and label them *shoulds, wants,* and *wills.*

Third, think about the ideas included under each section of the seven changes that need to be made now. Start writing down all the "shoulds" that come to mind. You may want to skim back through the pages of this book to refresh your memory.

Fourth, too often we get lost in a great list of things that we should do and lose our motivation and desire to make essential changes. When our personal agenda for change gets too long, we begin to lose hope of ever doing things well. So to counteract this proclivity, write in the second column the things that you truly want to change in relationship to becoming a stronger leader. Some people are not sure that they really want to do anything about improving their leading. That's fine. The important thing here is to be quite clear about what you really want to do about making changes.

Fifth, look over your list of "shoulds" and "wants" and in the last column write no more than three things that you are willing to undertake during the next three weeks.

If you had few listed in your want list, just figure out what it will take to move an item from the "should" list to the "will" list.

Then, as we have previously suggested, make a contract with yourself and share it with someone else so that you will have a person keeping track of your progress. This announcement of intentions is a good way to keep pressure on you.

What Do You Really Need to Change?

This approach to change will help you identify specific changes which may need to be on your top priority list and which may require personal attention and extra effort to change.

1. Take a piece of paper and write this sentence: "What I really need in my work life right now is more..."

2. Go back through the ideas presented in the "Where are You as a Powerful Leader" quiz and see if anything in any of the questions especially appeals to you. Jot down any ideas that you have. Remember, these are the most immediate things that seem to get in the way of helping others take the lead and allowing yourself to be more relaxed at work.

3. Ask your spouse or a close friend to look over your ideas and see if they agree or if they can add anything to what you have written.

4. At this point, make a plan to change these items as quickly as possible using the formats we have suggested. Most people that we consult find this to be a quick way to decide what to do first.

Using Mental Practice and Idealization

Using mental practice and idealization is the single most neglected tool to transform yourself from where you are now as a leader to where you would like to be. And this change process is quite simple to use:

- Write a statement about how you really act as a leader. You may want to consider how many people around you, who aren't "yes" men or women, see you as a leader. You may want to ask yourself, "How do my employees see me as a leader?" Their perceptions of how you really come across as a leader may be considerably less biased and more accurate than your own.

- Now visualize in your mind what you believe ideal leaders are like. What would they do? How would they speak? What would characterize ideal leaders? How would they come across to their cohorts?

- Write down a brief description of ideal leaders that you visualized.

- Now take one characteristic of the ideal leader, close your eyes, relax, and see yourself actually reaching that ideal. How does it feel? Do you feel more relaxed? What steps did you take to reach this ideal? Did you gain something good by taking this action and realizing this ideal?

- After visualizing and seeing yourself changing into the ideal leader, decide two or three things that you are going to do this week to realize your dream. And, this is most important, visualize yourself doing them successfully in your mind before you attempt to do them literally.

You will be amazed at how effective this whole process of visualization and mental practice is as you make changes in the way you attempt to lead people.

Encouraging Change in Others

One role of a leader is to encourage people to be open to change and to help them in every way possible to make changes. Notice the number of change process activities that take place as we relate the story of Lynne.

Also be aware of how her leader was able to help facilitate an important change in her work life behavior.

Lynne worked as an assistant to a manager of a specialty computer software manufacturer. Her main task was to keep the products flowing to the end of the assembly line. If the schedule slipped and eroded her lunch hour, her temper exploded. Having lunch on time was critical for her. Getting upset was easy for her, but it made life harder for her and those around her. She realized she needed to modify her episodes of irrational behavior.

At home one evening, Lynne reflected on some recent incidents in which she had become upset at work and said some things that she now regretted. The pain was beginning to surface. She decided that she had to do something and met with her leader to talk about it. As a leader, the manager drew her out and Lynne soon decided that her first task was to work without getting upset. She started to formulate a brief plan to stay on the peaceful path and retain a calm exterior in the face of adversity.

Much to her surprise, Lynne recognized that part of her problem was assuming that anyone working in a pressure situation was obligated to work with a short fuse. The leader was able to identify other people (potential models) who were working in stressful circumstances without any disruptive behaviors. She watched her models unobtrusively and responded with a calm resolve the next time the line lagged. With a calm and reassuring tone of voice, her leader instantly congratulated her and visited with her.

Lynne was on the way to making an important change in her behavior. The opportunity to get upset was still there, but the commitment to change, coupled with a positive model and regular reinforcement, stalled her traditional outbursts and led to dealing with unsettling situations in a calm and moderate manner. As she mastered her feelings and redirected her efforts, her enthusiasm for her new behavior increased. This intrinsic reward, along with the extrinsic rewards from her leader and coworkers, engendered considerable enthusiasm in Lynne to make her change long-lasting.

Fast Forward to the Basics

To encourage you to make some significant changes immediately in your approach to becoming a powerful leader, and to add a little more urgency to the importance of the essential changes explained in this book, we would like to conclude with an exhortation from William Cooper Proctor of Proctor and Gamble. This is going to be a little hard to believe, but over 100 years ago William Cooper Proctor confronted a world of unprecedented labor upheavals and strikes. Consequently, Proctor spent most of his tenure as the head of the first soap-producing giant in America trying to treat workers fairly. His initiatives included Saturday afternoons off with pay, comprehensive insurance benefits, stock options, and profit sharing. Now brace yourself for the lesson of a lifetime and remember that it was given a lifetime ago.

Proctor explained that businesspeople know that wages are higher and working conditions better in a large manufacturing plant than in a small one. Yet the people in the smaller plant—working longer hours, paid less, and not so well looked after—are usually more content. The reason, he said, lies largely in the fact that workers feel a more intimate personal interest in the smaller organization, and therefore a greater loyalty to it.

Notice now what Proctor says and compare it to what you have just been studying in this book and the changes that you are planning to make in your leadership style. He explained that the problem of "big business" today is to shape its policies so that each worker, whether in office or factory, will feel he or she is a vital part of the company with a personal responsibility for its success and a chance to share in that success. To bring this about, employers must take cohorts into their confidence. They should know why they are doing things, the relation of their work to other departments, and so far as practical, to the business as a whole. Cohorts should know those elements of cost of production associated with their work, or they cannot put intelligent effort into what they are doing. What is even more important is that the cohorts should have some means through which they can give expression to their ideas as to the general policy of the business, in accordance with their positions and abilities, and especially as it relates to their own work.

Proctor changed his approach to leading and made great things happen in the company. Now it's up to you to make some vital changes in your style of leading; stop doing things that don't work well and start doing things that do.

Return and Report

Once you have accurately defined your areas for improvement and made a plan for essential changes, you can concentrate on moving ahead and improving your leadership effectiveness. As a manager you should continually ask yourself, Am I playing to my strengths and shoring up my weakness? Are there some *occasional* leadership tendencies that I have that should be significantly strengthened? Should I devote more effort to helping others take the lead? As I consider strengthening myself as a leader, what are the first changes that I should make that would have the greatest positive impact upon my employees and allow me the most opportunity to do my own work?

Before you go to the next section, we want you to know that we are vitally interested in finding out how you are applying these essential changes in your daily activities. We would very much appreciate hearing from you. If there are concepts you find difficult to apply, let us know. If there are parts you found particularly helpful, let us know this as well.

If you would like further help in implementing these ideas in your organization, please give us a call and make arrangements to involve us in your plans. We are available and would enjoy helping you in any way possible.

Stephan can be reached at (801)378-3478, by email at *sstephan27@msn.com* by fax at (801)378-8098, or by writing to
Dr. Eric G. Stephan
464 West 300 South
Orem, Utah 84058

Pace can be reached at (435)688-8114 by phone or fax, by email at *wpace@redrock.net,* or by writing to
Dr. R. Wayne Pace
770 West Hampton Road
St. George, Utah 84770

Now, go to Appendix A and hear how three powerful leaders are adapting these seven essential changes to their special circumstances.

POWERFUL LEADERS ON POWERFUL LEADERSHIP

We would like you to hear what three contemporary powerful leaders have to say about principles of effective leadership. Charles A. Heimbold, Jr., chairman and CEO of Bristol-Myers Squibb Company, explains some rules of effective leadership and why leadership development is so critical. Julia Hughes Jones, auditor of the State of Arkansas, outlines the essentials of world-class leadership for women. Edward L. Moyers, CEO of Illinois Central Railroad, gives an A to H list detailing the necessary skills and activities of a successful leader.

What makes a powerful leader? Are powerful leaders born? If they are not born, then how do they survive the daily routine of organizational life to become a powerful influence in their organizations? What combination of skills do these leaders use to unite their followers and focus their performance on the achievement of organizational goals?

As you assimilate what each leader says, notice the various circumstances from which they each articulate their experience. Also, be sensitive to the excellent adaptations of the seven changes that these leaders made in their leadership opportunities.

Attributes and Formation of Good Leaders
Success Is Doing Things Right

Address by CHARLES A. HEIMBOLD, JR., Chairman and CEO, Bristol-Myers Squibb Company
Delivered to Rutgers School of Management, New Brunswick, New Jersey, November 9, 1998

Good afternoon, ladies and gentlemen, and thank you for that gracious welcome. It's delightful to be here with all of you. I was born here in New Jersey and for generations my family had lived here. So in a way, I'm returning to my roots.

I'd like to start off by reading from a *New York Times* article on successful business enterprises, written by two management experts: Jim Citrin and Tom Neff. I met them a few months ago as they were researching a book on leadership.

They said in this article, "Contrary to conventional wisdom, business success is not just defined by revenue and profit growth, superior returns on equity or increases in shareholder value. Rather, business success is doing the right things. Performance inevitably follows."

In other words, good managers do things right. But to be a truly good leader, you have to do the right things.

Doing the right things is not an easily quantifiable line item in a budget. But I agree with Mr. Citrin and Mr. Neff that it may be the single most important element of leadership.

"Leadership," of course, is a word that we CEOs use a great deal: We talk about leadership in markets, leadership in creating shareholder value, leadership in a competitive environment. But that's only one kind of leadership—to be in the top tier of your industry, to be a leader in the businesses in which you compete and in the service and value you provide to customers and shareholders.

There is another kind of leadership as well. And that's what I'd like to talk about for the next few minutes. Since it's a much more personal form of leadership, and more difficult to define, I think it might help to illustrate my points with a little bit of my own history at Bristol-Myers Squibb.

I've never been totally comfortable talking about myself. But that was my assignment. So, with apologies for the hubris, I'll get started. In so doing, I hope I can help you reflect on the experiences you might wish to seek out as you become leaders in your own right and, later, as you develop the leaders who will follow you.

I will touch on three things: first, the formative experiences that have helped me become a leader, a chief executive; second, drawing from those experiences, some general rules of what makes effective leaders; and third, why leadership development is so critical.

From the beginning of my career I have been extremely fortunate to have had great role models—admirable people who provided me with an example to follow. Those exemplars helped me to assume the role I have today. It is a role I cherish, the leadership of 55,000 organized and committed people around the world.

Someone once said that to acquire knowledge, one must study, but to acquire wisdom, one must observe. Making observations was a key element of my first position at Bristol-Myers some 35 years ago. And it still holds a prominent place as I view my job today.

When I joined what was then Bristol-Myers Company, as a young lawyer I was soon assigned to be secretary of the executive committee of the company. That afforded me the opportunity to listen to the deliberations of very senior, very experienced business people, including the men who would be my predecessors as chairman—Fred Schwartz, Gavin MacBain, and Dick Gelb. I had a chance to make my own judgments about their ideas and to see what worked, what didn't, and why.

The business decisions they arrived at were important. And the myriad ways they arrived at them were often fascinating. But what impressed me most of all was the set of values they used every day in making those decisions.

Observing these individuals gave me a fuller understanding of the critical importance of values in those people we term our leaders. Watching these men, I began to appreciate the difference between people with really terrific values and those who might not quite measure up. Understanding that difference gives you something to strive for as well as something with which to measure yourself and others.

Good leaders must be conscious always of the examples they set for others. Leaders must be role models. That's a big part of the job.

Dick Gelb, my immediate predecessor, has often said that one of the prime reasons Bristol-Myers Squibb has been successful is that the people who work there have high expectations of themselves and of one anther. I would add that our company culture of high expectation stems in part from the high expectations our leaders have had for, first, themselves, and then, for others.

The examples set by the leaders of a company are the examples that endure. They are the blueprints for the future.

What else is required of a leader? A leader must have a vision for the company he or she intends to lead. He or she must know the destination before taking others on the journey. My vision is of a company with a mission to extend and enhance human life—one which strives to be competitively superior in the quality and value of its products—with the result that its earnings grow faster than others and its shareholder value increases. To do this, I and my management group must develop leadership and talent at all levels of the company.

When I first took over as CEO in 1994, Bristol-Myers Squibb faced a number of thorny business issues, some of which were downright disheartening. My job was to turn people's attention and energy away from the risks and the downside, and redirect them so that we could address our challenges in a positive way as a cohesive, effective team. We worked through our problems by my setting goals that I knew were challenging but still attainable.

At my first management meeting in January 1994, just two weeks after I took over as CEO, I set a goal of doubling our sales, earnings, and earnings per share by the end of the year 2000. That implied a growth rate well beyond what we had managed in our recent history. That goal was greeted with general skepticism—both inside and outside the company.

My job was to overcome the disbelief, find energizing events for our company, and show people how we could achieve our goal.

We acquired a few smaller and medium-sized companies. We reinvested in businesses that had been lagging. We licensed in products. We spent heavily on R&D. We brought in new people and promoted many from within.

Now we are well on our way to meeting that once-distant goal—indeed, we are likely to attain it sooner than I had hoped. As a result, our company is in a position today that many wouldn't have dreamed possible just a few short years ago. Our shareholders have done well— our stock is up about four and a half times its level of five years ago. And all our employees have benefited through a stock option program I instituted about four years ago.

It just makes you feel terrific when everyone can benefit from the company's success. Sure, the senior executives usually do pretty well. But I would have felt pretty rotten if my people—the thousands of colleagues I have in the company—hadn't been able to share in the gains enjoyed by the executives and the shareholders.

As a leader you have to do four things—choose the right people, establish the right values, get your people focused on the right business goals and then communicate, communicate, communicate. The best communication is by your own example, in the field, with customers, shareholders, employees, with everyone and everywhere.

It's important that our employees know that I go out with the sales force and call on doctors. It's important that they know we reach out to help our colleagues in difficult moments—when the ice storms hit Quebec last year or when Hurricane Georges hit Puerto Rico this year. Right now, with Russia in dire straits and Central America battered by Mitch, my job is to look out for our people as well as our customers.

It's the responsible thing to do. But it's also a way of showing—by example—that all 55,000 of us in this company are connected; that we must be attentive to each other, be civil, helpful, caring. Setting that kind of example, creating that kind of expectation for our culture, makes a difference for our business.

So leaders must set a tone. Not only putting their minds into it but their bodies on occasion as well. You can't just set goals and say, "Okay everybody, now go for it."

I made a mistake like that early in my tenure, shortly after I became CEO. At the time, I determined that we needed to increase our productivity. So I called senior management together and said we needed a productivity effort to generate the resources to fund our growth. Everyone nodded in agreement—sure Charlie, right—good idea. Two months later, nothing was happening.

No one was trying to sabotage the productivity program. There simply was no productivity program. I hadn't given people the means to tackle the problem and they didn't know how to crash the obstacles on their own.

The lesson I learned then is that you cannot manage by exhortation. When you try to implement change in a large company, you have to put the machinery, the leaders, the process in place to drive it through the organization. And then you must carefully follow the progress.

Now what are some other attributes of leaders? Leaders ask lots of questions. Then they follow up on those questions to see the results. You don't want to drive people crazy with endless interrogating and probing. But as Peter Drucker has always maintained, people pay close attention to the things that get inspected and measured—in other words, the things they are regularly asked about.

Finally, while you want competitive people, you have to be careful how you manage them. I'm sure you've all heard the line that one of a CEO's biggest jobs is to keep the lions from eating one another. So you try to focus the natural competitive energies of people on the outside competition rather than on the inside.

You do that, first of all, by making sure you're not overstaffed. Turf battles are an opportunity to reduce redundant people. And you make sure people are clear about what they need to do, and that they are empowered to do it.

Now, I realize that "empowerment" is a management term that's been much in vogue. But, of course, it's not a magical concept. In fact, at Bristol-Myers Squibb, we believe empowerment only works when it's coupled with accountability. Yes, give people the responsibility to get things done. Yes, go on and get out of their way. But also let them understand that results are expected and they are accountable for those results.

So, bottom line: What is my advice to you as you seek to become leaders yourselves?

Have a vision of what you want to attain. It can be a general idea early on—like getting involved in finance and knowing that only later will you decide to become a CPA or a financial analyst or work in treasury. But at the same time, don't let your goals limit your options and opportunities. Picasso said that if you always know exactly what you want, you'll never find anything more than that.

Also, seek out an exemplar who does the right things. Find someone who will set the right examples for you, who will instruct you, someone you can observe and—if you are lucky—someone who will take an active interest in your future.

Finally, while you're out there trying to make your mark, stay in tune with your values—both your personal values and the things you value in others. Keep in mind the ancient prayer of the Persian soldier: "Give me the strength to tell the truth and pull the bow."

My objectives as CEO have been straightforward: to grow our company, add value for our shareholders, extend opportunity to our employees.

Today I am blessed with a workforce that is dedicated to making a difference in people's lives. They are proud they work for a company whose products help treat cancer, AIDS, heart disease, and other afflictions.

At Bristol-Myers Squibb we want people who are smart and focused. But we also want people with great values—people who care, people who are passionate about the future and the possibilities of our business, who take nothing for granted and understand that our goals are achievable if we work together. We want people who are highly creative, highly motivated, highly productive. Simply put, we want leaders.

That's why leadership development is at the top of our list of key business objectives. It is, in fact, objective number one.

In order to achieve competitive superiority in our industry, we determined we would have to develop greater depth and breadth of leadership talent at every level in our organization.

You can't do this job by yourself—not in an organization of 55,000 people. To be a successful leader in our organization, you must be continually creating other leaders. You exert enormous influence on an organization through the people you develop and put into leadership positions. That influence is probably greater than anything you can accomplish as an individual.

We have developed a rigorous program in which established leaders teach other leaders in the company, sharing their own stories, their own experiences, explaining their mistakes and triumphs. That program is now cascading down through all levels of the organization.

Only an organizational engine of the sort we're trying to build— one that creates new leaders and makes the leaders we have better and better—can tap the full potential of all our people.

Albert Schweitzer once said that example is not the main thing in influencing others—it is the only thing.

It is our job as leaders today—and your job as leaders tomorrow—to make certain that the examples we set are the right ones; that the values we hold are ones worth cherishing; that our vision of the future is one that inspires others to achieve and to build a growing, dynamic, vital business for many years to come.

I have been very, very fortunate in my own career. I wish all of you great success on your journeys of discovery and achievement. Thank you for your attention.

Tips For Effective Leadership
World Class Leadership for Women

Address by Julia Hughes Jones, Auditor of State of Arkansas, Retired and Sustaining Member of the Junior League of Little Rock, Arkansas
Delivered to the Junior League of Jacksonville, Florida, January 7, 1998

Most educated people know that worldwide, humanity faces three major threats: nuclear annihilation through war or accident, plague (such as AIDS), ecological catastrophe.

What has not been commonly recognized, however, is a fourth potential threat to civilization as we know it, and that is a leadership crisis, both nationally and worldwide. The failure of leaders to effectively address these nuclear, plague, and ecological issues is a threat far more dangerous because these problems cannot be solved without leadership.

That is my subject tonight: leadership for women. I hope to show you the connection between political, social, and economic concerns and the current leadership crisis in America. I plan to show you, as women and members of the Junior League of Jacksonville, what you can do to learn how to be more effective leaders in today's world.

As you know, Eleanor Roosevelt was one of the early members of the Junior League of New York City. She eventually took her training in voluntarism and community service all the way to the United Nations, where she was the chief architect of the Declaration of Human Rights. Her example must serve as a reminder that women have the capability of making tremendous changes in the way our world is operated, because women add an additional asset to the decision-making processes everywhere: We include the concerns of our hearts as well as those of our minds.

Why should women be more involved in these issues? Because there have been three significant political developments during the latter part of the 20th century:

> The growth of democracy.
>
> The growth of the corporation.
>
> The growth of propaganda as a means of protecting corporate power against democracy.

When you get right down to it, everything in a society revolves around money—the economy—the way we acquire our food, clothing, and shelter to survive. American corporations represent a symbol of American economic power to most people, and to corporate employees, the corporation has always been a major part of their existence and identity. With the downsizing occurring today, many dedicated corporate employees have suddenly been cut off from their sense of personal connectedness as well as losing their economic livelihood.

Many of us have forgotten that corporate charters were originally designed to serve the public interest. This concept has been replaced by the modern-day belief that corporations serve the stockholders and the bottom line only. In the past, corporate owners, managers, and directors were responsible for corporate debts as well as for any harm caused by the corporation. That is no longer the case.

Under the corporate leadership of the 1980s, the decade of greed, investment abroad today means that there is cheaper labor in third-world countries, and American companies avoid producing goods in the USA (and thereby take jobs away from Americans). Instead, corporations import these goods for us to buy after they have been made by underpaid workers in conditions similar to the early days of the 20th century. Recently publicized stories about sweatshops and child labor in third-world factories have included products linked with American celebrities.

Since few of the CEOs in the *Fortune* 500 are women, can it be assumed that male leadership has caused all this to occur? Is there a difference in male and female leadership? Are men truly smarter than woman as some say? Are women too emotional to handle leadership roles. Let's take a quick and cursory look at information from many recent books and reports about the differences in brain power between men and women.

For instance, after you adjust for women's lesser height and weight, men's brains are 10 to 11 percent larger than women's. And, there's evidence that size matters when it comes to brains, and that bulk normally equals intelligence.

But men and women perform equally on IQ tests, which suggests that larger brain mass does not always mean superior intelligence. One study found that women have a higher percentage of gray matter than men, with a conclusion that women may compensate for smaller brain size by an increased density of brain cells.

Another structural difference between male and female brains is in the bundle of nerves connecting the hemispheres of the brain. This area is larger and more bulbous in women and seems to confirm other recent findings that women are better at expressing feelings and accessing their emotions.

These studies have also shown that women have an easier time switching from verbal left brain to the emotional right brain than men do.

Additionally, other studies show that women's social savvy gives them a powerful evolutionary advantage despite their greater vulnerability to depression and anxiety. Many studies have shown that your chances of surviving a critical disease are much better if you are emotionally connected, as women are.

Finally, one report has revealed that men suffer from depression at a rate equal to women's but that they show distress differently: as workaholism, alcoholism, avoidance of intimacy, and aggressive or abusive behavior. In other words, they manifest the same disorders women do, but in a different manner. Women tend to internalize pain and distress, while men tend to externalize it. The solution one author recommended was to teach men the relational and empathetic skills that women have, and to teach women to distract themselves from intense relationships and problems as men do.

One of the most difficult lessons for me to learn as a politician was the lesson in distraction from constant work. Men have always known how to reduce tension and stress by playing golf, attending sports events, or other relaxing activities, but women seem to go from one work project to another with no break in between, which is a part of the Super Woman Complex. I learned from necessity to take time-outs when they were needed, yet always felt a sense of guilt for not being constantly productive.

As for the definition and meaning of leadership, regardless of gender and brain size, it is generally understood that leadership means having power over others. Power can be used or misused depending on the integrity and character of those who have power.

General George Patton once said, "Leadership is the thing that wins battles. I have it, but I'll be damned if I can define it."

Patton may not have been able to define leadership verbally but he did recognize it when he saw it. He knew that being a leader can be very difficult, because one is placed in a position to be a target for the problems of others. He knew that being a leader can bring blame when things go wrong and that leaders are the perfect justification for the insecurities of others. He also knew that the use and abuse of power in a position of influence meant that one is able to change conditions for better or worse, or to suit the leader's intentions.

What is a leader? Leaders know you can never make everyone happy unless you lie, to [yourself] or others. The nature of human behavior in our society is that to lie is to protect in some cases, and in other cases a lie achieves personal ends.

A leader who leads through tyranny or dictatorship wants followers to believe that nothing else has validity except the ideas and goals of the leader.

Being in control is defined as leadership by many, but real leaders do not try to control opposition and challenges to their authority, because they recognize that debate between opposing forces brings better and more long-lasting solutions to problems.

Real leaders recognize something may be wrong in their performance if they are challenged, and will set out to clarify and correct it through communicating more effectively. Real leaders have the capacity for self-doubt and humility, knowing these attributes will help keep them on track in times of trouble. Real leaders take their chances in the marketplace of ideas without threats of punishment and without attempting to control the process. Real leaders acknowledge mistakes openly and regretfully, then set out to correct them and move on. Real leaders will always solicit questions from others and will question themselves as well. A German philosopher once wrote that mediocre minds usually dismiss anything which reaches beyond their own understanding. When people are willing to accept what they are told without question, the danger of mediocrity becomes very real.

What is effective leadership? Effective leadership starts with being responsible, and being responsible is no more than the ability to respond and the willingness to be responsible for your actions. The best way to be responsible is through self-examination, confronting doubts and fears, and looking closely at the forces that have made you who you are, both personally and professionally.

An effective leader knows it is vital to leadership health to

Know yourself

Know your patterns of behavior

Know your strengths and weaknesses

Know your environment

Each of us is capable of becoming an effective leader by recognizing that leadership is not only responsibility, but character. Character has to do with who we are as human beings, and it has to do with the forces that have shaped us into who we are. Character continually evolves as we grow and develop through self-knowledge as well as continual self-assessment. People win and lose based not only on their knowledge of conditions but also on their knowledge of themselves.

There is power in self-discovery. Knowing yourself and recognizing where you are strong and where you are weak is a part of becoming a fully integrated human being as well as a leader. We do this by observing ourselves closely, reflecting on our experiences, and by actively seeking to change life patterns that do not serve us in becoming the person we want to be

Are women leaders different from men leaders? Yes and no. Women are different because they have the capacity for self-doubt as well as differing environmental and cultural influences on their performances. No, they are not different, because they have the same stakes as men in the pursuit of effective communication as leaders.

I have found that women's styles of leadership differ from men's in only one category, which is what I like to call the "mother hen" syndrome, where women nurture everyone else but themselves and gain no respect nor admiration from their employees or followers in the process. They sell themselves short in every way, put all other's needs ahead of their own, and generally spend more time taking care of people and their problems than taking care of the job. All of us know this is what has been expected of women in the home, and it has transferred itself to the workplace for those who have not yet learned better. The mother hen syndrome is a major reason for the lack of support for women in positions of power.

Another style of leadership women have been known for is what I call the "school marm" syndrome, where autocratic control with blame and punishment are the central themes. The school marm is the root cause of much fear and disgust where men, and many women, are concerned, because they associate this type of behavior with at least one female teacher from their school years. What isn't commonly recognized is that males have also been labeled with this same autocratic behavior as leaders and can be likened to dictators and tyranny.

These are two negative and extreme examples of the type of leadership attributed to women by most critics, but there are some examples from history of women leaders who have led their countries in times of crisis as effectively as any male leader could have done. In recent years, former Prime Minister Margaret Thatcher proved her effectiveness and mettle by showing the world she could be as tough in leading Great Britain to war against Argentina as she was in leading the fight on social issues.

From history, a classic example of women's leadership abilities is Queen Elizabeth I, who donned full armor and joined her troops on the shores of England in 1588 to fight King Phillip's Spanish Armada, the greatest fleet of ships the world had ever seen.

During the first 30 years of her reign, Elizabeth had avoided large-scale war, but was forced into it by the Catholic Church's efforts to restore its hold on England after the Reformation. The restoration of Catholicism and the abolition of King Henry the VIII's Church of England was seen by King Phillip as a Holy Crusade. But the Queen had other ideas, one of which included the possibility that her troops may have doubted her ability in war.

She resolved this doubt by announcing to her troops, "I know I have but the body of a weak and feeble woman: but I have the heart and stomach of a King—and a King of England, too!"

The Spanish were thwarted by what was interpreted by all to be the Hand of God when the Armada was met on the shores of Great Britain by a huge storm and the Queen's modest but feisty militia. Between the buffeting storm and the seasoned English vessels, the Armada was blown all the way around the rocky coast, where many were wrecked. Only a fraction survived to return to Spain, and the mystified King Phillip determined that is was a sign from God.

Queen Elizabeth knew her strengths and weaknesses and knew those of King Phillip. She recognized that the rocky coast of England and her small fleet of mostly fishing boats were assets. The coast itself was the strength of the fishing vessels, because they had learned to survive the treachery of the rocks in order to survive economically. She also knew that Phillip was her rejected suitor as well, and that his Armada would be hindered by the coastline.

But the storm gave to her an advantage neither King nor Queen had anticipated. The Chinese word for "crisis" is composed of two picture characters: One meaning danger and the other meaning opportunity. Queen Elizabeth converted the danger to England into an opportunity to show the world that England was invincible and she, a woman, was its leader. In fact, this was the beginning of England's reputation as a world naval power.

In the centuries-old book *The Art of War* Sun Tzu writes, "Know the enemy and know yourself, in a hundred battles you will never be in peril. When you are ignorant of the enemy but know yourself, your chances of winning or losing are equal. When you are ignorant both of your enemy and yourself, you are certain in every battle to be in peril."

Queen Elizabeth knew her enemy and she knew herself and she knew her country. Remember this anecdote while you prepare yourself to become better leaders, both personally and professionally.

Constant self-reflection and the persistent use of self-examination will help you to know yourself. That is the key to effective communication and world-class leadership.

According to Warren Bennis and Joan Goldsmith in their hallmark work, *Learning to Lead,* there are four demands that people want from their leaders:

> Purpose, Direction, and Meaning
>
> Trust
>
> Optimism
>
> Action and Results

They write that leaders must be committed and determined to achieve goals and be able to communicate that purpose in a way that galvanizes, energizes, and enthralls people. All involved must not only believe in the goals sought but also consider themselves a part of the process of achievement.

A leader must generate and sustain trust, because trust is the glue that binds commitment, promotes action, and produces results. Openness and dissent are a part of trust. To command and to control does not generate trust, and most situations require leadership that is shared and inclusive.

Leaders must be powerful purveyors of hope. They do not get stuck on mistakes, problems, wrong–turns, or mishaps, but see their efforts as opportunities to learn and change and grow. They have a clear vision of the future, are committed to getting there, and to bringing along their team.

Leaders have the capacity to convert purpose and vision into their action. It is not enough to have vision unless you have the ability to inspire people to produce results. Most leaders are pragmatic dreamers and practical idealists who step out to take their chances daily because they know they will miss out on the chances they don't take.

Successful organizations are run by effective leaders and are characterized by these elements:

Alignment

Empowerment

A Learning Culture

To be an effective leader in a successful organization, one must ensure that all participants are aligned with a common vision, with shared objectives and goals to which people can be dedicated. Alignment means everyone's work is part of pursuing a larger purpose embodied in the products or services of the organization.

Empowerment means that everyone has been convinced that they make a difference to the success of the organization. Empowered individuals feel that what they do has meaning and significance; that they have discretion as well as obligations; that they live in a culture of respect where they are encouraged to act on their own. Empowered organizations generate and sustain trust as well as communicate constantly.

A learning culture is a reflective organization where ideas, questions, and information are unhampered and not interfered with by people who are worried or fearful or feeling threatened. Learning cultures will look for problems and identify them before they become a crisis. They know how to change complexity into simplicity. They encourage discovery of new ideas and new information needed to solve problems, and are not afraid to test ideas. A leading culture simply means having the opportunity to reflect on and evaluate past actions and decisions.

Finally, leaders are the sum of all their experiences, just like all other people, but the difference is that effective leaders know that experience is not what happens *to* you, but what you *do* with what happens to you.

In other words, leadership begins and ends with the *self*. Leaders always know who they are, what their strengths and weaknesses are, and how fully to deploy their strengths and compensate for their weaknesses. They also know what they want, why they want it, and how to communicate what they want to others in order to gain cooperation and support.

Leaders are made, not born, and they are usually made or created by themselves rather than by someone else. Leaders continue to grow and develop throughout life. Self-examination and self-reflection help leaders to be alert to their own behavioral patterns and attributes that do not serve them well, and they do something about them. Effective leaders value clear communication, ethical practices, a diverse workforce, and participatory empowerment.

It is never too late to begin this process of transforming your *self* into what you want to be as a leader. I recommend you read *Learning to Lead* to find your own leadership style and potential. One of the worksheets included in this book is a questionnaire on your own personal leadership values. Here are some of the questions asked:

> How can I be clearer about my expectations of others' performances?
>
> What guidelines for results do I need to establish and communicate?
>
> What are my goals for communicating more effectively?
>
> What are my goals for supporting ethical behavior among my colleagues, team members, and others?

Contemplation, self-examination, and the constant reevaluation of your goals and communication skills will help you become a world-class leader. Knowing who you are and what forces have shaped you is a first step.

In closing, I would like to leave you with the following tips for women in leadership positions. These are some of the things I have learned while serving as a statewide elected official and as a woman leader. I hope they will help you in your pursuit of excellence.

> Be an optimist rather than a pessimist. Studies show that people who look on the bright side tend to do better on achievement tests, have more job success, live longer, and have better health.
>
> Do your homework. Be prepared by getting the facts and knowing what you are talking about. Good leaders don't waste other people's time.
>
> Knowledge may be power, but enthusiasm pulls the switch. The level of enthusiasm of a group rises no higher than the enthusiasm of the leader.

Remain poised, in control, and self-confident in the face of adversity. A self-assured leader instills confidence in others.

Have the courage to stand up for your beliefs, but always be open to other people's views.

Successful people are not necessarily the best and brightest, or the fastest and strongest. They are the ones with the most commitment.

Know yourself, your strengths and your weaknesses. Constantly evaluate your performance and behavior patterns in order to be the person you want to be.

I hope this information has given you a bit of encouragement in your pursuit of effective leadership. Thank you for giving me this opportunity to share my ideas, thoughts, and experiences with you.

Principles of Leadership
Think and Communicate

Address by Edward L. Moyers, Railroad Boss and CEO of Illinois Central Railroad
   Delivered to Millsaps College Commencement, Jackson, Mississippi, May 13, 2000

Mr. Chairman, Mr. President, Faculty, Graduates, Parents and Friends of the graduates: thank you for that kind introduction, Dr. Harmon. I am pleased to be back to the campus of Millsaps College. As Dr. Harmon said, I have been associated with the College since 1987, first, as a regular Trustee and more recently, since having reached the "age of presumed incompetence," as a Life Trustee. So I have watched Millsaps grow and progress for some time. With my wife, Helen, now an active Trustee on the Board, I will continue to be involved.

In the process of involvement with the College over the years, I have watched each class of graduates come and go. As in past years, I look out today and see another "changing of the guard," the past and the future—you, the face of the future—individuals in the sunrise ready to take their places in a world filled with opportunities. Today is a major stepping-stone for each of you in what I love to refer to as the American Dream.

What is the American Dream? Everyone knows that America is the land of opportunity. Each year, thousands of us, some native born, some arriving from elsewhere in search of a better life, some from great wealth, some from humble means, embark on an expedition to accomplish something that will lead to fulfillment and economic security, develop our potential, and contribute our skills to some enterprise that improves the lives of others. Most of those who truly want to make this journey end up succeeding. This experience, which has become so common and so emblematic in this country, has its own name, the American Dream.

In fact it was this term that led to my presence here today. A few years ago, during my second retirement, which was from the Southern Pacific Railroad—I am now in my third retirement and it may not be my last—I was persuaded by my wife to take time to record my experiences so that my family would not be ignorant of what I did in my professional life, or of the people and experiences that shaped my life, and in so doing allowed me to achieve my personal version of the "American Dream." I did so, in memoirs entitled "Six Roads, One Path" privately printed with only enough copies for my extended family and a few selected friends who expressed interest.

Dr. Harmon was one of those friends who asked for a copy. After reading it he asked me to deliver this address and in the process share with you some thoughts of how you too might achieve your own American Dream."

As I thought about this, I was reluctant, but also intrigued. I have never been one to talk about myself. On the other hand, in a world where a few high-profile 28-year-olds are running their own billion-dollar computer empires, where giant corporations in order to be competitive are merging and downsizing their workforce at dizzying speeds, throwing countless numbers of top and middle managers as well as lower level workers out of a job, and technology is drawing the industrialized nations of the world ever closer, you may be wondering where you will fit in. By sharing some aspects of my story, perhaps I might say something that will not only give you hope, but challenge you to achieve your own dream. So I agreed to do just that.

Everybody has some kind of life story, but no two life stories are exactly alike. But nobody's life story is unique, either; certain themes or motifs recur so often in human life that they become the subject matter of myths and folk tales and epics that hardly vary from one era to another or one culture to another. These stories keep being retold because people recognize that they have something important and enduring to tell us about human nature. What I will attempt to do is distill certain of those themes out of my life, or at least the professional part of my life.

First, I never planned my career. I never set out to become the chief executive officer of a railroad, or even a vice president, any more than that legendary ugly duckling "planned" to become a swan. All I ever tried to do was earn promotion to the next grade above me.

If I was assistant trainmaster, I just wanted to be the trainmaster. If I was assistant division manager, I just wanted to be division manager. Unlike many of today's whiz kids, I never set out to be a millionaire. All I wanted was to push on to the next level, to grow my skills and grow my rewards accordingly, and provide my family with a little more than they already had. Second, I emphasize that no person ever succeeds to achievement of his or her dream solely by their own efforts. Even before the individual is aware of his existence, powerful influences already are helping to shape his future. Parents, grandparents, siblings, friends, teachers, colleagues and mentors prepare the way, be it for good or ill. But there is one imperative to achieve the American Dream by anyone, and that imperative is education. My parents were firm believers in education. Their daily theme to me and my brother and sister was that education opened not only social and economic doors but opportunities to be of service to our fellow man. Fortunately, I took their advice and developed my own plan to pay my way though a respectable boarding school in Mississippi and later attend college in Louisiana.

It is often said that we are now in an era of lifelong learning that merges work and education, that to make progress one must not only be competent in the basic skills but also know how to think and communicate, adjust to change, and be able to absorb new ideas and transmit them to others.

But in reality, this is not new. My success is a direct result of continuing to learn throughout my career so as to be able to take advantage of opportunities as they opened up.

I will take a few minutes and share with you some of the management techniques that I used to make each of the three U.S. railroads I headed a success—as well as the three in Brazil. I have studied the management philosophies of such management gurus as Tom Peters, Frederick Herzberg, E. M. Goldratt, Peter Drucker, George Odiorne, and my good friend Bill Johnson. However, in order to be an outstanding manager, you must develop your own ideas and techniques. Sure, you can expose yourself to a host of different philosophies by studying people such as those mentioned, but in order to be successful, you must develop a style which is best suited to you and which will produce for you the desired results. Regardless of the type of activity you are involved in, these thoughts will certainly apply.

> I. One of the most difficult lessons for all leaders to learn is to develop your ability to listen and learn. I am sure you have heard the statement many times, but because it is so true to life, I will repeat it one more time—you never learned anything while you were talking. You will find that

people are anxious to share their thoughts and ideas with you if they believe you are interested. You will be surprised how many good suggestions you can acquire from people at all levels of your organization if you will only listen.

II. Leadership is not a popularity contest. Respect is what a true leader strives for—not to be just liked by all the people you are involved with. How do you accomplish that objective?

A. Always do what you say you are going to do. Never do those things you have promised people you will not do.

B. Take time to visit with those people at every level in your organization. The increased production, improvement in morale, and verbal support that you will receive as the result of such activities is amazing.

C. Spend enough time with those who report directly to you to determine what motivates them—then use that information to increase the output in your area of responsibility.

D. Don't be bound by past practices in your field. Who said that the people and the practices put in effect in the past fit today's environment? Don't be afraid to try new ideas—do things different. So what if you fail or you are wrong. You learn from mistakes, so try another method. Above all else, don't be discouraged. Never rest on your past performance.

E. Have a clear understanding with everyone as to what their objectives are. One of my first inquiries when arriving at a new company was to ask people to discuss their company objectives with me. After talking with several department heads when I took over one company, it was obvious that they did not have clearly defined objectives. I informed each of these executives that in 10 days we were going to have a meeting of all senior management people. They should be prepared to define their respective commitments and objectives for the remaining 6 months of the year which I had previously approved. In the meantime I hired a movie producing company to attend our meeting and film each executive as they outlined their objective. Needless to say, at the meeting, there were a lot of nervous people. You can imagine how you would feel if without any advanced notice you stood in front of a movie producing crew. The videos were made and each participant was given a copy of their presentation. I kept a copy and one went on their personal record file. Needless to say, from that day forward we had a clear understanding of what was expected from each individual and their department. Incidentally, I made my own commitments for the record and gave a copy to everyone present. Again, you should look for results in ways that have not been tried before.

F. Form a habit of checking on details in whatever you choose to become involved in. If you do this, the details will suddenly add up to success—in other words the big, major things will have collectively been taken care of—SUCCESS.

G. Spend time with your customers whether the customer is someone you sell to or provide service to [in] another department in your own company or profession. Listen to the customer. Try to adapt your operation to the customer's needs. It is possible that you are striving to fulfill what you believe are the customer's needs, but the customer may have no interest in what you are striving to produce. If you encourage the customer to share their thoughts with you, it is possible that you will be exposed to a different point of view and some helpful suggestions as to how you can improve your area of responsibility. I once had an interesting conversation with the CEO of one of the largest trucking companies in the U.S. Our company objective was to capture a very large account which was moving from the Port of Los Angeles—Long Beach—to the east coast. Our proposal was to move all of their trailers—containers—between these two points, on railroad flat cars. One of his major concerns was transit time and reliability. After much discussion, he asked me if we made an agreement would I give him my home telephone number and was it "okay" for his people to call me at home if they had a problem they could not get resolved. I answered yes—we got the contract and they never called me at home. What he really wanted was my assurance that we were committed to his operation. Isn't it strange how a simple thing like giving a customer your home telephone number could be the key to the opportunity to generate about $120,000,000 in annual revenue for your company.

H. A major responsibility of a successful manager is to take care of the employees who report to you—salary, recognition, awards, et cetera. After all, these are the people who have made you a success and they are the people who will insure your future success. You have a lot in common with these people. They are depending on you and you are depending on them.

In the world of business—whatever your business is—you will find what I describe as two kinds of people. They are the talkers and the doers. The talkers are always ready to talk about what should be done and, normally, who should do it, except them. The doer simply attacks the problem, solves it, then moves on to something else. He or she is always busy. Graduates, which are you going to be? Let me encourage you, urge you, to become a doer. Make a contribution to society and your organization.

Finally, a statement that causes me great concern and makes me give much thought as to the work ethics of the person making it is, "I did the best that I could." People approach their best, but they never do their best. No matter how much we do, we're always capable of more. No human being can declare with authority what his or her limits are, because our limits keep receding into the distance as we push for greater achievement. When someone makes this statement to me, I think what they really mean is "I decided to stop before I reached my limit."

Ladies and gentlemen, I have suggested some ways of thinking and acting which I am firmly convinced can help you succeed in whatever line of work you choose to follow. Now I want to challenge you. All of you, in your early years and especially during your years at Millsaps, have received as fine a formal education as can be had anywhere. You are well prepared to combine what you have learned at Millsaps with further "on-the-job" or self-education, and with the principles of leadership I have shared, to take advantage of the opportunities before you. You owe it not only to yourselves and your parents and friends who supported you to this point, but to this land of opportunity, to reach your potential as an individual and as a citizen. Along that line, remember that as you live the rest of your life, it will not do to assume that someone else will run for office, that someone else will care for the oppressed, that someone else will minister to the sick, ensure civil rights, enforce the law, preserve culture, transmit value, maintain civilization, and safeguard freedom.

You must never forget that what you do not cherish will not be treasured; what you do not remember will not be retained; what you do not alter will not be changed; what you do not do will not be accomplished. The heroes and heroines of yesterday have all vanished. But while history cites the death of Caesar, the execution of Joan of Arc, and the assassination of Abraham Lincoln, John and

Robert Kennedy, and Martin Luther King, it also records the fact that new heroes arise among us.

We are right to be wary of all pretenders to the throne of greatness, to be leery of even the notion of greatness itself. But for your generation, as for mine and for all others, such figures will surely emerge. It may be your privilege, your pain, to be such a person, to become in Shakespeare's phrase "the observed of all observers." Or it may be your destiny to observe. You should bear in mind, however, that to observe is also to bear witness and that, too, is an important role.

So I say, get involved, at whatever level. Give something back to this world, to this country, to this state, to this College. They're worth it.

Fact is, this country can likely do whatever it sets its mind to do. It always has. That's the American style and spirit; that's what led the Pilgrims to Plymouth Rock in the 1600s; that's what drove thousands in the 1800s across a continent in the great Westward movement. That's what enabled us to put humans on the moon and return them safely to earth. We've succeeded because we have grappled successfully with the problems we have faced.

In closing let me say that I hope that my sharing some of the story of my life will inspire you to carry on with yours. There is one more point I want to emphasize. I never used my career as a means to earn a reward. The career was the reward—and still is. The monetary rewards—though enjoyable—are not what drove me to pursue higher goals. As I lived my own American Dream, I was able to help an unknown number of others realize theirs. Thousands of shareholders who invested in the companies I headed saw the value of their investments rise as the properties entrusted to my care were rehabilitated and made profitable again.

Thousands of employees in these companies were able to feed, clothe, and house their families and send their children to college as a result of the success of the companies. Who knows how many other dreams came true, at least partially because of the value my work helped create for these investors and employees. And how many charities, schools, colleges and medical research institutions, and so on have shared and will continue to share in the results for the good of all. You can do the same.

My final thought is this. I had a lot of different jobs on the railroad, but never one I didn't like. I never had a morning where I got up and found myself saying, "I hate this job—why do I have to go to work?" I found something I loved, and as a result of that I feel as if I've never really done a hard day's work in my life. Gee, I've had a lot of fun! My hope is that you too will find something to do that you love, and that you will never have to do a day's work in your life, for it is work itself, not the reward at the end, that makes our lives truly rewarding. As the Romans used to say, "The journey is better than the inn."

Again, congratulation to each of you graduates. I join all your families and friends in wishing for you the best of everything this wonderful country has to offer. As you move out into society, we are confident that God will bless you in your journey. Thank you.

B

Essential Insights and Selected References

Included in this appendix are insights that amplify and enlarge your understanding of the seven essential changes that lead to powerful leadership and references beyond items mentioned in the body of the book.

We acknowledge in this section the prior understandings and wisdom of those scholars and leaders who preceded us, and whose special way of expressing ideas has attracted us and enlivened our own discourse.

Proclamation on Leadership

Insights

The curse of leadership is the failure of followers to sustain the critical drive coming from an internal fire of the soul that impels them to greatness. True leaders have that fire and recognize it in others. Many so-called leaders degrade their followers and push them into corrupt conceptions of the true nature of their potential. Powerful leaders grasp the significance of the human spirit and seek to exalt people.

References

Rand, Ayn. 1971, *The Fountainhead.* New York: Bobbs-Merrill Company.

Chapter 1

Houston, We Have a Problem!

Insights

The cause of most action may be attributed to the idea of goals that people have in their minds. When we lose our enthusiasm for working, we have lost key goals to achieve at work. Leaders have the responsibility to assist those with whom they work to identify, clarify, and achieve impelling goals that captivate the imagination of the workforce.

One of the most significant treatments of the effects of goals on human action is that of Edwin A. Locke and Gary P. Latham in a book called *A Theory of Goal Setting & Task Performance,* published by Prentice Hall in 1990. Locke and Latham summarize the main features of goal-directed action and observe, "it is the individual's idea of and desire for the goal or end that causes action" (p. 3). The failure to have clear and achievable goals as well as goals that make us stretch to reach them may be one of the most serious flaws in the management of human beings. Our inability to achieve impelling goals undermines our feelings of excitement and enthusiasm.

John Naisbitt and Patricia Aburdene, in their book called *Re-inventing the Corporation,* published by Warner Books in 1985, describe 10 guidelines to chart the course for those reinventing their companies. They suggest that the best and brightest people gravitate toward those corporations that foster personal growth. The evidence is clear that the achievement of personal growth goals is the most critical demand of employees in this era. Thus, an understanding of how leadership affects the achievement of personal growth goals may be the most important information powerful leaders need to be successful. As you may recognize, the seven essential changes that managers should make to fire up people and unleash organizational power are closely tied to personal growth goals.

References

Brandt, Steven C. *Entrepreneuring in Established Companies*. New York: New American Library, 1986.

Freudenberger, Herbert J. *Burn Out*. New York: Bantam Books, 1980.

Komarovsky, Mirra. *Blue-Collar Marriage*. New York: Vintage Books, 1967.

Macleod, Jennifer S. The Work Place as Prison. *Employment Relations Today*, Autumn 1985, 215–218.

Musselwhite, W. and Moran, J. On the Road to Self-Direction. *The Journal of Quality and Participation*, June 1990, 58.

Scott, William G., and David K. Hart. *Organizational Values in America*. New Brunswick, NJ: Transaction Press, 1989.

Sky Magazine. Comments by executives throughout this section were adapted from *Sky Magazine's* executive profiles. Atlanta, GA: Delta Airlines, 1981–1994.

Stephan, Mills, Pace, and Ralphs. HRD in the Fortune 500. *Training & Development Journal*. January 1988, pp 26–32.

Terkel, Studs. *Working*. New York: Avon Books, 1974.

Whyte, William H., Jr. *The Organization Man*. New York: Doubleday Anchor Books, 1957.

Wolfe, Alan. *America at Century's End*. Berkeley: University of California Press, 1991.

Chapter 2

The First Essential Change: Free People to Take the Lead

Insights

One of the most impelling goals associated with human existence is to be free. The emotions of people can be stirred to ultimate heights by appeals to the importance of freedom. We cannot underestimate the power of aspirations to be free in challenging the human spirit. Political, spiritual, and organizational acts have been inspired by the goal to be free. "Free my people" cried Martin Luther King.

In America, freedom is often associated with individualism. Philip Slater, in his book called *The Pursuit of Loneliness*, published by Beacon Press under the auspices of the Unitarian Universalist Association in 1970 and revised in 1976, provides a fascinating look at individualism. Slater argues persuasively that "the belief that everyone should pursue her own destiny autonomously has forced us to maintain an emotional detachment from our social and physical environment and aroused a vague guilt about our competitiveness and indifference to others." One of the goals of contemporary American culture is to "free us from the necessity of relating to, submitting to, depending upon, or controlling other people" (pp. 33–34). This challenging book probes a deep anxiety experienced by many even today.

References

Crosby, Philip B. *Quality is Free*. New York: Mentor Books. 1979.

Galagan, Patricia. Bringing Spirit Back to the Workplace. *Training and Development Journal*, September 1988, 37.

Locke, Edwin A., and Gary P. Latham. *A Theory of Goal Setting & Task Performance*. Englewood Cliffs, NJ: Prentice Hall, 1990.

Pace, R. Wayne, and Don F. Faules. *Organizational Communication*, 3rd ed. Englewood Cliffs, NJ: Prentice Hall.

Roessing, Walter. Blue Jean Boss. *Sky Magazine*, August 1994, 67.

Roosevelt, Franklin Delano. Four Essential Human Freedoms. Message to Congress, January 6, 1941.

Scott, William G., and David K. Hart. *Organizational Values in America*. New Brunswick, NJ: Transaction Publishers, 1990.

USA Today, Cover Story, September 23, 1991.

Yankelovich, Daniel. New Rules: Searching for Self-Fulfillment in a World Turned Upside Down. New York: Bantam New Age Book, 1982.

Chapter 3

The Second Essential Change: Promote Creativity, Innovation, and Fun at Work

Insights

Ultimate fulfillment is a function of the way in which circumstances encourage people to use their innate imaginative capabilities. Only human beings have the ability to imagine how things might be different from the way they actually exist. Oh, the thrill of creative fulfillment. Only next to freedom is creative activity essential to human living.

Norman R. F. Maier, in his book called *Problem Solving and Creativity*, published by the Brooks/Cole Publishing Company in 1970, explains that his research attempts to discover whether "processes higher than learning exist" and "whether behavior theory has overlooked some vital processes that are revealed in problem solving behavior" (pp. 4–5). Maier describes almost 40 research reports that explore all phases of creative problem solving

One of the most provocative conclusions offered by Maier is that "a good deal of discussion time is lost in group problem solving because of difficulties...[that] are purely artifacts created by interpersonal relations" (p. 457). Although this insight has been promulgated in most of the literature, its reinforcement by Maier in the form of empirical data is most gratifying and disturbing. It appears that interpersonal relations may be the source of too many barriers in solving problems.

References

Ackoff, Russell. *The Art of Problem Solving: Accompanied by Ackoff's Fables*. New York: John Wiley & Sons, 1978.

Baer, Jeanne. Unlocking Creativity: A Puzzle Game. *The 1996 McGraw-Hill Training & Performance Sourcebook*, Mel Silberman (Ed.). New York: McGraw-Hill.

Clegg, Brian. *Creativity and Innovation for Managers*. Oxford, England: Butterworth-Heinemann, 1999.

Clurman, Janice. More Than Just a Paycheck. *USA Weekend*, January 1990, 4–5.

Galagan, Patricia. Bringing Spirit Back to the Workplace. *Training and Development Journal*, September 1988, 37.

Garratt, Bob. *The Learning Organization and the Need for Directors Who Think*. London: Gower Publishing Co., 1987.

Ginn, Martin E. *The Creativity Challenge: Management of Innovation and Technology*. Greenwich, CT: JAI Press, 1995.

Hartman, Curtis, and Steven Pearlstein. The Joy of Working. *Inc. Magazine*, November 1987, 61.

Koestler, Albert. *The Act of Creation*. New York: Macmillan, 1969.

Koprowski, Eugene J. Toward Innovative Leadership. *Business Horizons*, Winter 1967, 25–33.

Maynard, Micheline. At Chrysler: The Bob's Management Style Spells Success. *USA Today*, February 5, 1997, 5.

Naisbitt, John, and Patricia Aburdene. *Re-Inventing the Corporation*. New York: Warner Books, 1985.

Osborn, Alex. *Applied Imagination*. New York: Scribner and Sons, 1950.

Parnes, Sidney. *Creative Problem Solving Workbook*. Buffalo, NY: Creative Problem Solving Institute, 1961.

Parnes, Sidney. *Creative Behavior Guidebook*. Buffalo, NY: Creative Problem Solving Institute, 1967.

Seligman, Martin E. P. *Learned Optimism*. New York: Alfred A. Knopf, 1991.

Stern, Sam. Are You Sitting on a Gold Mine? *Utah Business*, February 2000, 74–75.

Chapter 4

The Third Essential Change: Switch from Boss to Cohort

Insights

Nothing is more fundamental to achieving personal and organizational goals than people who willingly cooperate and become allies. The concept of cohort describes a unity between manager and employee that brings about great victories and celebrates successes that routine leadership doesn't. A cohort relationship strikes a chord of common sense. Being a cohort captures the sense of freedom and imagination in relationships among people that transcends typical superior–subordinate connections. A cohort juggernaut triggers salient human emotions and releases stirring and sustained actions.

One of the most difficult tasks managers face is changing their style of working with others. Alterations in people's habitual ways of interacting with others are made most effectively when they recognize a simpler, more direct, more appealing approach. The change from boss to cohort produces the most uncomplicated way of leading people.

In their provocative and insightful book, *Managing the New Organization*, David Limerick and Bert Cunnington, both of Griffith University in Brisbane, Queensland, Australia, describe the management styles of those who will survive the transition to network-based organizations—the wave of the future. They assert that "the very intangible issues of trust and reciprocity that are so problematic in choosing partners in the first place require constant reinforcement and management over the life of the alliance" (p. 102). Interestingly, they suggest that a concept nearer the idea of amicability be substituted for trust in the new organization. If you look up amicable in a dictionary, you will read synonyms such as neighborly and friendly, and a definition explaining that amicable means exhibiting goodwill and an absence of antagonism, and stresses cordiality, warmth, and intimacy of personal relations. The concept of cohort encompasses amicability and trust, supporting our premises that leaders should change from boss to cohort.

References

Ackoff, Russell L. *The Democratic Corporation*. New York: Oxford University Press, 1994.

Bennis, Warren, and Burt Nanus. *Leaders: The Strategies for Taking Charge*. New York: Harper & Row, 1985.

Burton, Terence T., and John W. Moran. *The Future Focused Organization*. Englewood Cliffs, NJ: Prentice Hall, 1995.

Davidow, William H., and Michael S. Malone. *The Virtual Corporation*. New York: Harper Collins, 1992.

Hersey, Paul, and Kenneth H. Blanchard. *Management of Organizational Behavior*. Englewood Cliffs, NJ: Prentice Hall, 1993.

Limerick, David, and Bert Cunnington. *Managing the New Organisation*. Chatswood, NSW, Australia: Business and Professional Publishing, 1993.

Mackay, Hugh. *Reinventing Australia*. Pymble, NSW, Australia: Collins Angus & Robertson Publishers, 1993.

Oakley, Ed, and Doug Krug. *Enlightened Leadership*. New York: Simon & Schuster, 1991.

Roberts, Wess. *Leadership Secrets of Attila the Hun*. New York: Warner Books, 1985.

Schumann, Paul A., Jr., Donna C. L. Prestwood, Alvin H. Tong, and John H. Vanston. *Innovate*. New York: McGraw-Hill, 1994.

Staub, Robert E., II. *The Heart of Leadership*. Provo, UT: Executive Excellence Publishing, 1996.

Stephan, Eric, and R. Wayne Pace. *The Perfect Leader*. Salt Lake City: Deseret Book Company, 1990.

Yukl, Gary. *Leadership in Organizations*, 3rd ed. Englewood Cliffs, NJ: Prentice Hall, 1994.

Chapter 5

The Fourth Essential Change: Master the 4E's of Involvement

Insights

Powerful leaders reveal their abilities by the way in which they involve, inspire, and activate those with whom they work. The power of the organization is released when people feel that they are free to take the lead, use their imaginations to achieve goals, and participate as cohorts in the activities that sustain productivity. This power is released through the 4E's of Involvement: Envision, Enable, Energize, and Ensure.

The cardinal concept that melds the 4E's into a coherent whole is involvement. Eric Hoffer, in his book *The True Believer*, provides an additional perspective on the power of involvement. Hoffer talks about the critical role of *hope* in instigating and sustaining action. Everyone who contemplates engaging in successful and effective leadership must take into account the driving force of hope as a central requirement in preparing followers for full and total involvement. The work of Hoffer describes involvement in a daring and provocative manner.

References

Case, John. *Open-Book Management*. New York: HarperBusiness, 1995.

Collins, Jim. Level 5 Leadership. *Harvard Business Review*, January 2001, 70–72.

Conger, Jay A. and Kanungo, Rabindra N. The Empowerment Process: Integrating Theory and Practice. *Academy of Management Review*, July 1988, 471–82.

DuBrin, Andrew J. *Essentials of Management*, 4th ed. Cincinnati, Ohio: South-Western College Publishing, 1997, 339–346.

Harrison, Roger. Harnessing Personal Energy: How Companies Can Inspire Employees. *Organizational Dynamics*, Fall 1987, 5–20.

Hoffer, Eric. *The True Believer*. New York: The New American Library, 1951.

Humphrey, John W. A Time of 10,000 Leaders. In *A New Paradigm of Leadership*. Ken Shelton (Ed.). Provo, UT: Executive Excellence Publishing, 1997.

Moorhead, Gregory, and Ricky W. Griffin. *Organizational Behavior: Managing People and Organizations*. Boston: Houghton Mifflin, 1995.

Nahavandi, Afsaneh. *The Art and Science of Leadership*. Englewood Cliffs, NJ: Prentice Hall, 1997.

Schermerhorn, John R., Jr. *Management and Organizational Behavior Essentials*. New York: John Wiley & Sons, 1996.

Schulze, Horst, and Dimond, Kevin. The Essence of Leadership. In *A New Paradigm of Leadership*. Ken Shelton (Ed.). Provo, UT: Executive Excellence Publishing, 1997.

Shriberg, Arthur, Carol Lloyd, David Shriberg, and Mary Lynn Williamson. *Practicing Leadership: Principles and Applications*. New York: John Wiley & Sons, 1997.

Townsend, Robert. *Up the Organization*. Greenwich, CT: Fawcett Publishing, 1977.

Walsh, Pam. Management Mavericks: Good Managers March to the Beat of a Different Drum. *Utah Business*, June 2000, 50–51.

Welch, John F. Big is Beautiful. In *A New Paradigm of Leadership*. Ken Shelton (Ed.). Provo, UT: Executive Excellence Publishing.

Whetten, David, and Kim Cameron. *Developing Management Skills*, 3rd ed. New York: Harper Collins, 1995.

242 POWERFUL LEADERSHIP

W. W. Burke. Leadership as Empowering Others. In S. Srivastva and
Associates, *Executive Power*. San Francisco: Jossey-Bass, 1986.

Zemke, Ron. Stalking the Elusive Corporate Credo. *Training*, June 1985,
44–51.

Chapter 6

The Fifth Essential Change: Stop Criticizing and Start Applauding

Insights

Nothing inspires the human spirit like applause. Performers—actors,
politicians, athletes, musicians—live for the response of the audience. By
applause, we know that people appreciate us. By applause, we are invigorated. By applause, we stretch and strain to achieve great things. We love
the uplifting feeling of wild and riotous applause.

One can hardly comprehend the enormous impact of applause on
human beings without an understanding of the place of optimism in
human relations. Martin Seligman, writing in his book called *Learned
Optimism*, provides a scholarly explication of the basic conditions underlying optimism. Those conditions are concerned mostly with having a
positive view of your ability to achieve goals. Hope and optimism are
intimately intertwined; optimism is hoping for the best and acting upon
that hope. Truly inspiring, visionary, enabling, and energizing leadership
is grounded in a happy confidence in the future. Pessimists, who seldom
achieve the status of effective leaders, have a negative, unfavorable,
depressing, cynical, discouraging, disheartening view of the possibility of
accomplishments. Powerful leaders make the 4E's more effective by
grounding them in a milieu of optimism.

References

Cameron, David, and Kim Cameron. *Developing Management Skills*, 3rd
ed. New York: HarperCollins, 1995.

Case, John. *Open-Book Management*. New York: HarperBusiness, 1995.

Caudron, S. The Top 20 Ways to Motivate Employees. *Industry Week*,
April 3, 1995, 14.

Conger, Jay A. and Kanungo, Rabindra N. The Empowerment Process: Integrating Theory and Practice. *Academy of Management Review*, July 1988, 471-482.

Gibb, Jack R. Defensive Communication. *Journal of Communication*, 1961, 141-148.

Glasser, William. *Reality Therapy: A New Approach to Psychiatry.* New York: Harper and Row.

Johnson, David W. Effects of Warmth of Interaction, Accuracy of Understanding, and the Proposal of Compromises on Listener's Behavior. *Journal of Counseling Psychology*, 1971, 207-216.

Johnson, David W. *Reaching Out: Interpersonal Effectiveness and Self-Actualization.* Englewood Cliffs, NJ: Prentice Hall, 1972.

McConnell, James V. *Understanding Human Behavior*, 2nd ed. New York: Holt, Rinehart, Winston, 1974.

Pace, R. Wayne, Robert R. Boren, and Brent D. Peterson. *Communication Behavior and Experiments: A Scientific Approach.* Belmont, CA: Wadsworth Publishing Company, 1975.

Pace, R. Wayne, and Robert R. Boren. *The Human Transaction.* Glenview, IL: Scott, Foresman Co., 1973.

Seligman, Martin E. P. *Learned Optimism.* New York: Alfred A. Knopf, 1991.

Stein, Joel. Bosses From Hell. *Time*, December 7, 1998, 181.

Tobia, Peter M. and Shari Johnson. Chrysler Harnesses Brainpower. *Industry Week*, September 21, 16-22.

Thibaut,John W. and John Coules. The Role of Communication in the Reduction of Interpersonal Hostility. *Journal of Abnormal and Social Psychology*, f1952, 770-777.

Chapter 7

The Sixth Essential Change: Take the High Road

Insights

The human spirit flourishes best in an atmosphere of trust, calmness, supportiveness, and integrity. The code of ethics to which individuals subscribe creates the atmosphere of trust and integrity in which they live. This idea of ethics is embodied in the Greek concept of *ethos*, which refers to the character of a person. In many ways ethics concerns the character of organizations. Organizational character is revealed by the way in which individual ethics govern the lives of workforce members.

The high road represents more than just being ethical. The high road is a concept that transcends simple rights and wrongs and being a good scout. The high road represents the path of ennobling decisions and actions, doing what is best for all concerned, rising above the expected by maintaining standards of thinking, deciding, and acting that enrich the lives of those with whom you are associated. In fact, the high road encompasses the other six essentials that every manager should make to fire up employees and become a powerful leader.

Jesus, Mohammed, Gandhi, and Martin Luther King, the great compassionate leaders of all time, epitomize the high road in leadership. Eric G. Stephan and R. Wayne Pace have written about the leadership of Jesus in a book called *The Perfect Leader: Following Christ's Example to Leadership Success,* Salt Lake City, UT: Deseret Book Company, 1990. This book strives to position leadership in terms of the high road.

References

Covey, Stephen R., A. Roger Merrill, and Rebecca A. Merrill. *First Things First.* New York: Simon & Schuster, 1994.

Dass, Ram, and Paul Gorman. *How Can I Serve?* New York: Alfred A. Knopf, 1985.

Hines, Frederick L. *Scout Handbook.* North Brunswick, NJ: Boy Scouts of America, 1975.

Jensen, Larry C. *What's Right? What's Wrong?: A Psychological Analysis of Moral Behavior.* Washington, DC: Public Affairs Press, 1975.

Jick, Todd J. *Managing Change: Cases and Concepts.* Homewood, Ill: Irwin, 1993.

Pace, R. Wayne, and Don Faules. Ethical Issues in Organizations, *Organizational Communication.* Englewood Cliffs, NJ: Prentice Hall. 1994.

Saxon, Charles D. *Honesty is One of the Better Policies: Saxon's World of Business.* New York: Viking Press, 1984.

Shaw, William, and Vincent Barry. *Moral Issues in Business,* 4th ed. Belmont, CA: Wadsworth Publishing Company, 1989.

Solomon, Robert C., and Kristine Hanson. *It's Good Business.* New York: Atheneum Publishers, 1985.

Chapter 8

The Seventh Essential Change: Stay on the Peaceful Path

Insights

Though enthusiasm, vigor, and focus undergird goal achievement in organizations, sustained growth and continued strength is a function of how well every individual in the workforce is able to renew himself or herself. The mental, moral, physical, financial, and spiritual regeneration of employees is fundamental to organizational success. The major deterrent to staying on the peaceful path is stress, especially mental stress. Worksite stress has been linked to such effects as job anxiety, tension, and dissatisfaction and to more serious consequences like depression, ulcers, heart disease, and death. Staying on the peaceful path is critical for every manager.

The most common source of stress is the feeling of powerlessness. Every point being made in this book cries out for leaders to help their cohorts to avoid the feeling of powerlessness. Freeing people to take the lead gives them more perceived power; encouraging creativity, innovation, and fun at work gives them more perceived power; changing from boss to cohort gives them more perceived power; mastering and using the 4E's of involvement gives them more perceived power; stopping criticism and starting applause gives them more perceived power; and, of course, taking the high road gives them more perceived power. If you can stay on the peaceful path, you will gain strength and an increased sense of power, and reduce the amount of stress you experience in the workplace.

A comprehensive treatment of stress, its consequences, and the values of staying on the peaceful path is presented in Edward A. Charlesworth and Ronald G. Nathan's book called *Stress Management: A Comprehensive Guide to Wellness*, published by Ballantine Books in 1985. They discuss not only ways to relax when you feel stressed, but how to make changes in your lifestyle so as to attack stressful behaviors, thoughts, and attitudes.

References

Albrecht, Karl. *Stress and the Manager: Making It Work for You.* Englewood Cliffs, NJ: Prentice Hall, 1979.

Angel, Sherry. Stress Without Distress. *The Toastmaster*, July 1979, 16–20.

Baker, Beth. The Mind Body Connection. *AARP Bulletin*, July/August, 1997, 17, 20.

Dass, Ram and Gorman, Paul. *How Can I Help?* New York: Alfred A. Knopf, 1986.

Greenberg, Jerald. *Managing Behavior in Organizations*. Englewood Cliffs, NJ: Prentice Hall, 1996.

Heaney, Catherine A., and Michelle van Ryn. Broadening the Scope of Worksite Stress Programs: A Guiding Framework. *American Journal of Health Promotion*, July/August, 1990, 413–420.

Krass, Peter (Ed.). *The Book of Leadership Wisdom*. New York: John Wiley & Sons, 1998.

Moorhead, Gregory, and Ricky W. Griffin. *Organizational Behavior: Managing People and Organizations*, 3rd ed. Boston: Houghton Mifflin, 1992.

Rosch, Paul J. Stress and Illness: Fact or Fantasy? *The Practical Clinical Journal for Physician Assistants*, 1984, 13–16.

Wallis, C. Stress: Can We Cope? *Time*, June 6, 1983, 48–54.

Chapter 9

Where are You as a Powerful Leader?

Insights

Shiftlessness, laziness, lackadaisicalness, and slothfulness lead to extraordinarily calumnious conditions that plague people in organizations. Organizations prize individuals who are ambitious, willing to work, energetic, industrious, active, conscientious, and scrupulous. Powerful leadership creates a climate in which workers freely, openly, and willingly exhibit features that are prized in people. Leadership that results in slothfulness and inactivity is deemed inappropriate and undesirable.

The greatest insight to be derived from this book is that slothfulness at work isn't a natural state of existence; it is created by leaders. Scrupulousness isn't a natural state of existence; it is also cultivated by leaders. Creativeness and innovativeness aren't natural states of existence, but they evolve from the acts of leaders. This insight places a heavy burden on anyone who seeks the role of leader, who has leadership responsibilities thrust upon them.

Another insight to be derived from the totality of this book is that your approach to leadership must become consistent with the changes outlined. You must commit yourself to free people to take the lead; promote creativity, innovation, and fun at work; switch from boss to cohort; master the 4E's of involvement; stop criticizing and start applauding; take the high road; and stay on the peaceful path. There can be no shiftlessness on your part concerning these changes. We entreat you to accept the challenge and pursue the goal of making the necessary changes, for your own survival and also for the ennobling experience you can bring to those with whom you work.

References

Bandura, Albert, and D. Cervone. Self-Evaluative and Self-Efficacy Mechanisms Governing the Motivational Effects of Goal Systems. *Journal of Personality and Social Psychology,* 45 (1983), 1017–1028.

Berger, M. L. and P. J. Berger. *Group Training Techniques.* New York: John Wiley & Sons, n.d., circa 1970.

Birch, D., and J. Veroff. *Motivation: A Study of Action.* Belmont, CA: Wadsworth Publishing Co., 1966.

Chamberlain, Jonathan M. *Eliminate Your SDBs.* Provo, UT: Brigham Young University Press, 1978.

Gorman, Walter. *Selling: Personality, Persuasion, Strategy.* New York: Random House, 1979.

Hill, Napolean. *Think and Grow Rich.* New York: Hawthorn Books, 1967.

Hill, Richard L. *Role Negotiation: Participant Workbook.* Plymouth, MI: Human Synergistics, 1983.

King, Stephen W. *Communication and Social Influence.* Reading, MA: Addison-Wesley, 1975.

Maltz, Maxwell. *Psycho-Cybernetics.* Hollywood, CA: Wilshire Book Co., 1975.

Matsui, T., A. Okada, and T. Kakuyama. Influence and Achievement Need on Goal Setting, Performance, and Feedback on Effectiveness. *Journal of Applied Psychology,* 1982, 645–648.

McClelland, David C., J. W. Atkinson, R. A. Clark, and E. L. Lowell. *The Achievement Motive.* New York: Appleton-Century-Crofts, 1953.

McGuire, William J. The Nature of Attitudes and Attitude Change. In *The Handbook of Social Psychology*, Vol. III, 2nd ed., Gardener Lindzey and Elliott Aronson (Eds.). Reading, MA: Addison-Wesley, 1969.

Peale, Norman V. *The Positive Principle Today*. Englewood Cliffs, NJ: Prentice Hall, 1976.

Spice, Martha B. The Thought Selection Process: A Tool Worth Exploring. *Training and Development Journal*, May 1982, 54–59.

INDEX

The *Financial Times* delivers a world of business news.

Use the Risk-Free Trial Voucher below!

To stay ahead in today's business world you need to be well-informed on a daily basis. And not just on the national level. You need a news source that closely monitors the entire world of business, and then delivers it in a concise, quick-read format.

With the *Financial Times* you get the major stories from every region of the world. Reports found nowhere else. You get business, management, politics, economics, technology and more.

Now you can try the *Financial Times* for 4 weeks, absolutely risk free. And better yet, if you wish to continue receiving the *Financial Times* you'll get great savings off the regular subscription rate. Just use the voucher below.

8 reasons why you should read the Financial Times for 4 weeks RISK-FREE!

To help you stay current with significant
developments in the world economy ...
and to assist you to make informed business
decisions — the Financial Times brings you:

❶ Fast, meaningful overviews of international affairs ... plus daily
briefings on major world news.

❷ Perceptive coverage of economic, business, financial and political
developments with special focus on emerging markets.

❸ More international business news than any other publication.

❹ Sophisticated financial analysis and commentary on world market
activity plus stock quotes from over 30 countries.

❺ Reports on international companies and a section on global investing.

❻ Specialized pages on management, marketing, advertising and
technological innovations from all parts of the world.

❼ Highly valued single-topic special reports (over 200 annually)
on countries, industries, investment opportunities, technology and more.

❽ The Saturday Weekend FT section — a globetrotter's guide to
leisure-time activities around the world: the arts, fine dining, travel,
sports and more.

For Special Offer See Over

FINANCIAL TIMES
World business newspaper

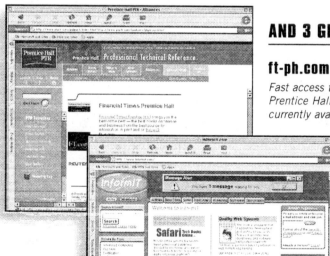